Cambridge Studies in Biological and Evolutionary Anthropology 31

Paleodemography: age distributions from skeletal samples

Paleodemography is the field of inquiry that attempts to identify demographic parameters from past populations (usually skeletal samples) derived from archaeological contexts, and then to make interpretations regarding the health and well-being of those populations. However, paleodemographic theory relies on several assumptions that cannot easily be validated by the researcher and, if incorrect, can lead to large errors or biases. In this book, physical anthropologists, mathematical demographers and statisticians tackle these methodological issues for reconstructing demographic structure for skeletal samples. Topics discussed include how skeletal morphology is linked to chronological age, assessment of age from the skeleton, demographic models of mortality and their interpretation, and biostatistical approaches to age structure estimation from archaeological samples. This work will be of immense importance to anyone interested in paleodemography, including biological anthropologists, demographers, geographers, evolutionary biologists and statisticians.

ROBERT D. HOPPA is a physical anthropologist in the Department of Anthropology at the University of Manitoba. His research interests include historical demography, epidemiology, human skeletal biology, growth and development and forensic anthropology. He has also coedited *Human growth in the past: studies from bones and teeth* (1999; ISBN 0 521 63153 X).

JAMES W. VAUPEL is a demographer and is currently Director of the Max Planck Institute for Demographic Research in Rostock, Germany. He is also Professor of Demography and Epidemiology at the Institute of Public Health, University of Southern Denmark, Odense, and Senior Research Scientist at the Sanford Institute at Duke University in North Carolina. His research focuses on human biodemography, human longevity, and centenarian research. He has authored or edited numerous books in the field of demography, particularly oldest old mortality, including *Population data at a glance* (1997), *The force of mortality at ages 80 to 120* (1998), and *Validation of exceptional longevity* (1999).

Cambridge Studies in Biological and Evolutionary Anthropology

Series Editors

HUMAN ECOLOGY
C. G. Nicholas Mascie-Taylor, University of Cambridge
Michael A. Little, State University of New York, Binghamton
GENETICS
Kenneth M. Weiss, Pennsylvania State University
HUMAN EVOLUTION
Robert A. Foley, University of Cambridge
Nina G. Jablonski, California Academy of Science
PRIMATOLOGY
Karen B. Strier, University of Wisconsin, Madison

Consulting Editors
Emeritus Professor Derek F. Roberts
Emeritus Professor Gabriel W. Lasker

Paleodemography

age distributions from skeletal samples

EDITED BY

ROBERT D. HOPPA

University of Manitoba,
Winnipeg, Manitoba, Canada

JAMES W. VAUPEL

Max Planck Institute for Demographic Research,
Rostock, Germany

CAMBRIDGE UNIVERSITY PRESS

PUBLISHED BY THE PRESS SYNDICATE OF THE UNIVERSITY OF CAMBRIDGE
The Pitt Building, Trumpington Street, Cambridge, United Kingdom

CAMBRIDGE UNIVERSITY PRESS
The Edinburgh Building, Cambridge CB2 2RU, UK
40 West 20th Street, New York NY 10011-4211, USA
477 Williamstown Road, Port Melbourne, VIC 3207, Australia
Ruiz de Alarcón 13, 28014 Madrid, Spain
Dock House, The Waterfront, Cape Town 8001, South Africa

http://www.cambridge.org

First published 2002

Printed in the United Kingdom at the University Press, Cambridge

Typeface Times 10/12.5pt   *System* Poltype® [VN]

A catalogue record for this book is available from the British Library

ISBN 0 521 80063 3 hardback

To our families

Contents

Contributors

Jesper L. Boldsen
Anthropological Data Base Odense University (ADBOU) and Danish Center for Demographic Research, Odense University, Sdr. Boulevard 23 A, DK 5000 Odense C, Denmark

Helene Buba
Institute for Anthropology, Department of Biology, University of Geissen, Wartweg 49, D-35392 Geissen, Germany

Rebecca J. Ferrell
Department of Anthropology and Population Research Institute, Pennsylvania State University, University Park, PA 16802, USA

Nicholas P. Herrmann
Department of Anthropology, University of Tennessee, Knoxville, TN 37996, USA

Darryl J. Holman
Department of Anthropology and Center for Studies in Demography and Ecology, University of Washington, Seattle, WA 98195, USA

Robert D. Hoppa
Department of Anthropology, University of Manitoba, Winnipeg, Manitoba, Canada R3T 5V5

Ariane Kemkes-Grottenthaler
Fachbereich Biologie (21), Institut für Anthropologie, Johannes Gutenberg-Universität, Colonel-Kleinmann-Weg 2, SB II, 2.Stock, D-55099 Mainz, Germany

Lyle W. Konigsberg
Department of Anthropology, University of Tennessee, Knoxville, TN 37996, USA

Bradley Love
Molecular Dynamics Inc., 928 East Arques Avenue, Sunnyvale, CA 94085-4520, USA

George R. Milner
Department of Anthropology, Pennsylvania State University, 409 Carpenter Building, University Park, PA 16802, USA

Hans-Georg Müller
Division of Statistics, University of California, Davis, CA 95616, USA

Kathleen A. O'Connor
Department of Anthropology and Center for Studies of Demography and Ecology, University of Washington, Seattle, WA 98195, USA

Richard R. Paine
Department of Anthropology, University of Utah, Salt Lake City, UT 84112-0060, USA

Bethany M. Usher
Department of Anthropology, SUNY Potsdam, 44 Pierrepont Avenue, Potsdam, NY 13676, USA

James W. Vaupel
Max Planck Institute for Demographic Research, Doberaner Strasse 114, Rostock 18057, Germany

Ursula Wittwer-Backofen
Max Planck Institute for Demographic Research, Doberaner Strasse 114, Rostock 18057, Germany

James W. Wood
Department of Anthropology and Population Research Institute, Pennsylvania State University, 409 Carpenter Building, University Park, PA 16802, USA

Acknowledgments

This volume represents the cumulative efforts of those who participated in the workshops on paleodemography hosted in June 1999 and August 2000 at the Max Planck Institute for Demographic Research. We would like to extend our gratitude to all of our contributors who have taken the time and effort to provide us with exciting and original perspectives on paleo-demogaphic reconstructions. As with any project that brings together experts from many fields, finding common ground for notation was not a simple task. All contributors are to be acknowledged for their tolerance of having to comply with the group compromise for notation. At Cambridge University Press, Tracey Sanderson, as always, was supportive of this project from its inception. For her skillful editorial eye, we are again indebted to Sandi Irvine for her meticulous copy-editing of the volume. The workshops that led to the production of this work were facilitated by the conscientious efforts of many of the administrative staff at the Max Planck Institute for Demographic Research including Rene Flibotte-Lüskow, Gunde Paetrow, Dirk Vieregg, Holger Schwadtze, Rainer Walke, Christine Röpke and Jutta Gampe. This work was supported in part by the Max Planck Institute for Demographic Research, the Social Sciences and Humanities Research Council of Canada and the University of Manitoba.

Rob Hoppa
Jim Vaupel

1 The Rostock Manifesto for paleodemography:
the way from stage to age

ROBERT D. HOPPA AND JAMES W. VAUPEL

Introduction

In June 1999, the Laboratory of Survival and Longevity at the Max Planck Institute for Demographic Research in Rostock, Germany, hosted a three-day workshop entitled "Mathematical Modelling for Palaeodemography: Coming to Consensus". The title chosen reflected two issues the workshop was meant to deal with. First, the use of biostatistical methods as a means for estimating demographic profiles from skeletal data was clearly emerging as the right direction for the future. A number of individuals were invited who had published such techniques. Second, coming to consensus was a play on words for evaluating and finding a methodological approach that best did the job for paleodemography.

The initial workshop focused specifically on adult aging techniques. This was partly a reflection of the need to find methods that could capture the right-most tail of the age distribution in archaeological populations – the oldest old. Although nonadult aging techniques have increased levels of accuracy and precision, assessing the complete age structure of the population is absolutely imperative. The statistical approaches presented in this volume, while presented in the context of adult age estimation, are more broadly applicable to age indicator methods for any group (see e.g., Konigsberg and Holman 1999).

The purpose of the workshop was to provide individuals with an identical dataset on which to test their techniques. Thus everyone would be able to use their methods to estimate the demographic profile for a real target sample using a series of skeletal age indicator stages for which known-age data were associated, but not revealed. The assumption here was that, for the first time, the presentation of these newly emerging statistical techniques could be evaluated in terms of their accuracy and reliability in estimating age profiles on a level playing field – comparing apples with apples, if you will.

As it turns out, the outcome of the workshop resulted in a realization that statistical methods might vary, but it was the theoretical framework in which such methods were placed that was critical. Thus, on conclusion of the workshop, there was unanimous acceptance of a theoretical approach – what became known amongst attendees as the "Rostock Manifesto", a collegial call for new directions in paleodemographic research. While this theoretical framework represents the primary basis for which this project was developed, we nevertheless recognized that there are several interconnected issues in the reconstruction of population parameters from skeletal samples that should be addressed. Subsequently, in August 2000, a follow-up workshop was held in Rostock, in which attendees presented and discussed a variety of issues directly relevant to the field of paleodemography. This book represents the cumulative efforts of those who participated in these meetings.

The Rostock Manifesto has four major elements:

1. Working more meticulously with existing and new reference collections of skeletons of known age, osteologists must develop more reliable and more vigorously validated age indicator stages or categories that relate skeletal morphology to known chronological age.
2. Using these osteological data, anthropologists, demographers and statisticians must develop models and methods to estimate $\Pr(c|a)$, the probability of observing a suite of skeletal characteristics c, given known age a.
3. Osteologists must recognize that what is of interest in paleodemographic research is $\Pr(a|c)$, the probability that the skeletal remains are from a person who died at age a, given the evidence concerning c, the characteristics of the skeletal remains. This probability, $\Pr(a|c)$, is NOT equal to $\Pr(c|a)$, the latter being known from reference samples. Rather $\Pr(a|c)$ must be calculated from $\Pr(c|a)$ using Bayes' theorem. Even the most experienced and intelligent osteologists cannot make this calculation in their heads. Pencil and paper or a computer is required, as well as information concerning $f(a)$, the probability distribution of ages-at-death (i.e., lifespan) in the target population of interest.
4. This means that $f(a)$ must be estimated *before* $\Pr(a|c)$ can be assessed. That is to say, to calculate $\Pr(a|c)$ it is necessary to first estimate $f(a)$, the probability distribution of lifespans in the target population. To

estimate $f(a)$ a model is needed of how the chance of death varies with age. Furthermore a method is needed to relate empirical observations of skeletal characteristics in the target population to the probability of observing the skeletal characteristics in this population. The empirical observations generally will be counts of how many skeletons are classified into each of the stages or categories c. The probability of these characteristics, $\Pr(c)$, is given by

$$\Pr(c) = \int_0^\omega \Pr(c\,|\,a)f(a)\mathrm{d}a, \qquad (1.1)$$

where ω is the upper limit of the human lifespan. The basic strategy is to choose the parameters of the model of the lifespan distribution $f(a)$, or the levels of mortality in various age categories in a nonparametric model, to maximize the "fit" between the observed frequencies of the morphological characteristics and the underlying probabilities of these characteristics.

The various chapters of this book pertain to these four precepts. In the following discussion we explain each of the dictums in more detail and adumbrate how the chapters relate to them.

The need for better osteological methods

Paleodemographic reconstructions of past populations depend on accurate determination of age-at-death distributions, sorted by sex, within skeletal samples. The accuracy and reliability of age estimation techniques have been central concerns in critiques of paleodemography. In particular, the underestimation of ages for older adults and age mimicry have invited strong criticism (Bocquet-Appel and Masset 1982, 1985, 1996; Sattenspiel and Harpending 1983; Van Gerven and Armelagos 1983; Buikstra and Konigsberg 1985; Masset and Parzysz 1985; Bocquet-Appel 1986; Greene et al. 1986; Wittwer-Backofen 1987; Horowitz et al. 1988; Konigsberg and Frankenberg 1992, 2001). While there are a variety of methodological approaches to scoring age-related changes in the skeleton, many (although not all) commonly employed methods are based on an osteological age indicator staging system where the stages serve as proxies for age. In Chapter 4, Kemkes-Grottenthaler provides an excellent historical overview of age indicator methods for assessing age-at-death in the skeleton, contrasting the historical division between European and North American methods, and the need for true multivariate techniques. Such methods are used both in forensic investigations where the age of an individual is of primary interest, and in paleodemographic investigations where the mortality schedule of a population is of interest. The subsequent two chapters present two new osteological techniques relevant to estimating age-at-death from the skeleton. In Chapter 5, Boldsen and colleagues present a new multivariate method that incorporates morphological assessments of the pubic symphysis, auricular surface, and cranial suture closures. Estimating age for an individual requires, as noted above, information about the population mortality schedule. Different statistical approaches to estimating this schedule may be appropriate when the number of individuals to be aged is a handful or less or thousands or more. Chapter 5 by Boldsen and colleagues demonstrates the applicability of transition analysis for estimating age in a single individual or a small sample for which estimating of age structures from the target sample is impossible. In Chapter 6, Wittwer-Backofen and Buba present the preliminary results of a validation study of a refined method for estimating age-at-death directly from teeth, using cementum annulation.

The need for better reference samples

As noted above, the information that osteologists have regarding age and stages pertains to the probability of being in a specific stage given age, $\Pr(c|a)$. This is based on comparisons of stage and age in documentary reference samples. It is important that the reported ages in such reference samples be carefully validated. Age misreporting is common, so care must be taken to document and verify ages. This is particularly important when a person's age is given by a proxy source (because, e.g., the person has died). The reference collection used in Chapter 5 by Boldsen and coworkers includes three black females who are reported to have reached their 90s. They almost certainly died at younger ages and either their reported ages should be checked or they should be excluded from any future analysis. For further discussion of age validation, see Jeune and Vaupel (1999).

It became abundantly clear both from discussions that developed during the workshops and from the practical difficulties in providing attendees with real data on which to test their methods – specifically the paucity of published reference sample data – that there was a need to explore the existence of known-age skeletal samples for which methods have and can be developed and/or tested. Usher addresses this issue in Chapter 3, where she provides an overview of the use of known-age reference samples as a means for developing osteological aging techniques, and a general assessment of those collections that are known to exist.

The need to use Bayes' theorem

The concept of estimating age from a skeleton is fundamental to any skeletal biologist. Training in osteology means learning rigorously how to "read" biological information from the skeleton related to age, sex, pathology, and personal identification. The specific means of any one study will be tied to the questions being asked, but ultimately age and sex have formed a fundamental first step for any anthropologist examining a series of skeletons. Because these two features are so important to further analyses, and to some extent codependent on one another (many aging criteria are sex specific), they have formed an intrinsic expertise for all experienced researchers.

The concept of age estimation has, despite a variety of possible techniques, followed the same series of short steps: (a) assess skeletal morphology, (b) link skeletal morphology to chronological age through a reference collection, and (c) estimate age. While in principle these steps are correct, there is some issue over how the second step is executed. The second step is tied critically to the reference population on which a method, or series of methods, has been developed. In this step, morphological aging criteria are established, given known age in the reference sample. Thus we have some understanding of the probability of what stage a skeleton should be, conditional on age, or in mathematical notation $\Pr(c|a)$, where c represents the morphological age indicator stage or category, and a represents chronological age-at-death. However, the ultimate goal of using this relationship is to estimate the age of an individual or group of individuals within an archaeological sample: that is to say, to estimate the probability of age conditional on stage, or $\Pr(a|c)$. This probability is not equivalent to $\Pr(c|a)$ but can be solved using Bayes' theorem as follows:

$$\Pr(a|c) = \frac{\Pr(c|a)f(a)}{\displaystyle\int_0^\omega \Pr(c|a)f(a)\mathrm{d}a}. \tag{1.2}$$

As noted by Konigsberg and Frankenberg (1994), it is a paradox that the very distribution that one is trying to estimate, $f(a)$, is required before individual age estimation can proceed. This seems counterintuitive to osteological training – how can one estimate a population structure before knowing the age of the individuals? But again, the problem is based, in part, on the notion that we can easily invert the relationship between stage and age, which is not correct. The question then arises as to how to make use of information in the reference sample without biasing our estimates of the age distribution or making faulty assumptions.

While, ultimately, the goal would be to proceed without the need to impose any predefined patterns of mortality, currently the kinds of osteological data available are not adequate to allow for nonparametric approaches, at least for intervals of reasonable length. As a result, there is a need to incorporate parametric models of mortality into paleodemographic reconstructions. Given the limited information available from current skeletal age indicator methods and relatively small target samples sizes, only a handful of parameters can reasonably be estimated. As Konigsberg and Frankenberg (2001) note, this has plagued a variety of statistical exercises that have attempted to estimate more age intervals than age indicator categories, resulting in negative degrees of freedom in their models.

Chapters 7 (Wood et al.) and 8 (Paine and Boldsen) both deal with the process of modeling population dynamics in paleodemography. First, Wood and colleagues summarize for the reader various models that can be used to fit to paleodemographic data, and the advantages and disadvantages of differing approaches. In Chapter 8, Paine and Boldsen illustrate how one can link the mortality patterns in paleodemographic analyses to the broader questions of population processes, including disease, migration, and fertility.

The need to assess the distribution of lifespans in the target population

There are four approaches to estimating $f(a)$, the probability distribution of ages at death (i.e., lifespan) in the target population of interest. First, the distribution can be specified based on some convenient assumption, such as the assumption that all lifespans between age 20 years, say, and age 100 years, say, are equally likely. Second, the distribution can be assessed using the subjective judgments of experts who have ancillary knowledge. Third, a known distribution of lifespans, from some population assumed to be similar to the target population of interest, can be appropriated. Fourth, empirical data on the frequency of characteristics c in the skeletons of the target population together with information about $\Pr(c|a)$ from the reference population can be used in a mortality model to estimate the parameters or values of $f(a)$. The first three of these approaches are discussed briefly in Chapter 5, where Boldsen and colleagues argue that, when a flat or uniform prior is assumed, $\Pr(a|c)$ is related proportionally to $\Pr(c|a)$ and can be estimated relatively easily. However, a uniform prior is not reflective of real mortality distributions. The last, and most appealing, approach is discussed in Chapters 9 to 12.

First, Love and Müller (Chapter 9) use a semiparametric approach and estimate weight functions in order to estimate age structure from age indicator data in the target sample. The next two chapters present parametric approaches to estimating age profiles – Holman and colleagues (Chapter 10) use a logit and Konigsberg and Herrman (Chapter 11) a probit approach. An example of how these methods can be applied to archaeological data follows with Herrmann and Konigsberg (Chapter 12) re-examining the Indian Knoll site, using the statistical approach outlined in Chapter 11 to make new inferences about this Archaic population.

Paleodemographic studies have the potential to provide important information regarding past population dynamics. However, the tools with which this task has been traditionally undertaken have not been sufficient. If we are interested in understanding demographic processes in archaeological populations, it is necessary to adopt a new framework in which to estimate age distributions from skeletal samples. It was once argued that, to be successful, paleodemographers should work more closely with researchers in the field of demography (Petersen 1975). This book answers that challenge, bringing together physical anthropologists, demographers, and statisticians to tackle theoretical and methodological issues related to reconstructing demographic structure from skeletal samples.

References

Bocquet-Appel JP (1986) Once upon a time: palaeodemography. *Mitteilungen der Berliner Gesellschaft für Anthropologie, Ethnologie und Urgeschichte* **7**, 127–133.

Bocquet-Appel JP and Masset C (1982) Farewell to palaeodemography. *Journal of Human Evolution* **11**, 321–333.

Bocquet-Appel JP and Masset C (1985) Palaeodemography: resurrection or ghost? *Journal of Human Evolution* **14**, 107–111.

Bocquet-Appel JP and Masset C (1996) Paleodemography: expectancy and false hope. *American Journal of Physical Anthropology* **99**, 571–583.

Buikstra JE and Konigsberg LW (1985) Palaeodemography: critiques and controversies. *American Anthropologist* **87**, 316–334.

Greene DL, Van Gerven DP, and Armelagos GJ (1986) Life and death in ancient populations: bones of contention in palaeodemography. *Human Evolution* **1**, 193–207.

Horowitz S, Armelagos G, and Wachter K (1988) On generating birth rates from skeletal populations. *American Journal of Physical Anthropology* **76**, 189–196.

Jeune BE and Vaupel JW (eds.) (1999) *Validation of exceptional longevity.* Monographs on Population Aging no. 6. Odense: Odense University Press.

Konigsberg LW and Frankenberg SR (1992) Estimation of age structure in anthropological demography. *American Journal of Physical Anthropology* **89**, 235–256.

Konigsberg LW and Frankenberg SR (1994) Palaeodemography: "Not quite dead". *Evolutionary Anthropology* **3**, 92–105.

Konigsberg LW and Frankenberg SR (2001) Deconstructing death in paleodemography. *American Journal of Physical Anthropology*, in press.

Konigsberg L and Holman D (1999) Estimation of age at death from dental emergence and implications for studies of prehistoric somatic growth. In RD Hoppa and CM FitzGerald (eds.): *Human growth in the past: studies from bones and teeth*. Cambridge Studies in Biological and Evolutionary Anthropology, 25. Cambridge: Cambridge University Press, pp. 264–289.

Masset C and Parzysz B (1985) Démographie des cimetières? Incertitude des estimateurs en paléodemographie. *L'Homme* **25**, 147–154.

Petersen W (1975) A demographer's view of prehistoric demography. *Current Anthropology* **16**, 227–237.

Sattenspiel L and Harpending H (1983) Stable populations and skeletal age. *American Antiquity* **48**, 489–498.

Van Gerven DP and Armelagos GJ (1983) "Farewell to paleodemography?" Rumors of its death have been greatly exaggerated. *Journal of Human Evolution* **12**, 353–360.

Wittwer-Backofen U (1987). Überblick über den aktuellen Stand paläodemographischer Forschung. *Homo* **38**, 151–160.

2   *Paleodemography:*
looking back and thinking ahead

ROBERT D. HOPPA

Introduction

Paleodemography is the field of inquiry that attempts to identify demographic parameters from past populations derived from archaeological contexts. Questions have been explored primarily by physical anthropologists through the analysis of skeletal remains, although such information can be augmented with associated documentary information available from epigraphy, census and parish records, or, sometimes, primary literary sources.

When demographic parameters are known or can be estimated, it is argued that the resultant population structure is predictable and can be extended either forward or backward in time to examine the significance of sets of parameters (Howell 1986:219). However, paleodemographic theory relies upon several assumptions that cannot be readily validated by the researcher. The primary assumption of paleodemographic reconstructions is that the age and sex profiles seen within the sample of dead individuals provide a clear and accurate reflection of those parameters within the once-living population – that is, the numbers, ages and sexes of the mortality sample accurately reflect the death rate of the population. Second, any bias that may affect the data can be recognized and taken into account (Ubelaker 1989).

Historical perspectives

By 1950, the subject of human longevity in the past had been tackled by the occasional inquiry (e.g., Lankester 1870; Pearson 1902; MacDonnell 1913; Hooton 1930; Vallois, 1937; Willcox 1938; Weidenreich 1939; Senyürek 1947). However, it was the writings of J. Lawrence Angel, in the mid 20th century, on life expectancy in ancient Greece (e.g., Angel 1947, 1954) that many cite as the beginnings of paleodemography as an emerging area of specialization within physical anthropology (for a more detailed overview of the history of the field, see Konigsberg and Frankenberg 2001).

9

Following Angel's early papers, paleodemography became standard practice in physical anthropological studies of human skeletal samples from the archaeological record. Initially, such studies made use of the abridged life table as a tool for interpreting age-at-death profiles in ancient populations (e.g. Vallois 1960; Kobayashi 1967; Angel 1968, 1969a,b, 1972, 1975; Kennedy 1969; Swedlund and Armelagos 1969; Acsádi and Nemeskéri 1970; Blakely 1971, 1977; Brothwell 1971; Lovejoy 1971; McKinley 1971; Bennet 1973; Masset 1973; Weiss 1973,1975; Ubelaker 1974; Moore *et al.* 1975; Piasecki 1975; Plog 1975; Asch 1976; Armelagos and Medina 1977; Bocquet-Appel 1977, 1978, 1979; Bocquet-Appel and Masset 1977; Clarke 1977; Henneberg 1977; Lovejoy *et al.* 1977; Passarello 1977; Palkovich 1978; Owsley and Bass 1979; Piontek 1979; Welinder 1979; Hassan 1981; Piontek and Henneberg 1981; Van Gerven *et al.* 1981; Pardini *et al.* 1983). Using osteological age indicator methods, individuals were assigned to age groups and distributed into an abridged life table. That is to say, individual ages were estimated first and those estimates were aggregated for demographic analysis. Because of the differences in precision for differing ages, and the desire to try to standardize the demographic data into five-year cohorts, individuals were often redistributed across multiple cohorts within the life table.

In the mid 1970s Howell (1976) noted that demographic analyses of past populations rely on the assumption of biological uniformitarianism. This principle asserts that past and present regularities are crucial to future events and that, under similar circumstances, similar phenomena will have behaved in the past as they do in the present, and will do so in the future (Watson *et al.* 1984:5). The law of uniformitarianism is a fundamental assumption made by biologists working on skeletons at a variety of analytical levels. Estimates of demographic parameters in past populations necessarily assume that the biological processes related to mortality and fertility in humans were the same in the past as they are in the present (Weiss 1973, 1975; Howell 1976; see also Paine 1997). However, it is not only the broader issues of demographic structure that must conform to this assumption. Techniques for assessing age from skeletal remains must also assume uniformitarianism in the use of biological aging criteria, such that the pattern of age-progressive changes observed in modern reference populations is not significantly different from the pattern observed in past populations.

This assumption has implications at two levels for paleodemography. The first issue relates to application of this theory to biological processes, particularly those relevant to population structure, and assumes that humans have not changed over time with respect to their biological responses to the environment (Howell 1976). This assumption is critical in order for us to be able to relate our current understanding of the impact of demographic changes on past populations (e.g. see, Gage 1989, 1990; Paine and Harpending 1998; Wood 1998; see also Paine and Boldsen, Chapter 8, Wood *et al.*, Chapter 7, this volume). Wood and colleagues (1992b; see also Chapter 7, this volume) noted that an important goal of paleodemography is to find models of population dynamics that facilitate etiological ways of thinking about mortality profiles and allow for meaningful biological interpretation and insight. As these authors commented, there seems to be some agreement that there is a common pattern of mortality among human populations and that alterations in its shape and trajectory can be captured by parametric models. Nevertheless, there is still debate regarding which parametric models can best fit the force of human aging and mortality, or whether in fact we should be applying nonparametric approaches first to explore the data.

Second, it assumes that the biological development of age-related morphology in humans is the same in populations that are separated in either time or space. While the rate at which these changes occur may be different, the general pattern should be the same. Several studies in fact have examined this issue for osteological aging techniques. We know that the rate of change in various age indicator techniques is different between males and females, and has been shown to be different when applied to populations with a background different from that of the original reference samples. Lovejoy and colleagues (1997:44) have recently noted that, while great strides have been made in our ability to estimate "basic demographic parameters from human skeletal remains . . . [further] progress will require investigations that improve our understanding of the fundamental *biology* of human skeletal aging in contrast to most previous studies which have been largely typological" (see also Lovejoy *et al.* 1995). The point here is that variation inherent in the biological process of aging in the skeleton continues to be a fundamental source of error for current osteological aging criteria (Lovejoy *et al.* 1997; Bocquet-Appel and Masset 1997; see also Kemkes-Grottenthaler, Chapter 4, this volume). As such, differences in age-related changes in the human skeleton may impede the use of these criteria on skeletal samples that differ significantly in time from the reference (Bocquet-Appel and Masset 1982; Angel *et al.* 1986; İşcan and Loth 1989; Kemkes-Grottenthaler 1996). Hoppa (2000) has even suggested that there may be distinct differences between populations with similar backgrounds, although others have suggested this is a product of interobserver error, rather than population differences (Konigsberg and Frankenberg 2001).

If we presuppose the validity of biological uniformitarianism proposed by Howell (1976), the basic premise for using the abridged life table in demographic reconstructions from skeletal samples is that the population from which the sample is from is "stationary". A stationary population is a special form of "stable" population (Acsádi and Nemeskéri 1970). A stable population is defined as a "population which is closed to migration and has an unchanging age–sex structure that increases (or decreases) in size at a constant rate" (Wilson 1985:210). In reality, paleodemographic analyses do not expect this assumption to be true, since changes in composition over time are a central focus – temporal analyses would be meaningless if we truly assumed that the intrinsic growth rate was zero over time. However, errors introduced by failure of the population to meet stationary conditions will depend on the extent to which the population deviates from the assumed conditions (Gage 1985).

> In nonstationary populations, age-at-death distributions are extremely sensitive to changes in fertility but not to changes in mortality . . .. Thus, if a population is not stationary – and changing populations never are – small variations in fertility have large effects on its age-at-death distribution, while even quite large modifications of mortality have virtually none.
>
> (Wood *et al.* 1992a:344)

Acsádi and Nemeskéri (1970) once argued that the long-term rate of growth within populations has been very close to zero. Weiss (1975) similarly noted that in most animal populations, including humans, there is a tendency toward an approximate zero-growth equilibrium, with significant deviations often being corrected through natural ecological processes. Even with the apparent rapid growth in the world population over the last 10 000 years, Hassan (1981) argued that it is likely that intervals of rapid growth in human prehistory were infrequent and easily defined against a general trend of very slow growth. Whether this claim is applicable in the short term with respect to various local populations, which are for the most part the primary focus of paleodemographic analyses, is difficult to assess (Johansson and Horowitz 1986). Moore and colleagues (1975) attempted to estimate the effects of stochastic fluctuations within small populations. Using computer simulations, these authors suggested that, since an individual cemetery represents only one of many possible outcomes within a dynamic system, interpretations based on such samples are questionable.

In the late 1970s, demographers issued a call to arms regarding paleodemography (Petersen 1975; Howell 1976). Petersen (1975) argued that the demographic analyses of past population by anthropologists are undertaken without a firm understanding of demographic theory and method. "Very little of the demographic analysis in [archaeology and anthropology] has reached the level of professional competence that is almost routine in historical studies" (Petersen 1975:228). Petersen's (1975) primary critique is that anthropologists do not have a firm grasp of the fundamentals of demographic theory. Secondarily, he noted that the paucity of evidence from which to make statements regarding paleodemographic parameters forces extrapolations from models derived from other sources (e.g., ethnographic analogy).

Following an earlier critique of paleodemography in which she highlighted the importance of uniformitarianism, Howell (1982) undertook an analysis of the Libben site (Lovejoy *et al.* 1977) using the program AMBUSH (Howell and Lehotay 1978). On the basis of the mortality structure and assumptions about fertility in this large skeletal sample, Howell concluded that serious social consequences would have been occurring within the Libben population for the demographic structure implied from the skeletal sample to have developed. Such elements included unstable marriage patterns and a two- rather than three-person generation as a result of abnormally high adult mortality, a high proportion of orphaned children, and a high dependency ratio (Howell 1982). This led Howell to conclude that either biocultural interactions in prehistoric societies were very different from those observed in ethnographic populations or that the sample was unrepresentative of the true mortality sample.

Ethnographic analogy for prehistoric demography

The primary question is whether skeletal data alone are sufficient for accurate demographic reconstructions of past populations. Petersen's (1975) concern over the paucity of evidence from which to make statements regarding paleodemographic parameters forced many investigators to extrapolate from models derived from other sources. Coale and Demeny's (1966) classic compendium of model life tables for modern demographic studies was the probable impetus for anthropological demographers to develop model life tables for past populations (e.g., Weiss 1973). Weiss (1973) provided model life tables for various fertility schedules based on probability of death, q_x. Relating probability of death to life expectancy at age 10 years by least squares linear regression and logarithmic regression equations from a variety of relatively contemporary populations based on vital statistics, Coale and Demeny (1966) produced age-specific mortality rates for males and females presented as regional model life tables. These authors asserted that the use of life expectancy at age 10 years, rather than birth, is an unbiased general index of differences that can result from fitting model life tables. Many investigators have agreed that demographic statistics derived from contemporary non-Western societies represent an effective means of assessing skeletal age profiles of past populations (Weiss 1973; Petersen 1975; Milner et al. 1989; Paine 1989). On the other hand, given the variety of conditions under which many contemporary populations live, it is difficult to be certain that ethnographic analogies for demographic statistics will always be appropriate. Further, the application of ethnographic estimators to samples for which related sociocultural information is sparse serves only to compound the problem. However, "comparing data from different groups, understanding the cultural context of the population, and critically evaluating the sources of the data can minimize some of the potential errors" (Hassan 1981:5).

Although a potentially powerful tool for anthropological and, particularly, paleodemographic analyses, model life table fitting techniques are still subject to potential biases resulting from the use of inappropriate model populations (Gage 1988). As such, Gage (1988, 1989, 1990) has proposed the use of a hazard model of age-at-death patterns that can be fitted to survivorship, death rate, and age structure data. This technique provides a method of estimating age-specific mortality and fertility directly from anthropological data, and will smooth demographic data from a variety of populations without imposing a predetermined age structure (Gage 1988). Gage (1990) later constructed a new set of model life tables using hazard models, for which there were no equivalent corresponding models in Coale and Demeny (1966), noting that the greatest variation between these models resulted from differences in adult mortality.

Looking to what we know from small, contemporary hunter–gatherer and foraging societies must surely provide some insight. However, arguments that prehistoric patterns of mortality are unlike their observed contemporary analogy are difficult to assess. Meindl and Russel (1998:393) assert that paleodemographic data should not be forced into modern industrialized demographic profiles without some empirical justification. If the demographic patterns of prehistory were fundamentally different, archaeological demographers should reserve the opportunity to detect them.

The great debate: paleodemography on trial

The 1980s marked a pivotal point for paleodemography. While there had been the occasional critique prior to the 1980s (e.g., Petersen 1975; Howell 1976) it was not until 1982 that the great debate ensued regarding the validity of the methods on which paleodemographic reconstructions were based (Bocquet-Appel and Masset 1982, 1985; Sattenspiel and Harpending 1983; Van Gerven and Armelagos 1983; Buikstra and Konigsberg 1985; Masset and Parzysz 1985; Bocquet-Appel 1986; Greene *et al.* 1986; Horowitz *et al.* 1988). In 1982 Bocquet-Appel and Masset (1982) attacked paleodemography on two fronts: (1) that age-at-death profiles obtained from prehistoric skeletal samples are artifacts of the age distributions of the reference samples employed for estimating chronological age from human skeletal remains, and (2) there is inherent inaccuracy and unreliability of *all* age estimation techniques because of the low correlation between skeletal age and chronological age. These authors noted that the mean ages for various skeletal stages are a product of both the biological process of aging and the age structure of the reference population. They further suggested that paleodemographers assume that age-related changes in the human skeleton are constant through time. Despite the fervor of publications critical of the relative merit of paleodemography, studies of demography from excavated skeletal samples continue to flourish (e.g., Wittwer-Backofen 1989, 1991; Balteanu and Cantemir 1991; Grauer 1991; Miu and Botezatu 1991; Parsche 1991; Alekseeva and Fedosova 1992; Berner 1992; Cunha *et al.* 1992; Srejic *et al.* 1992; Cesnys 1993; Rewekant 1993; Henneberg & Steyn 1994; Macchiarelli & Salvadei 1994; Saldavei and Macchiarelli 1994; Coppa *et al.* 1995; Alekseeva and Buzhilova 1996, 1997; Della Casa 1996; Kozak 1996; Leben-Seljak 1996; Piontek *et al.* 1996; Sciulli *et al.* 1996; Pietrusewsky *et al.* 1997; Alesan *et al.* 1999; Buzhilova and Mednikova 1999; Bocquet-Appel and Demars 2000).

Nevertheless, the next 15 years saw researchers refocusing their attention on testing the accuracy and bias of the age indicator techniques used in osteological investigations. Initial studies examined this problem by utilizing cadaver samples to test the relationship between estimated age and known chronological age (see Usher, Chapter 3, this volume). Later, with the increased availability of archaeological skeletal samples from with documented individuals, researchers were able to examine the reliability of these methods (e.g., Lovejoy *et al.* 1985; Meindl *et al.* 1985, 1990; Gruspier and Mullen 1991; Saunders *et al.* 1992, 1993; Aiello and Molleson 1993; Bedford *et al.* 1993; Rogers and Saunders 1994; Lucy *et al.* 1995). During this period paleodemography saw a revival of model life table fitting techniques and the development of more sophisticated mathematical approaches that attempted to compensate for known biases in skeletal samples (Gage 1985, 1988, 1989, 1990; Jackes 1985; Boldsen 1988; Milner *et al.* 1989; Paine 1989; Siven 1991a,b; Konigsberg and Frankenberg 1992, 1994; Roth 1992; Wood *et al.* 1992a; Skytthe and Boldsen 1993; Lucy *et al.* 1995, 1996). However, in recent years, much of the debate regarding paleodemography has moved away from the methodological issues of sample reconstruction, to the more theoretical concern of sample representativeness (Lovejoy 1971; Piontek and Henneberg 1981; Milner *et al.* 1989; Paine 1989; Wood *et al.* 1992a; Hoppa 1996; Paine & Harpending 1996, 1998; Hoppa and Saunders 1998). With the more recent, detailed studies of historic cemetery skeletal samples, researchers have begun to test the representativeness of their samples by comparing the mortality data derived from the skeletal sample with the documentary mortality data associated with the cemetery from which the sample was drawn (Walker *et al.* 1988; Lanphear 1989; Herring *et al.* 1991; Molleson *et al.* 1993; Grauer and McNamara 1995; Higgins and Sirianni 1995; Molleson 1995; Saunders *et al.* 1995a,b; Scheuer and Bowman 1995; Sirianni and Higgins 1995). Infant underrepresentation and older adult underrepresentation, the two most commonly recognized biases in paleodemographic studies have been the focus of many investigations (e.g., Cipriano-Bechtle *et al.* 1996; Guy *et al.* 1997; Paine and Harpending 1998). Reiterating the impact of adult underenumeration on paleodemographic studies (Jackes 1992; Hoppa and Saunders 1998) Paine and Harpending (1998) observed that a deficiency in older adults (45 +) serves to inflate estimates of crude birth rate by 10 to 20%. At the other end of the spectrum, infant underrepresentation decreased both fertility and crude birth estimates by 20 to 25%.

While methodological issues relating to age determination and representativeness in skeletal samples remain a primary focus for refining answers to this problem, the current approach to understanding demographic structure in past populations has begun to shift. Ultimately, the focus of physical anthropology has been to refine estimates at the individual level in order to get some aggregate estimate of the population level. More recently, however, borrowing heavily from biostatistical sources, researchers have begun directly to estimate the mortality distribution of samples on the basis of the distribution of age indicator stages. While the difference is subtle, it is important, in that approaches try to avoid the broad range of error associated with estimates at the individual level. This, of course, means that there is now a distinction between methods most appropriate for estimating error in individual assessments of age, as would be important for forensic anthropology, and those for estimating error in aggregate assessments of demographic structure.

Recognizing that age estimation techniques in skeletal biology are less than 100% accurate, paleodemographic reconstructions of age structures have had to compensate for the possible error, or range of confidence, that is attributable to individual assessments. Jackes (1985, 1992) has suggested that probability distributions derived using this concept are preferable to previously used methods of smoothing. Konigsberg and Frankenberg (1992:239) demonstrated that techniques typically used to recast skeletal age distributions result in "an estimated age distribution which is neither a complete 'mimic' of the reference sample nor completely independent of the reference".

While Konigsberg and Frankenberg (1992) focused on age estimation with the life table and series of discrete age groups, they and a few others (e.g., Gage 1988; Wood *et al.* 1992a) anticipated that future directions would include the use of hazards analysis for estimating the age structure of skeletal samples. Indeed a variety of recent reviews (e.g., Konigsberg and Frankenberg 2001; Milner *et al.* 2000) all recognize that hazards analysis is now a practical and essential procedure for reconstruction paleodemo-graphic profiles. Hazards analysis provides a way of dealing with the age ranges associated with various methods, while at the same time easily incorporating related factors such as population growth (see Konigsberg and Frankenberg 2001; see also Wood *et al.*, Chapter 7, this volume).

Of particular interest to this approach is a return to bases for paleodemography. Angel (1969a,b) was a strong proponent of using age indicator groups and not assigning those groups mean ages based on the distribution in a reference sample. This same approach has been reiterated recently by osteologists. Jackes (2000) argues that, given the problems of accuracy in aging methods, we should be comparing the distribution of age indicator stages themselves between populations, rather that translating those into estimates of chronological age first. It seems clear, now, that the central tenet of paleodemography – the analysis of the life table – cannot be used. Rather, demographic profiles must be estimated directly from the distributions of age indicator data themselves.

Answering Petersen's challenge

The field of paleodemography has survived a series of battles over the last 25 years. The debates have continued spouting such publications as "Fare-well to Paleodemography", "Paleodemography: Resurrection or Ghost?",

"Paleodemography: Not Quite Dead" and most recently "Deconstructing Death in Paleodemography" (Bocquet-Appel and Masset 1982; Buikstra and Konigsberg 1985; Konigsberg and Frankenberg 1994, 2001). Dealing with critiques from both within and outside the anthropological community, the field has strived and struggled in order to better understand human survival in the past. This volume represents a true multidisciplinary endeavor between physical anthropologists, demographers, and biostatisticians to bring together their expertise to the problem of assessing human survivorship in the past.

Like any multidisciplinary project, there is a considerable amount of time spent educating one another in the relevant strengths and weaknesses of each others' fields. While many of our contributors are extremely versed in osteological, demographic, and statistical methods and theory, this repertoire of scholarly hats is not one that is often interchanged so comfortably by many physical anthropologists. While we do not believe that we have solved all the problems associated with this field of inquiry, we do believe that this volume provides new hope for really understanding demographic structure in populations in which skeletal samples have been found. Clearly there remain several issues that can be explored further.

By its very nature the question of human survival in the past falls within the purview of the historical sciences. Unlike many sciences in which an hypothesis is proposed and an experiment conducted to collect data to accept or reject that hypothesis, osteological studies by necessity or circumstance collect the data first and then put forward a number of questions and hypotheses. Since archaeological samples are collected retrospectively, there can be no premeditated control over factors of interest. As a result, interpretations are made that best fit with observable data. When these data change, so too must our interpretations. What does this mean for the story of human life expectancy? It remains a work in progress, but one for which there is now new hope for accurately answering this question.

References

Acsádi Gy and Nemeskéri J (1970) *History of human lifespan and mortality.* Budapest: Akadémiai Kiadó.
Aiello LC and Molleson T (1993) Are microscopic ageing techniques more accurate than macroscopic ageing techniques? *Journal of Archaeological Science* **20**, 689–704.

Alekseeva TI and Buzhilova AP (1996) [Medieval urban Russians according to anthropological data: origins, paleodemography, paleoecology.] In Russian. *Rossiiskaia Arkheologiia* **3**, 58–72.

Alekseeva TI and Buzhilova AP (1997) Medieval urban Russians according to anthropological data: origins, paleodemography, paleoecology. *Anthropology and Archeology of Eurasia* **35**, 42–62.

Alekseeva TI and Fedosova VN (1992) [The early stages of Slavic colonization of the Russian north. 1, Anthropological composition and paleodemography.] In Russian. *Voprosy antropologii* **86**, 8–23.

Alesan A, Malgosa A, and Simo C (1999) Looking into the demography of an Iron Age population in the western Mediterranean (1): mortality. *American Journal of Physical Anthropology* **110**, 285–301.

Angel JL (1947) The length of life in ancient Greece. *Journal of Gerontology* **2**, 18–24.

Angel JL (1954) Human biology, health and history in Greece from the first settlement until now. *Yearbook of American Philosophical Society* **98**, 168–174.

Angel JL (1968) Ecological aspects of paleodemography. In DR Brothwell (ed.): *The skeletal biology of earlier human populations.* London: Pergamon Press, pp. 263–270.

Angel JL (1969a) Paleodemography and human evolution. *American Journal of Physical Anthropology* **31**, 343–354.

Angel JL (1969b) The bases of paleodemography. *American Journal of Physical Anthropology* **30**, 427–438.

Angel JL (1972) Ecology and population in the eastern Mediterranean. *World Archaeology* **4**, 88–105.

Angel JL (1975) Paleoecology, palaeodemography and health. In S Polgar (ed.): *Population, ecology and social evolution.* Mouton: The Hague, pp. 167–190.

Angel JL, Suchey JM, İşcan MY, and Zimmerman MR (1986) Age at death estimated from the skeleton and viscera. In MR Zimmerman and J Lawrence (eds.): *Dating and age determination of biological materials.* London: Croom Helm, pp. 179–220.

Armelagos GJ and Medina C (1977) The demography of prehistoric populations. *Eugenics Society Bulletin* **9**, 8–14.

Asch DL (1976) *The Middle Woodland population of the Lower Illinois Valley: a study in paleodemographic methods.* Evanston, IL: Northwestern University Archeological Program.

Balteanu CA and Cantemir P (1991) Contributions à la connaissance de quelques aspects paléodémographiques chez la population néolithique de Chirnogi-Suvita. *Studi si cercetari de antropologie* **28**, 3–7.

Bedford ME, Russel KF, Lovejoy CO, Meindl RS, Simpson SW, and Stuart-Macadam PL (1993) Test of the multifactorial aging method using skeletons with known age-at-death from the Grant collection. *American Journal of Physical Anthropology* **91**, 287–297.

Bennett KA (1973) On the estimation of some demographic characteristics of a prehistoric population from the American Southwest. *American Journal of Physical Anthropology* **39**, 723–731.

Berner M (1992) Das frühbronzezeitliche Gräberfeld von Franzhausen I, Niederösterreich 2. Demographische Analyse. *Anthropologischer Anzeiger* **50**, 13–26.

Blakely L (1971) Comparison of the mortality profiles of Archaic, Middle Woodland, and Middle Mississippian skeletal populations. *American Journal of Physical Anthropology* **34**, 43–53.

Blakely L (1977) Sociocultural implications of demographic data from Etowah, Georgia. In R Blakely (ed.): *Biocultural Adaptation in Prehistoric America.* Athens, GA: University of Georgia Press, pp. 45–66.

Bocquet-Appel JP (1977) Perspectives paléodémographiques. Thèse d'Anthropologie Historique, École des Hautes Études en Sciences Sociales, Paris.

Bocquet-Appel JP (1978) Méthodes d'estimation de l'age au décès des squelettes d'adults et structure démographique des populations passés. In MD Garralda and RM Grande (eds.): *I Simposio de Antropologia Biologica de España*, Madrid, pp. 37–47.

Bocquet-Appel JP (1979) Une approche de la fécondité des populations inhumanées. *Bulletins et Mémoirs de la Société d'Anthropologie de Paris* **6**, 261–268.

Bocquet-Appel JP (1986) Once upon a time: paleodemography. *Mitteilungen der Berliner Gesellschaft für Anthropologie, Ethnologie und Urgeschichte* **7**, 127–133.

Bocquet-Appel JP and Demars PY (2000) Population kinetics in the upper Paleolithic in western Europe. *Journal of Archaeological Science* **27**, 551–570.

Bocquet-Appel JP and Masset C (1977) Estimateurs en paléodémographie. *L'Homme* **27**, 65–90.

Bocquet-Appel JP and Masset C (1982) Farwell to paleodemography. *Journal of Human Evolution* **11**, 321–333.

Bocquet-Appel JP and Masset C (1985) Paleodemography: resurrection or ghost? *Journal of Human Evolution* **14**, 107–111.

Brothwell DR (1971) Paleodemography. In W Brass (ed.) *Biological aspects of demography.* London: Taylor Francis, pp. 111–130.

Buikstra JE and Konigsberg LW (1985) Paleodemography: critiques and controversies. *American Anthropologist* **87**, 316–334.

Buzhilova AP and Mednikova MB (1999) [Koasar, an ancient population from the eastern Aral region: paleodemography, osteometry, growth arrest.] In Russian. *Homo* **50**, 66–79.

Cesnys G (1993). [Paleodemography, anthropology and population genetics of the Plinkaigalis population.] In Lithuanian. *Lietuvos Archeologija* **10**, 182–196, 213–218.

Cipriano-Bechtle A, Grupe G, and Schroter P (1996) Ageing and life expectancy in the early Middle Ages. *Homo*, **46**, 267–279.

Clarke S (1977) Mortality trends in prehistoric populations. *Human Biology* **49**, 181–186.

Coale AJ and Demeny P (1966) *Regional model life tables and stable populations.*

Princeton, NJ: Princeton University Press.

Coppa A, Cucina A, Chiarelli B, Luna Calderon F, and Mancinelli D (1995) Dental anthropology and paleodemography of the Precolumbian populations of Hispaniola from the third millennium B.C. to the Spanish conquest. *Human Evolution* **10**, 153–167.

Cunha E, Araújo T, Marrafa C, Santos A, and Silva A (1992) Paléodémographie de la population médiévale portugaise de Fão: résultats préliminaires. *Rivista di Antropologia* **70**, 237–245.

Della Casa P (1996) Linking anthropological and archaeological evidence: notes on the demographic structure and social organization of the Bronze Age necropolis Velika Gruda in Montenegro. *Arheoloski vestnik* **47**, 135–143.

Gage TB (1985) Demographic estimation from anthropological data: new methods. *Current Anthropology* **26**, 644–647.

Gage TB (1988) Mathematical hazards models of mortality: an alternative to model life tables. *American Journal of Physical Anthropology* **86**, 429–441.

Gage TB (1989) Bio-mathematical approaches to the study of human variation and mortality. *Yearbook of Physical Anthropology* **32**, 185–214.

Gage TB (1990) Variation and classification of human age patterns of mortality: analysis using competing hazards models. *Human Biology* **62**, 589–617.

Grauer AL (1991) Patterns of life and death: the palaeodemography of Medieval York. In H Bush and M Zvelebil (eds.): *Health in past societies*. British Archaeological Reports International Series no. 567. Oxford: Tempus Reparatum, pp. 67–80.

Grauer AL and McNamara EM (1995) A piece of Chicago's past: exploring childhood mortality in the Dunning Poorhouse Cemetery. In AL Grauer (ed.): *The not too distant past: reconstructing the past through skeletal analysis*. New York: Wiley-Liss Inc., pp. 91–103.

Greene DL, Van Gerven DP, and Armelagos GJ (1986) Life and death in ancient populations: bones of contention in paleodemography. *Human Evolution* **1**, 193–207.

Gruspier KL and Mullen GJ (1991) Maxillary suture obliteration: a test of the Mann method. *Journal of Forensic Sciences* **36**, 512–519.

Guy H, Masset C and Baud C (1997) Infant taphonomy. *International Journal of Osteoarchaeology* **7**, 221–229.

Hassan FA (1981) *Demographic archaeology*. New York: Academic Press.

Henneberg M (1977) Proportion of dying children in paleodemographic studies: estimation by guess or by methodological approach. *Przeglad Antropologiczny* **43**, 105–114.

Henneberg M and Steyn M (1994) Preliminary report on the paleodemography of the K2 and Mapungubwe populations (South Africa). *Human Biology* **66**, 105–120.

Herring DA, Saunders SR, and Boyce G (1991) Bones and burial registers: infant mortality in a nineteenth century cemetery from Upper Canada. *Northeast Historical Archaeology* **20**, 54–70.

Higgins RL and Sirianni JE (1995) An assessment of health and mortality of

22   R. D. Hoppa

nineteenth century Rochester, New York using historic records and the Highland Park skeletal collection. In AL Grauer (ed.): *The not too distant past: reconstructing the past through skeletal analysis.* New York: Wiley-Liss Inc., pp. 121–136.

Hooton, EA (1930) *The Indians of Pecos Pueblo: a study of their skeletal remains.* New Haven, CT: Yale University Press.

Hoppa RD (1996) Representativeness and bias in cemetery samples: implications for palaeodemographic reconstructions of past populations. PhD dissertation, McMaster University.

Hoppa RD and Saunders SR (1998) The MAD legacy: how meaningful is mean age-at-death in skeletal samples. *Human Evolution* **13**, 1–14.

Horowitz S, Armelagos G, and Wachter K (1988) On generating birth rates from skeletal populations. *American Journal of Physical Anthropology* **76**, 189–196.

Howell N (1976) Toward a uniformitarian theory of human paleodemography. In RH Ward and KM Weiss (eds.): *The demographic evolution of human populations.* New York: Academic Press, pp. 25–40.

Howell N (1979) *The demography of the Dobe !Kung.* New York: Academic Press.

Howell N (1982) Village compostition implied by a paleodemographic life table: the Libben site. *American Journal of Physical Anthropology* **59**, 263–269.

Howell N (1986) Demographic anthropology. *Annual Reviews of Anthropology* **15**, 219–246.

Howell N and Lehotay V (1978) AMBUSH: a computer program for stochastic microsimulation of small human populations. *American Anthropologist* **15**, 219–246.

İşcan MY and Loth SR (1989) Osteological manifestations of age in the adult. In MY İşcan and KAR Kennedy (eds.): *Reconstruction of life from the skeleton.* New York: Wiley-Liss, pp. 23–40.

Jackes MK (1985) Pubic symphysis age distributions. *American Journal of Physical Anthropology* **68**, 281–299.

Jackes MK (1992) Paleodemography: problems and techniques. In SR Saunders and MA Katzenberg (eds.): *Skeletal biology of past peoples: research methods.* New York: Wiley-Liss, pp. 189–224.

Jackes MK (2000) Building the bases for paleodemographic analysis: adult age determination. In MA Katzenberg and SR Saunders (eds.): *Biological anthropology of the human skeleton.* New York: Wiley-Liss, pp. 417–466.

Johansson SR and Horowitz S (1986) Estimating mortality in skeletal populations: influence of the growth rate on the interpretations of levels and trends during the transition to agriculture. *American Journal of Physical Anthropology* **71**, 233–250.

Kemkes-Grottenthaler A (1996) Critical evaluation of osteomorphognostic methods to estimate adult age at death: a test of the "complex method". *Homo* **46**, 280–292.

Kennedy KA (1969) Paleodemography of India and Ceylon since 3000 B.C. *American Journal of Physical Anthropology* **31**, 315–319.

Kobayashi K (1967) Trends in the length of life based on human skeletons from prehistoric to modern times in Japan. *Journal of the Faculty of Science, University of Tokyo*, section V, *Anthropology* **2**, 109–160.

Konigsberg LW and Frankenberg SR (1992) Estimation of age structure in anthropological demography. *American Journal of Physical Anthropology* **89**, 235–256.

Konigsberg LW and Frankenberg SR (1994) Paleodemography: "Not quite dead". *Evolutionary Anthropology* **3**, 92–105.

Konigsberg LW and Frankenberg SR (2001) Deconstructing death in paleodemography. *American Journal of Physical Anthropology*, in press.

Kozak J (1996) [An early mediaeval cemetery at Sowinki – anthropological and paleodemographic analysis.] In Polish. *Przeglad Antropologiczny* **59**, 91–96.

Lankester ER (1870) *On comparative longevity in man and the lower animals.* London: Macmillan.

Lanphear KM (1989) Testing the value of skeletal samples in demographic research: a comparison with vital registration samples. *International Journal of Anthropology* **4**, 185–193.

Leben-Seljak P (1996) [Paleodemographic analysis of the necropolis at the parish church in Kranj.] In Slovenian. *Antropoloski Zvezki* **4**, 95–107.

Liversidge HM (1994) Accuracy of age estimation from developing teeth of a population of known age. *International Journal of Osteoarchaeology* **4**, 37–45.

Lovejoy CO (1971) Methods for the detection of census error. *American Anthropologist* **73**, 101–109.

Lovejoy CO, Meindl RS, Pryzbeck TR, Barton TS, Heiple KG, and Kotting D (1977) Paleodemography of the Libben site, Ottawa county, Ohio. *Science* **198**, 291–293.

Lovejoy CO, Meindl RS, Pryzbeck TR, and Mensforth RP (1985) Chronological metamorphosis of the auricular surface of the ilium: a new method for the determination of adult skeletal age. *American Journal of Physical Anthropology* **68**, 15–28.

Lovejoy CO, Meindl RS, Tague RG, and Latimer B (1995) The senescent biology of the hominoid pelvis: its bearing on the pubic symphysis and auricular surface as age-at-death indicators in the human skeleton. *Rivista di Antropologia* **73**, 31–49.

Lovejoy CO, Meindl RS, Tague RG, and Latimer B (1997) The comparative senescent biology of the hominoid pelvis and its implications for the use of age-at-death indicators in the human skeleton. In RR Paine (ed.): *Integrating archaeological demography: in multidisciplinary approaches to prehistoric population.* Occasional Papers 24, Center for Archaeological Investigations, Carbondale, IL: Southern Illinois University, pp. 43–63.

Lucy D, Aykroyd RG, Pollard AM, and Solheim T (1996) A Bayesian approach to adult age estimation from dental observations by Johanson's age changes. *Journal of Forensic Science* **41**, 189–194.

Lucy D, Pollard AM, and Roberts CA (1995) A comparison of three dental techniques for estimating age at death in humans. *Journal of Archaeological Science* **22**, 417–428.

Macchiarelli R and Salvadei L (1994) Paleodemography and selective funerary practices at "Latium Vetus", middle-Tyrrhenian Italy. *Anthropologischer Anzeiger* **52**, 37–52.

MacDonnell WR (1913) On the expectation of life in ancient Rome and in the Provinces of Hispania and Lusitania and Africa. *Biometrika* **9**, 366–380.

Masset C (1973) La démographie des populations inhumées. Essai de paléodémographie. *L'Homme* **13**, 95–131.

Masset C and Parzysz B (1985) Démographie des cimitières? Incertitude des estimateurs en paléodemographie. *L'Homme* **25**, 147–154.

McKinley K (1971) Survivorship in gracile and robust australopithecines: a demographic comparison and proposed birth model. *American Journal of Physical Anthropology* **34**, 417–426.

Meindl R and Russel KF (1998) Recent advances in method and theory in paleodemography. *Annual Review of Anthropology* **27**, 375–399.

Meindl RS, Lovejoy CO, Mensforth RP, and Walker RA (1985) A revised method of age determination using the os pubis, with a review of tests of accuracy of other current methods of pubic symphyseal aging. *American Journal of Physical Anthropology* **68**, 29–45.

Meindl RS, Russel KF, and Lovejoy CO (1990) Reliability of age at death in the Hamann–Todd collection: validity of subselection procedures used in blind tests of the summary age technique. *American Journal of Physical Anthropology* **83**, 349–357.

Milner GR, Humpf DA, and Harpending HC (1989) Pattern matching of age-at-death distributions in paleodemographic analysis. *American Journal of Physical Anthropology* **80**, 49–58.

Miu G and Botezatu D (1991) Considerations sur les caracteristiques paléodémographiques chez quelques populations qui ont veçu sur notre territoire (IIIe–Ve siècles n.e). *Studi si cercetari de antropologie* **28**, 13–18.

Molleson TI (1995) Rates of ageing in the eighteenth century. In SR Saunders and DA Herring (eds.): *Grave reflections: portraying the past through cemetery studies*. Toronto: Canadian Scholars' Press, pp. 199–222.

Molleson T, Cox M, Waldron A, and Whittaker DK (1993) *The Spitalfields report*, vol. 2, *The middling sort*. York: CBA Research Report no. 86.

Moore JA, Swedlund AC, and Armelagos GJ (1975) The use of life tables in paleodemography. *American Antiquity*, vol. 40 Part 2[2], Memoir 30, AC Swedlund (ed.), pp. 57–70.

Owsley D and Bass W (1979) A demographic analysis of skeletons from the Larson Site (39WWZ), Walworth County, South Dakota: vital statistics. *American Journal of Physical Anthropology* **51**, 145–154.

Paine RR (1989) Model life table fitting by maximum likelihood estimation: a procedure to reconstruct paleodemographic characteristics from skeletal age distributions. *American Journal of Physical Anthropology* **79**, 51–61.

Paine RR (ed.) (1997) *Integrating archaeological demography: multidisciplinary ap-*

proaches to prehistoric population. Carbondale, IL: Southern Illinois University.

Paine RR and Harpending HC (1996) Assessing the reliability of palaeodemographic fertility estimators using simulated skeletal distributions. *American Journal of Physical Anthropology* **101**, 151–160.

Paine RR and Harpending HC (1998) Effect of sampling bias on paleodemographic fertility estimates. *American Journal of Physical Anthropology* **105**, 231–240.

Palkovich A (1978) A model of the dimensions of mortality and its application to paleodemography. Ph.D. dissertation, Northwestern University.

Pardini E, Mannucci P, and Lombardi Pardini EC (1983) Sex ratio, età media di vita, mortalità differenziale per età e per sesso in una popolazione campana vissuta a Pontecagnano, Salerno, nei secoli VII–IV a.C. *Archivo per l'Antropologia e la Etnologia* **113**, 269–285.

Parsche F (1991) Paläodemographische und Kulturhistorische Untersuchungen an Skelettfunden der vor- und Frühdynastischen Nekropole in Minshat Abu Omar (östliches Nildelta). *Anthropologischer Anzeiger* **49**, 49–64.

Passarello P (1977) Paleodemographic aspects of the Iron Age in Italy: the Veio's Villa-novians. *Journal of Human Evolution* **6**, 175–179.

Pearson K (1902) On the change in expectation of life in man during a period of circa 2000 years. *Biometrika* **1**, 261–264.

Petersen W (1975) A demographer's view of prehistoric demography. *Current Anthropology* **16**, 227–237.

Piasecki E (1975) [An endeavour to characterize the age-structure of the population of Kom el-Dikka in Alexandria in the 13–14th century, based on data of a skeletal population.] In Polish. *Materiały i Prace Antopologiczne* **89**, 117–146.

Pietrusewsky M, Douglas MT, and Ikehara-Quebral RM (1997) An assessment of health and disease in the prehistoric inhabitants of the Mariana Islands. *American Journal of Physical Anthropology* **104**, 315–342.

Piontek J (1979) Procesy mikroewolucyine w europejskich populajach ludzkich. *Uniwersytet im. Adama Mickiewicza, Series Anthropology*, No. 6, Pozna.

Piontek J and Henneberg M (1981) Mortality changes in a Polish rural community (1350–1972), and estimation of their evolutionary significance. *American Journal of Physical Anthropology* **54**, 129–138.

Piontek J, Wiercinska A, and Wiercinska A (1996) Mortality structure in Mesolithic, Neolithic and Early Bronze Age populations of Central Europe and Ukraine: a new methodological approach. *Anthropologie* **34**, 307–313.

Plog F (1975) Demographic studies in southwestern prehistory. In AC Swedlund (ed.): Population studies in archaeology and biological anthropology. *Society of American Archaeology Memoir* **30**, 94–103.

Rewekant A (1993) Mortality changes in central European populations from Bronze Age to Iron Age: comparative analysis. *International Journal of Anthropology* **8**, 73–81.

Rogers TL and Saunders SR (1994) Accuracy of sex determination using morphological traits of the human pelvis. *Journal of Forensic Science* **39**, 1047–1056.

Roth EA (1992) Applications of demographic models to paleodemography. In SR Saunders and MA Katzenberg (eds.): *Skeletal biology of past peoples: research methods.* New York: Wiley-Liss, pp. 175–188.

Saldavei L and Macchiarelli R (1994) Insiemi di mortalità e realisticità delle stime paleodemografiche per l'età del Ferro dell'Italia centro-meridionale. *Bullettino di Paletnologia Italiana (Roma)* **85**, 431–448.

Sattenspiel L and Harpending H (1983) Stable populations and skeletal age. *American Antiquity* **48**, 489–498.

Saunders SR, FitzGerald C, Rogers T, Dudar C, and McKillop H (1992) A test of several methods of skeletal age estimation using a documented archaeological sample. *Canadian Society for Forensic Science Journal* **25**, 97–118.

Saunders SR, DeVito C, Herring DA, Southern R, and Hoppa RD (1993) Accuracy tests of tooth formation age estimations for human skeletal remains. *American Journal of Physical Anthropology* **92**, 173–188.

Saunders SR, Herring DA, and Boyce G (1995a) Can skeletal samples accurately represent the living populations they come from? The St. Thomas' cemetery site, Belleville, Ontario. In AL Grauer (ed.): *The not too distant past: reconstructing the past through skeletal analysis.* New York: Wiley-Liss, pp. 69–89.

Saunders SR, Herring DA, Sawchuk LA, and Boyce G (1995b) The nineteenth-century cemetery at St. Thomas' Anglican Church Belleville: skeletal remains, parish records and censuses. In SR Saunders and DA Herring (eds.): *Grave reflections. Portraying the past through cemetery studies.* Toronto: Canadian Scholars Press, pp. 93–118.

Scheuer JL and Bowman JE (1995) Correlation of documentary and skeletal evidence in the St. Bride's crypt population. In SR Saunders and DA Herring (eds.): *Grave reflections. Portraying the past through cemetery studies.* Toronto: Canadian Scholars Press, pp. 49–70.

Sciulli PW, Giesen MJ, and Paine RR (1996). Paleodemography of the Pearson complex (33SA9) Eiden phase cemetery. *Archaeology of Eastern North America* **24**, 81–94.

Senyürek MS (1947) A note on the duration of life on the ancient inhabitants of Anatolia. *American Journal of Physical Anthropology* **5**, 55–66.

Sirianni JE and Higgins RL (1995) A comparison of death records from the Monroe County Almshouse with skeletal remains from the associated Highland Park cemetery. In SR Saunders and DA Herring (eds.): *Grave reflections. Portraying the past through cemetery studies.* Toronto: Canadian Scholars Press, pp. 71–92.

Siven CH (1991a) On estimating mortalities from osteological age data. *International Journal of Anthropology* **6**, 97–110.

Siven CH (1991b) On reconstructing the (once) living population from osteological data. *International Journal of Anthropology* **6**, 111–118.

Skytthe A and Boldsen JL (1993) A method for construction of standards for determination of skeletal age at death. *American Journal of Physical Anthropology Supplement* **16**, 182.

Srejic MD, Zivanovic S, and Letic V (1992). [A contribution to the medieval

Serbian paleodemography.] In Serbian. *Rivista di Antropologia* **70**, 171–173.

Swedlund AC and Armelagos GJ (1969) Un recherche en paléodémographie: la Nubia Soudanaise. *Annales: Économie, Sociétés, Civilization* **24**, 1287–1298.

Ubelaker DH (1974) Reconstruction of demographic profiles from ossuary samples. A case study from the Tidewater Potomac. *Smithsonian Contributions to Anthropology* no. 18. Washington, DC: Smithsonian Institution Press.

Ubelaker DH (1989) *Human skeletal remains: excavation, analysis and interpretation* 2nd edn. Washington: Smithsonian Institution, Manuals on Archaeology, 2.

Vallois HV (1937) La durée de la vie chez l'homme fossile. *Anthropologie* **47**, 499–532.

Vallois HV (1960) Vital statistics in prehistoric populations as determined from archaeological data. In RF Heizer and SF Cook (eds.): *The application of quantitative methods in archaeology*. Chicago: Viking Fund Publications in Anthropology no. 28, pp. 186–222.

Van Gerven DP and Armelagos GJ (1983) "Farewell to paleodemography?" Rumors of its death have been greatly exaggerated. *Journal of Human Evolution* **12**, 353–360.

Van Gerven DP, Sandford MK, and Hummert JR (1981) Mortality and culture change in Nubia's Batn el Hajar. *Journal of Human Evolution* **10**, 395–408.

Walker PL, Johnson JR, and Lambert PM (1988) Age and sex biases in the preservation of human skeletal remains. *American Journal of Physical Anthropology* **76**, 183–188.

Watson PJ, LeBlanc SA, and Redman CL (1984) *Archaeological explanation: the scientific method in archaeology*. New York: Columbia University Press.

Weidenreich F (1939) The duration of life of fossil man in China and the pathological lesions found on his skeleton. *Chinese Medical Journal* **55**, 34–44.

Weiss KM (1973) Demographic models for anthropology. *Memoirs of the Society for American Archaeology* no. 27.

Weiss KM (1975) Demographic disturbance and the use of life tables in anthropology. *American Antiquity*, vol. 40 Part 2[2], Memoir 30, AC Swedlund (ed.), pp. 46–56.

Welinder S (1979) Prehistoric demography. *Acta Archaeologica Lundensia* Series 8.

Willcox WF (1938) Length of life in the early Roman Empire. *Congrès International de la Population* **2**, 14–22.

Wilson C (ed.) (1985) *The dictionary of demography*. Oxford: Basil Blackwell Ltd.

Wittwer-Backofen U (1989). Zur Paläodemographie des Neolithikums. *Homo* **40**, 64–81.

Wittwer-Backofen U (1991). Nekropole und Siedlung: Moglichkeiten und Grenzen der Rekonstruktion prahistorischer Bevolkerungsstrukturen. *Mitteilungen der Berliner Gesellschaft für Anthropologie, Ethnologie und Urgeschichte* **12**, 31–37.

Wood JW (1998) A theory of preindustrial population dynamics: demography, economy, and well-being in Malthusian systems. *Current Anthropology* **39**, 99–135.

Wood JW, Milner GR, Harpending HC, and Weiss KM (1992a) The osteological paradox: problems of inferring prehistoric health from skeletal samples. *Current Anthropology* **33**, 343–370.

Wood JW, Holman DJ, Weiss KM, Buchanan AV, and LeFor B (1992b) Hazards models for human population biology. *Yearbook of Physical Anthropology* **35**, 43–87.

3   *Reference samples:*
the first step in linking biology and age in the human skeleton

BETHANY M. USHER

Introduction

One of the most overlooked, but basic, sources of error in skeletal age estimation comes from problems with the human osteological reference collection on which the method is based. The purpose of this chapter is to review the need for known-age and sex human skeletal collections to be used both for testing current age estimation methods and for developing new ones, and to present a database of such reference collections world-wide.

Bocquet-Appel and Masset (1982) were the first researchers to stress the importance of the reference sample. They showed that, because of the simple regression methods being used for age estimation methods, the age structure of the reference population was reflected in the estimated age distribution in the target (unknown or archaeological) sample. The authors saw this as one of the fatal flaws of paleodemography, and although many did not agree that it was insurmountable, the paper did spur a reanalysis of age estimation methods (see e.g., Konigsberg and Frankenberg 1992, 1994; Milner *et al.* 1997). However, none of these concentrated on the reliability and representativeness of reference collections, which are usually taken for granted.

There are two ways to deal with the problems with the structure of the reference population. The first is to use a reference collection of skeletons with a uniform distribution of ages. This has been the most logical method in new age estimation methods (see e.g., Boldsen *et al.*, Chapter 5, this volume). However, this procedure assumes that the skeletons in the target population have an equal chance of being all ages (Konigsberg and Frank-enberg 1994). While not necessarily wrong, this method means that the information about the age distribution in the target sample is discarded (Konigsberg and Frankenberg 1992). The second method of dealing with the reference collection structure is to use statistical methods, such as those presented in the other chapters in this volume, to avoid the affect of the age structure of the reference population. In these cases, a reference population that adequately represents all ages for the features being used in the method is all that is needed. In either case, good reference collections provide the foundation of any age estimation method.

Methods

A major portion of this research has consisted of compiling a database of worldwide reference collections (Table 3.1). The preference has been for anthropologists to use a small number of collections, because they are well known and easily accessed. The most studied collections are the Terry Collection, housed in Washington, DC, at the Smithsonian Institution's National Museum of Natural History, and the Hamann–Todd Collection at the Cleveland Museum of Natural History. An astonishing amount of all age and sex estimation research, published both in the USA and in other countries, has been based on these collections, despite their known discrepancies. A search of PubMed (http://www.ncbi.nlm.nih.gov/entrez/query.fcg) in October 2000, resulted in 73 references to the Terry Collection, 32 to the Hamann–Todd Collection, 23 to the English Spitalfield Collection, and fewer than 10 for any other collection. Therefore, it is important to compile a list of known-age skeletons that are directly available or have data available for research.

Information about reference collections was gathered through literature searches in MedLine, PubMed, Anthropological Literature, and Anthropological Index Online, and through searches on the Internet concentrating on museums and departments of anthropology and anatomy at universities and medical schools. Additional information came through personal communication with curators, who were often able to refer me to additional collections. Most collections listed here contain complete skeletons. However, because different collections meet different needs, there are several collections included that do not contain the entire skeleton, or a complete age range. There are several fetal and child skeletal collections listed, including the Smithsonian fetal and infant, and the Johns Hopkins Fetal Collection. There are also collections that include only certain elements. The Florence and Amsterdam anatomy collections comprise mostly skulls, and the Okamoto Research Laboratory of Dentistry Collection has collections of human teeth with known identification. Several collections consist of radiographs of human bones (e.g., the Brush–Bolton Collection), and others have only selected elements. For example, St Thomas Anglican Church has only written records, measurements, and tissue samples, and the Suchey collection has pubic symphyses of known individuals. The Forensic Anthropology Data Bank contains extensive, standardized data about modern forensic cases (Jantz and Jantz 1999).

This research is ongoing. The table is not complete; new collections and additional information are being added regularly. Therefore, the table presented here is for initial information only. A more complete table, with contact and access information, links to email addresses and web sites, and updated information about the collections is available at the Reference Collection website (www2.potsdam.edu/usherbm/reference).

Discussion

Despite the fact that no one collection is "ideal", a set of characteristics of an ideal sample was compiled to highlight the strengths and weaknesses of the different collections, and to provide a standard for new collections. An ideal reference collection has several characteristics. The first is that the ages-at-death of the skeletons are known. Many collections, including the Terry Collection, that are called "known age" have some or all skeletons with ages that were self-reported. Demographers have ample data that people do not always give accurate information about their ages, because either they do not know their true age or they choose for cultural reasons to misrepresent their age (Howell 1976a). Therefore, a good reference collection will have verified ages that have used vital records to collaborate a self-reported age.

The second issue of concern with reference collections is that most real collections contain a select subset of individuals. An ideal reference collection would also have a good representation of the variation present in the population of interest. This would include individuals of various socioeconomic statuses, races, and health. Because these real collections are based on one of several collection strategies that produce biased samples, most do not fit the ideal description. The first collection strategy is epitomized by the Terry and Hamann–Todd Osteological Collections, where anatomy departments curated all skeletons from their dissection laboratories. These individuals included both unclaimed or indigent bodies from the state, and the bodies of people who willed that their bodies be used for research. A study by Ericksen (1982) showed, that while there were differences between the "regular" (unclaimed body) collection and the willed bodies in the Terry Collection, presumably reflecting differences in socioeconomic status, these differences were not ubiquitous and did not show clearly that the "regular" skeletons were different enough to invalidate most age estimation procedures.

Table 3.1. *List of known-age human osteological reference collections. For additional information, see the Reference Collection website (www2.potsdam.edu/usherbm/reference)*

Name	Number of skeletons	Ages (years)	Males	Females	Origin	Location	Example references
Amsterdam Laboratory of Anatomy and Embryology	256 crania					Amsterdam, Netherlands	Perizonious 1984
Banaras Hindu University	>244	Adult	>176	>68	Varanasi zone, India	Department of Anatomy, Institute of Medical Sciences, Banaras Hindu University, Varanasi, India	Singh *et al.* 1974, 1975; Singh and Singh 1972
Belgian femurs	>416					Belgium	Defrise-Gussenhoven and Orban-Segebarth 1984
Brush–Bolton Collection		Children				Case Western Reserve University, USA	Scoles *et al.* 1988
Chiang Mai University	104	18–90	70	34	Donated remains from individuals who died at Chiang Mai University hospital	Chiang Mai City, Thailand	King 1997; King *et al.* 1998
Coimbra	>121					Coimbra University, Coimbra, Portugal	Cogoluenhes 1984

Collection					Description	Institution	Reference
Dart Collection, Department of Anatomical Sciences						Faculty of Health Sciences, University of Witwatersrand, South Africa	Kieser et al. 1987, 1992, 1996; Loth and Henneberg 1996
Department of Anatomy and Cell Biology						Philipps University, Marburg, South Africa	
Duckworth Osteological Collection						University of Cambridge, UK	
FACES Laboratory Collection					Forensic cases	Department of Geography and Anthropology, Louisiana State University, USA	Trudell 1999
Ferraz de Macedo						Lisbon, Portugal	Hauser and De Stefano 1985
Florence skull	83	13–62	44	39	Unclaimed indigents from Florence hospital	Museo Nazionale di Antropologia e Etnologia, Florence, Italy	Moggi-Cecchi et al. 1994
Florida Atlantic University Forensic Anthropology Data Bank	0				Forensic cases	Boca Raton, FL, USA	
					Forensic cases	University of Tennessee, USA	Jantz and Jantz 1999
Frasetto Collection	>200	19 to >65	>100	>100	Sardinian, exhumed around 1900 from Sassari cemetery	Dipartimento di Biologia Evoluzionistica Sperimentale, Bologna, Italy	Gualdi-Russo and Russo 1995; Gualdi-Russo 1998; Gualdi-Russo et al. 1999

Table 3.1. (cont.)

Name	Number of skeletons	Ages (years)	Males	Females	Origin	Location	Example references
Grant Collection	202	Majority (147) >40	175	27	Unclaimed bodies	University of Toronto, Department of Anthropology, Canada	Bedford et al. 1993; Rogers 1999
Hamann–Todd Collection	>3000				Cadaver	Cleveland Museum of Natural History, OH, USA	Scoles et al. 1991; Holland 1991; Marino 1995; Simms 1989; Hershkovitz et al. 1999
Hanged men[a]	3	17–26	3	0	Southern Ontario		Pfeiffer 1992
Harvia family cemetery[a]	6	25–98	2	4	Southern Ontario		Pfeiffer 1992
Hong Kong Collection	94	24–88	68	26	Southern China, excavation of known individuals from Wo Hop Shick cemetery	Department of Anatomy, Hong Kong	King 1997
Hungarian Natural History Museum, Anthropology Department	>10				Excavation of church basement	Natural History Museum, Budapest, Hungary	Hershkovitz et al. 1999
I. Gemmerich Collection	151	6–95	48	103	Modern cemeteries of the Vaud Canton	Department of Anthropology and Ecology, University of Geneva, Switzerland	Gemmerich 1999

Collection	No.	Age	Males	Females	Sample	Institution	Reference
Institute of Anatomy	101	36–100	57	44	Body donors	Institute of Anatomy, University of Technology, Aachen, Germany	Prescher and Bohndorf 1993
Institute of Forensic Medicine	Large number >205	All	205		Cadaver donors	University of Vienna, Austria	Szilvassy and Kritscher 1990
Institute of Forensic Sciences					Modern Chinese	Ministry of Public Security, Beijing, PRC	Liu et al. 1988
Institute of Legal Medicine	>80	25–80	>40	>40	Southern Italian	Institute of Legal Medicine, University of Bari, Italy	Introna et al. 1998
Istituto di Anatomia	742	All	424	317	General and mental hospital in Siena	Istituto di Anatomia, Siena, Italy	Guidotti 1984; Bastianini et al. 1985; Susanne 1985; Guidotti et al. 1986; Brasili-Gualandi and Gualdi-Russo 1989
Jikei University School of Medicine	>90				Japan	Jikei University, Japan	Tanaka 1999; Işcan et al. 1994
Johns Hopkins Fetal Collection						Case Western Reserve University, Cleveland, OH, USA	Hershkovitz et al. 1999
M.R. Drennan Museum and Departmental Specimen Collection	~250				Cadaver	University of Cape Town, South Africa	
Morphology Collection	236	30–80s			Cadavers from NYU Medical School, Long Island Medical College, and the Cornell Medical School	American Museum of Natural History, New York, USA	

Table 3.1. (*cont.*)

Name	Number of skeletons	Ages (years)	Males	Females	Origin	Location	Example references
Musée d'Anatomie Delmas-Orfila-Rouvière						V. René Descartes University, Paris, France	
Museo do Departamento de Anatomia	492	Adult				Instituto de Ciencias Biomedicas da Universidade de São Paul, Brazil	de Francisco *et al.* 1990
Museum of Pathological Anatomy	>50 000	All			Mostly pathological	Rome, Italy	Beighton *et al.* 1994
Museum Vrolik, Department of Medicine, Academic Medical Centre					Private collection	Department of Medicine, Academic Medical Centre, Amsterdam, Netherlands	Oostra *et al.* 1998a–e; Baljet and Oostra 1999
National Museum of Health and Medicine					Fetal, Civil War, forensic, pathological	Washington, DC, USA	Barbian *et al.* 2000
Okamoto Research Laboratory of Dentistry	0					Yonago, Japan	Aoki 1990; Morita 1990
Palmer Collection Quakers	2200	All			Pathological	Davenport, IA, USA Bournemouth, England	
Royal College of Surgeons of England Museums						London, UK	

Smithsonian Institution Fetal and Infant Collection	>300			Fetal and infant		Smithsonian Institution, Washington, DC, USA	Curran and Weaver 1983; Ubelaker 1989; Weaver 1980
Spitalfields Collection				All	Christ Church, Spitalfields	Natural History Museum, London, UK	Schutkowski 1993; Humphrey 1998; Liversidge 1994; Scheuer and Maclaughlin-Black 1994
Spitalfried Hof St Johann	83	42	41	17–75		Basel, Switzerland	Stout et al. 1996
SR Atkinson Library of Applied Anatomy and the P&S Comparative Anatomy Collections	>1500			*In utero* to adult	Autopsies and biological warehouses	University of the Pacific School Dentistry, San Francisco, USA	Eversole et al. 1986
St Bride's, London	56	30	26	22–90	Church of St Bride, Fleet Street, London	British Museum (Natural History), London, UK	Scheuer and Maclaughlin-Black 1994; Day and Pitcher-Wilmott 1975
St Thomas Anglican Church	80			All	Partial excavation of St Thomas Anglican Church cemetery, burials 1821–1874	London, UK	Saunders et al. 1992
Stirrup Court Cemetery[a]	6	2	4	45–76	Southern Ontario		Pfeiffer 1992

Table 3.1. (cont.)

Name	Number of skeletons	Ages (years)	Males	Females	Origin	Location	Example references
Suchey Public Collection	1225	14 to 99	739	273	Modern individuals autopsied at the Office of the Chief Medical Examiner, County of Los Angeles	California State University, Fullerton, USA	Klepinger et al. 1992; Sutherland and Suchey 1991
Terry Collection	>1500				Unclaimed bodies and donated	National Museum of Natural History, Smithsonian Institution, Washington, DC, USA	Dibennardo and Taylor 1982; Holman and Bennett 1991; İşcan and Miller-Shaivitz 1984; Marino 1995; Smith 1996; Simms 1989; Steele 1976; Ericksen 1976, 1982; Holland 1986
Trotter Collection	>133	Fetal				Washington State University, USA	Holcomb and Konigsberg 1995
Tubingen, Germany	>108	4–86	67	41	Southwest Germany	?	Graw et al. 1999
Universidad Complutense	>132	34–97	>60	>72	Exhumed from cemetery in Madrid	Complutense University of Madrid, Department of Biology, Spain	Trancho et al. 1997
University Museum, University of Tokyo	~300				Japan	University Museum, University of Tokyo, Japan	Suwa 1981

University of Florida Collection					Forensic cases	CA Pound Human Identification Laboratory, University of Florida, USA	Trudell 1999
University of Indianapolis						Indianapolis, USA	
University of New Mexico Maxwell Museum Documented Collection	Up to 100	~120	77	45	Body donation program (on-going)	University of New Mexico, Albuquerque, USA	Stojanowski 1999; Tomczak and Buikstra 1999; Rogers 1999
University of Pretoria		>196			South Africa (white and black)	Department of Anatomy, University of Pretoria, South Africa	
University of Torino	All	1064	384	680	Italian, cadavers from city prisons and hospitals	Department of Human Anatomy, University of Torino, Italy	Giraudi et al. 1984
William M. Bass Donated Skeletal Collection	25–89	235			Forensic cases and donated bodies	Anthropology Department, University of Tennessee at Knoxville, USA	Mann et al. 1987, 1991; Trudell 1999; Rogers 1999
Wise family cemetery[a]	66	1	1	0	Southern Ontario		Spence 1996; Pfeiffer 1992
Wistar Institute of Anatomy and Biology	All				Private collection	Philadelphia, USA	Brosco 1991

[a]Skeletons reburied; only extensive records left.

Another collection strategy used to produce human osteological collections was to save bodies that showed "interesting" or pathological features, usually for teaching purposes. The National Museum of Health and Medicine in Washington, DC, and the Museum of Pathological Anatomy in Vienna, Austria, have extensive collections of this type. Several collections, particularly those housed at universities in the USA, have collections based on forensic cases, where the skeletal materials have been donated for further study. The collections of the University of Tennessee William M. Bass Donated Collection and Forensic Anthropology Data Bank, the Louisiana State University FACES Laboratory Collection, and some of the material from the US National Museum of Health and Medicine were accessioned this way. The final method of collecting skeletons comes from disinterment of skeletons of known individuals from cemeteries. Examples of this type of collection strategy are the Spitalfields, Frasetto, Hong Kong, and I. Gemmerich Collections.

The next characteristic of an ideal reference sample is that all ages and both sexes are well represented. For adult age estimation techniques, this normally means a skeletal collection that includes male and female individuals from their mid or late teenage years up through the 80s and 90s. Many skeletal collections are oversampled at certain years, depending on the origin of the sample. For instance, the sample that McKern and Stewart used for their pubic symphysis aging method (McKern and Stewart 1957) was based on dead soldiers from the Korean War, oversampling young men. In contrast, because the Terry Collection of the Smithsonian National Museum of Natural History consists primarily of the remains of indigents from St Louis, Missouri, in the first half of the twentieth century, it has an overabundance of older black and white males and fewer young women (http://nmnhwww.si.edu/anthro/Collmgt/terry.htm).

The final criterion for an ideal reference collection is that it is easily accessed. All of the collections mentioned in this chapter have opportunities for researchers to access the collections, although some may require more preliminary permission and planning than others. In all cases, it is important to contact the curator of the collection before research begins; some may require a copy of a research proposal before allowing access.

Even though many of the collections have some or many of the "ideal" characteristics, the most important part of choosing a research collection is that it meets the criteria needed for the specific research project. Populations should be closely matched for ages, ethnic origin, socioeconomic status, etc. A reference collection that is perfect for one study may be impractical for another.

Because no real reference population is "ideal", two assumptions have to be made when using one as the basis of an age estimation method. The first is the assumption that the reported ages are correct biological ages. This has been an unacknowledged underlying assumption of most of the age estimation methods that are currently used. The researcher has to accept that the ages, if incorrect, are "close enough", but this does add an additional amount of uncertainty to the final individual age estimation. Noting whether the ages of the sample have been verified will help to alleviate most of the uncertainty.

The second assumption that must be made is that senescent processes are uniform. The uniformitarian principle, on which much of our paleodemographic research is based, states that the demographic processes we see in the present are the same as they were in the past (Howell 1976b). Extending this idea to skeletal age estimation, it means that a biological marker of a certain age in one individual will be a marker of the same age in a different person, regardless of sex, origin, health, or socioeconomic status. This assumption, again, is known to be untrue (Boldsen 1997). It is partially corrected by looking at males and females separately, ethnic groups separately, and usually discarding skeletons that were clearly from unhealthy individuals. After correcting for these other differences, it still must be assumed that people of similar background have biological aging processes that proceed in similar ways, regardless of when that person was alive. In other words, a reference sample of skeletons from European-derived individuals who died in the early 20th century will give valid information for estimating the ages of medieval European peasants. Without this assumption, no paleodemographic data would be valid.

One of the goals of identifying collections of known-age human skeletal material is to test these assumptions about biological aging of the skeleton. By comparing populations with different collection strategies and in different parts of the world, questions about the uniformity of biological aging patterns can be answered. It will be important to determine which aging methods can be validated across cultures, and which biological characteristics are always reliable indicators of age. If there are significant differences between populations, quantifying the variation present will also be important, and will give us a baseline to evaluate how the differences affect the ability to estimate ages of skeletons from preindustrial times.

Acknowledgments

This research has been conducted with the help of many people. Conversations with Jim Wood, George Milner, Jesper Boldsen, Jaimin Weets,

Darryl Holman, D. Troy Case, and Rob Hoppa helped to clarify my ideas about the importance of this research. The Interlibrary Loan services at Pennsylvania State University and SUNY Potsdam have found articles in far-flung journals and at least 10 different languages. Special thanks go out to the numerous curators and researchers who have taken the time to supply information about their collections and provide references and encouragement. This research was supported by a Hill Grant from the Pennsylvania State University Department of Anthropology, and web hosting is provided by the Computer Department at SUNY Potsdam.

References

Aoki K (1990) Morphological studies on the roots of maxillary premolars in Japanese. Shika Gakuho. *Journal of the Tokyo Dental College Society* **90**, 79–97.

Baljet B and Oostra RJ (1999) Digital data and the 19th century teratology collection. *Journal of Audiovisual Media in Medicine* **22**, 186–194.

Barbian LT, Sledzik PS, and Nelson AM (2000) Case studies in pathology from the National Museum of Health and Medicine, Armed Forces Institute of Pathology. *Annals of Diagnostic Pathology* **4**, 170–173.

Bastianini A, Guidotti A, Hauser G, and De Stefano GF (1985) Variations in the method of the division of the hypoglossal canal in Sienese skulls of known age and sex. *Acta Anatomica* **123**, 21–24.

Bedford ME, Russell KF, Lovejoy CO, Meindle RS, Simpson SW, and Stuart-Macadam PL (1993) Test of the multifactorial aging method using skeletons with known ages-at-death from the Grant Collection. *American Journal of Physical Anthropology* **97**, 113–125.

Beighton P, Sujansky E, Patzak B, and Portele KA (1994) Bone dysplasias of infancy in the Vienna collection. *Pediatric Radiology* **24**, 384–386.

Bocquet-Appel J-P and Masset C (1982) Farewell to paleodemography. *Journal of Human Evolution* **11**, 321–333.

Boldsen JL (1997) Transitional analysis: a method for unbiased age estimation from skeletal traits. *American Journal of Physical Anthropology Supplement* **24**, 78.

Brasili-Gualandi P and Gualdi-Russo E (1989) Discontinuous traits of the skull: variations on sex, age, laterality. *Anthropologischer Anzeiger* **47**, 239–250.

Brosco JP (1991) Anatomy and ambition: the evolution of a research institute. *Transactions and Studies of the College of Physicians of Philadelphia* **13**, 1–28.

Cogoluenhes A (1984) Travail sur les humerus de la collection anthropologique de l'Université de Coimbra. *Antropologia Portuguesa*, **2**, 5–8.

Curran BK and Weaver DS (1982) The use of the coefficient of agreement and likelihood ratio test to examine the development of the tympanic plate using a known-age sample of fetal and infant skeletons. *American Journal of Physical Anthropology* **58**, 343–346.

Day MH and Pitcher-Wilmott RW (1975) Sexual differentiation in the innominate bone studied by multivariate analysis. *Annals of Human Biology* **2**, 143–151.

de Francisco M, Lemos JLR, Liberri Ea, Adamo J, Jacomo AL, and Matson E (1990) Contribution to the study of anatomical hypoglossal canal variations. *Revista de ondontologia da Universidade de São Paulo* **4**, 38–42.

Defrise-Gussenhoven E and Orban-Segebarth R (1984) Generalized distance between different thigh-bones and a reference population. In GN van Vark and WW Howells (eds.): *Multivariate statistical methods in physical anthropology*. Dordrecht: D. Reidel Publishing Company, pp. 89–99.

Dibennardo R and Taylor JV (1982) Classification and misclassification in sexing the black femur by discriminant function analysis. *American Journal of Physical Anthropology* **58**, 145–151.

Ericksen MF (1976) Some aspects of aging in the lumbar spine. *American Journal of Physical Anthropology* **45**, 575–580.

Ericksen MF (1982) How "representative" is the Terry collection? Evidence from the proximal femur. *American Journal of Physical Anthropology* **59**, 345–350.

Eversole LR, Pappas JR, and Graham R (1986) Dental occlusal wear and degenerative disease of the temporomandibular joint: a correlation study utilizing skeletal material from a contemporary population. *Journal of Oral Rehabilitation* **12**, 401–406.

Gemmerich I (1999) Creation of an anthropological collection of reference and use of discrete traits in the case of known genealogy. Dissertation, University of Geneva, Geneva.

Giraudi R, Fissore F, and Giacobini G (1984) The collection of human skulls and postcranial skeletons at the Department of Human Anatomy of the University of Torino (Italy). *American Journal of Physical Anthropology* **65**, 105–107.

Graw M, Czarnetzki A, and Haffner HT (1999) The form of the supraorbital margin as a criterion in identification of sex from the skull: investigations based on modern human skulls. *American Journal of Physical Anthropology* **108**, 91–96.

Gualdi-Russo E (1998) Study on long bones: variation in angular traits with sex, age, and laterality. *Anthropologischer Anzeiger* **56**, 289–299.

Gualdi-Russo E and Russo P (1995) A new technique for measurements on long bones: development of a new instument and techniques compared. *Anthropologischer Anzeiger* **53**, 153–182.

Gualdi-Russo E, Tasca MA, and Brasili P (1999) Scoring of nonmetric traits: a methodological approach. *Journal of Anatomy* **195**, 543–550.

Guidotti A (1984) Morphometrical considerations on occipital condyles. *Anthropologischer Anzeiger* **42**, 117–119.

Guidotti A, Bastianini A, De Stefano GF, and Hauser G (1986) Variations of supraorbital bony structures in Sienese skulls. *Acta Anatomica* **127**, 1–6.

Hauser G and De Stefano GF (1985) Variations in the form of the hypoglossal canal. *American Journal of Physical Anthropology* **67**, 7–11.

Hershkovitz I, Greenwald C, Rothschild BM, Latimer B, Dutour O, Jellema LM, Wish-Baratz S, Pap I, and Leonetti G (1999) The elusive diploic veins: anthropological and anatomical perspective. *American Journal of Physical Anthropology* **108**, 345–358.

Holcomb SM and Konigsberg LW (1995) Statistical study of sexual dimorphism in the human fetal sciatic notch. *American Journal of Physical Anthropology* **97**, 113–125.

Holland TD (1986) Sex determination of fragmentary crania by analysis of the cranial base. *American Journal of Physical Anthropology* **70**, 203–208.

Holland TD (1991) Sex assessment using the proximal tibia. *American Journal of Physical Anthropology* **85**, 221–227.

Holman DJ and Bennett KA (1991) Determination of sex from arm bone measurements. *American Journal of Physical Anthropology* **84**, 421–426.

Howell N (1976a) Notes on collection and analysis of demographic field data. In JF Marshall and S Polgar (eds.): *Culture, natality, and family planning.* Chapel Hill, NC: University of North Carolina, pp. 221–240.

Howell N (1976b) Toward a uniformitarian theory of human paleodemography. In RH Ward and KM Weiss (eds.): *The demographic evolution of human populations.* London: Academic Press, pp. 25–40.

Humphrey LT (1998) Growth patterns in the modern human sample. *American Journal of Physical Anthropology* **105**, 57–72.

Introna F, Di Vella G, and Campobasso CP (1998) Sex determination by discriminant analysis of patella measurements. *Forensic Science International* **95**, 39–45.

İşcan M, Yoshino M, and Kato S (1994) Sex determination from the tibia: standards for contemporary Japan. *Journal of Forensic Sciences* **39**, 785–792.

İşcan MY and Miller-Shaivitz P (1984) Determination of sex from the tibia. *American Journal of Physical Anthropology* **64**, 53–57.

Jantz LM and Jantz RL (1999) Secular change in long bone length and proportion in the United States, 1800–1970. *American Journal of Physical Anthropology* **110**, 57–67.

Kieser J, Gebbie T, and Ksiezycka K (1996) A mathematical model for hypothetical force distribution between opposing jaws. *Journal of the Dental Association of South Africa* **51**, 701–705.

Kieser JA, Cameron N, and Groeneveld HT (1987) Evidence for a secular trend in the Negro dentition. *Annals of Human Biology* **14**, 517–532.

Kieser JA, Moggi-Cecchi J, and Groeneveld HT (1992) Sex allocation of skeletal material by analysis of the proximal tibia. *Forensic Science International* **56**, 29–36.

King CA (1997) Osteometric assessment of 20th century skeletons from Thailand and Hong Kong. MA thesis, Florida Atlantic University, Boca Raton, FL.

King CA, İşcan MY, and Loth SR (1998) Metric and comparative analysis of sexual dimorphism in the Thai femur. *Journal of Forensic Sciences* **43**, 954–958.

Klepinger LL, Katz D, Micozzi MS, and Carroll L (1992) Evaluation of cast methods for estimating age from the os pubis. *Journal of Forensic Science* **37**, 763–770.

Konigsberg LW and Frankenberg SR (1992) Estimation of age structure in anthropological demography. *American Journal of Physical Anthropology* **89**, 235–256.

Konigsberg LW and Frankenberg SR (1994) Paleodemography: not quite dead. *Evolutionary Anthropology* **3**, 92–105.

Liu W, Chen S, and Xu Z (1988) Estimation of age from the pubic symphysis of Chinese males by means of multiple analysis. *Acta Anthropologica Sinica* **VII**, 147–153.

Liversidge HM (1994) Accuracy of age estimation from developing teeth of a population of known age (0–5.4 years). *International Journal of Osteoarchaeology* **4**, 37–45.

Loth SR and Henneberg M (1996) Mandibular ramus flexure: a new morphological indicator of sexual dimorphism in the human skeleton. *American Journal of Physical Anthropology* **99**, 473–485.

Mann RW, Symes SA, and Bass WM (1987) Maxillary suture obliteration: aging the human skeleton based on intact or fragmentary maxilla. *Journal of Forensic Sciences* **32**, 148–157.

Mann RW, Jantz RL, Bass WM, and Willey PS (1991) Maxillary suture obliteration: a visual method for estimating skeletal age. *Journal of Forensic Sciences* **36**, 781–791.

Marino EA (1995) Sex estimation using the first cervical vertebra. *American Journal of Physical Anthropology* **97**, 127–133.

McKern TW and Stewart SD (1957) *Skeletal age changes in young American males. Analyzed from the skeletal standpoint of age identification.* Natick, MA: US Army Quartermaster Research and Development Center.

Milner G, Boldsen J, and Usher BM (1997) Age at death determination using revised scoring procedures for age-progressive skeletal traits (abstract). *American Journal of Physical Anthropology Supplement* **24**, 170.

Moggi-Cecchi J, Pacciani E, and Pinto-Cisternas J (1994) Enamel hypoplasia and age at weaning in 19th-century Florence, Italy. *American Journal of Physical Anthropology* **93**, 299–306.

Morita M (1990) Morphological studies on the roots of lower first molars in Japanese. Shika Gakuho. *Journal of the Tokyo Dental College Society* **90**, 55–71.

Oostra RJ, Baljet B, Dijkstra PF, and Hennekam RC (1998a) Congenital anomalies in the teratological collection of the Museum Vrolik in Amsterdam, The Netherlands. I: Syndromes with multiple congenital anomalies. *American Journal of Medical Genetics* **77**, 100–115.

Oostra RJ, Baljet B, Dijkstra PF, and Hennekam RC (1998b) Congenital anomalies in the teratological collection of the Museum Vrolik in Amsterdam, The Netherlands. II: Skeletal dysplasias. *American Journal of Medical Genetics* **77**, 116–134.

Oostra RJ, Baljet B, and Hennekam RC (1998c) Congenital anomalies in the teratological collection of the Museum Vrolik in Amsterdam, The Netherlands. IV: Closure defects of the neural tube. *American Journal of Medical Genetics* **80**, 60–73.

Oostra RJ, Baljet B, Verbeeten BW, and Hennekam RC (1998d) Congenital anomalies in the teratological collection of the Museum Vrolik in Amsterdam, The Netherlands. III: Primary field defects, sequences, and other complex anomalies. *American Journal of Medical Genetics* **80**, 45–59.

Oostra RJ, Baljet B, Verbeeten BW, and Hennekam RC (1998e) Congenital anomalies in the teratological collection of the Museum Vrolik in Amsterdam,

The Netherlands. V: Conjoined and acardiac twins. *American Journal of Medical Genetics* **80**, 74–89.

Perizonius WRK (1984) Closing and non-closing sutures in 256 crania of known age and sex from Amsterdam (AD 1883–1909). *Journal of Human Evolution* **13**, 201–216.

Pfeiffer S (1992) Cortical bone age estimates from historically known adults. *Zeitschrift für Morphologie und Anthropologie* **79**, 1–10.

Prescher A and Bohndorf K (1993) Anatomical and radiological observations concerning ossification of the sacrotuberous ligament: is there a relation to spinal diffuse idiopathic skeletal hyperostosis (DISH)? *Skeletal Radiology* **22**, 581–585.

Rogers TL (1999) A visual method of determining the sex of skeletal remains using the distal humerus. *Journal of Forensic Sciences* **44**, 57–60.

Saunders SR, FitzGerald C, Rogers T, Dudar C, and McKillop H (1992) A test of several methods of skeletal age estimation using a documented archaeological sample. *Canadian Society of Forensic Science Journal* **25**, 97–118.

Scheuer L and Maclaughlin-Black S (1994) Age estimation from the pars basilaris of the fetal and juvenile occipital bone. *International Journal of Osteoarchaeology* **4**, 377–380.

Schutkowski H (1993) Sex determination of infant and juvenile skeletons. I. Morphological features. *American Journal of Physical Anthropology* **90**, 199–205.

Scoles PV, Salvagno R, Villalba K, and Riew D (1988) Relationship of iliac crest maturation to skeletal and chronological age. *Journal of Pediatric Orthopedics* **8**, 639–644.

Scoles PV, Latimer BM, DiGiovanni BF, Vargo E, Bauza S, and Jellema LM (1991) Vertebral alterations in Scheuermann's kyphosis. *Spine* **16**, 509–515.

Simms DL (1989) Thickness of the lateral surface of the temporal bone in children. *Annals of Otology, Rhinology, and Laryngology* **98**, 726–731.

Singh G, Singh S, and Singh SP (1975) Identification of sex from tibia. *Journal of the Anatomical Society of India* **24**, 20–24.

Singh S and Singh SP (1972) Identification of sex from the humerus. *Indian Journal of Medical Research* **60**, 1061–1066.

Singh S, Singh G, and Singh SP (1974) Identification of sex from the ulna. *Indian Journal of Medical Research* **62**, 731–735.

Smith SL (1996) Attribution of hand bones to sex and population groups. *Journal of Forensic Sciences* **41**, 469–477.

Spence MW (1996) Nonmetric trait distribution and the expression of familial relationships in a nineteeth century cemetery. *Northeast Anthropology* **52**, 53–67.

Steele DG (1976) The estimation of sex on the basis of the talus and calcaneus. *American Journal of Physical Anthropology* **45**, 581–588.

Stojanowski CM (1999) Sexing potential of fragmentary and pathological metacarpals. *American Journal of Physical Anthropology* **109**, 245–252.

Stout SD, Porro MA, and Perotti B (1996) Brief communication: a test and correction of the clavicle method of Stout and Paine for histological age estimation of skeletal remains. *American Journal of Physical Anthropology* **100**, 139–142.

Susanne C, Guidotti A, and Hauspie R (1985) Age changes of skull dimensions. *Anthropologischer Anzeiger* **43**, 31–36.

Sutherland LD and Suchey JM (1991) Use of the ventral arc in pubic sex determination. *Journal of Forensic Sciences* **36**, 501–511.

Suwa G (1981) A morphological analysis of Japanese crania by means of the vestibular coordinate system. *Journal of the Anthropological Society of Tokyo* **89**, 329–350.

Szilvassy J and Kritscher H (1990) Estimation of chronological age in man based on the spongy structure of long bones. *Anthropologischer Anzeiger* **48**, 289–298.

Tanaka H (1999) Numeral analysis of the proximal humeral outline: bilateral shape differences. *American Journal of Human Biology* **11**, 343–357.

Tomczak PD and Buikstra JE (1999) Analysis of blunt trauma injuries: vertical deceleration versus horizontal deceleration injuries. *Journal of Forensic Sciences* **44**, 253–262.

Trancho GJ, Robledo B, Lopez-Bueis I, and Sanchez JA (1997) Sexual determination of the femur using discriminant functions: Analysis of a Spanish population of known sex. *Journal of Forensic Science* **42**, 181–185.

Trudell MB (1999) Anterior femoral curvature revisited: race assessment from the femur. *Journal of Forensic Sciences* **44**, 700–707.

Ubelaker DH (1989) The estimation of age at death from immature human bone. In MY İşcan (ed.): *Age markers in the human skeleton.* Springfield, IL: C. C. Thomas Publisher, pp. 55–70.

Weaver DS (1980) Sex differences in the ilia of a known sex and age sample of fetal and infant skeletons. *American Journal of Physical Anthropology* **52**, 191–195.

4   *Aging through the ages:*
historical perspectives on age indicator methods

ARIANE KEMKES-GROTTENTHALER

Introduction

Due to its resistance to decomposition, the human skeleton proves to be an extremely valuable source for the reconstruction of past life parameters. Archaeologists, historians, and anthropologists alike rely on these biological building blocks for many paleodemographic inferences and, not surprisingly, there is a longstanding tradition of establishing mortality profiles from prehistoric cemetery populations. These death structures serve as indicators of overall life expectancy, fertility, and even population growth. Moreover, historical patterns of health, disease, and ontogenesis are used to isolate biological as well as social life history factors.

However, the principal source of error – the accuracy of the osteologically derived vital statistics – needs to be critically addressed. Unfortunately, given the desire to make paleodemographic inferences, it is all too often forgotten that the attribution of individual biological profiles merely represents a well-founded estimate. While sexing methods, when applied to sufficiently preserved adult skeletons, may reach an overall precision of up to 90% (St Hoyme and İşcan 1989), postmaturity age assessment still remains one of the most difficult tasks. Although bones and teeth undergo a lifelong age-related metamorphosis, each part of the skeleton, depending on its location, structure and function, reflects a different aspect of the aging phenomenon (Figure 4.1).

In spite of the strong overall association between maturational and skeletal changes, the aging process is merely universal to the extent that it applies to both sexes and all populations. Beyond that, there is remarkable interpersonal heterogeneity due to distinctive genetic differences, behavior variation, diverse predispositions, and the individual's lifetime interaction with the environment. Making matters worse, there is evidence of notable within-subject variability (Spirduso 1995). Consequently, the terms "biological age" and "chronological age" are not synonymous. Rather, the determination of biological age is inferred from variables that are correlated with chronological aging (Arking 1998). Biological age markers

48

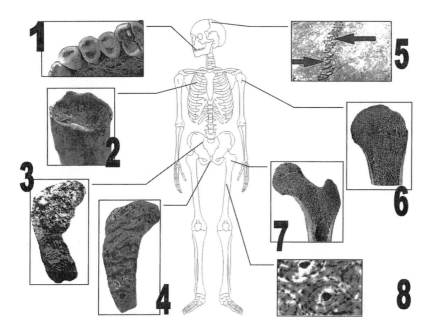

Figure 4.1. The lifelong sequential metamorphosis of the human skeleton;
depicted are some of the most often used age indicators (young male,
approximately 20–25 years old, Early Medieval cemetery). 1, dental attrition;
2, sternal rib end; 3, auricular surface; 4, pubic symphysis; 5, (ecto)cranial sutures;
6, proximal humerus; 7, proximal femur; 8, bone histology. Although all bone
markers point towards early adulthood, the specific "age windows" may vary
according to the trait employed and the influence of confounding factors. Thus
some indicators will provide an accelerated estimate.

therefore do not represent chronological age, but are merely an estimate of
the physiological status of the individual (Figure 4.2).

Whereas early research into skeletal biology focused exclusively on a
few select traits, the rise of the prominent subdiscipline of forensic osteology has undisputedly elevated classical individualization techniques to a
new level of scientific inquiry. Continuous retesting, modification, and
calibration of existing methods as well the development of new techniques
has coincidentally promoted a dramatic shift from single-trait to multiple-
trait approaches. Beyond that, the multitude of confounding factors of the
aging process has shattered the long-held assumption that age estimation
requires merely the routine application of textbook standards. In retro-
spect, and not surprisingly, the past two decades have been characterized
by a critical rebuttal of such long-held concepts, ultimately culminating in

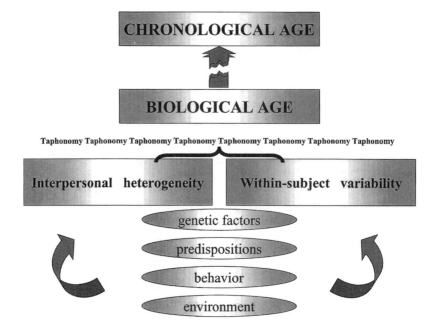

Figure 4.2. From biological to chronological age estimates: the effect of confounding factors on the final age estimation.

an undeserved and untimely "farewell to paleodemography" (Bocquet-Appel and Masset 1982).

However, instead of prematurely hailing the demise of paleodemography, innovative research avenues, novel traits, and new techniques need to be explored. Admittedly, because of the plasticity of the aging process, valid improvements in our knowledge of age progression may remain elusive. Nevertheless, the conceptualization of genuinely polysymptomatic procedures may provide us with a valid research alternative.

The evolution of age markers: single-trait systems

Any recapitulation of current and past research traditions in skeletal biology brings to light a longstanding and strong adherence to a select few age markers. However wide the span of possible features presenting itself today, past strategies almost exclusively focused on the fusion of cranial sutures, the process of dental wear, or the metamorphosis of the pubic

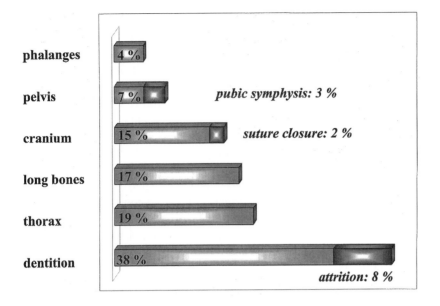

Figure 4.3. Current divergence of skeletal age markers, with emphasis on the relative share of pubic, sutural, and dental wear standards; 435 distinct methodical approaches surveyed; (Kemkes-Grottenthaler 1993). Summarized markers include "*dentition*", i.e., enamel, color, dentine, pulp, racemization, translucency, cement, third molar; "*thorax*", i.e., thyroid cartilage, clavicle, scapula, sternum, ribs, vertebrae; "*long bones*", i.e., humerus, radius, ulna, femur, tibia, fibula.

symphysis (see Figure 4.3). Some historically oriented reviews even go so far as to claim that "from the 1920's on, most skeletal biologists have relied almost solely on the cranial sutures and pubic symphysis for age estimation in the adult" (İşcan 1989:7). Thus generations of physical anthropologists – completely oblivious to the fact that individual bones are not isolates – erroneously believed that skeletal age could be adequately calculated from a small pool of available traits, when in truth the human skeleton, i.e., its composition, physical appearance, and aging pattern, is influenced by a myriad intrinsic and extrinsic factors. Once it was understood that a single age marker merely provided a narrow window into a specific age segment, a general picture of the sequential aging process arose and consequently multiple-trait assessment became routine.

With hindsight, the obvious preponderance of certain traits cannot simply be attributed to a commonly shared belief in these age markers' relative accuracy (see Table 4.3). Instead, other reasons come to mind. For one, from the standpoint of practicality, these traits are easy to examine and exhibit a very distinctive metamorphosis. Furthermore, the human cranium has always been of exceptional fascination (Henschen 1966) and is often the best-preserved portion of an archaeologically recovered skeleton. Thus the preference for age markers of the skull seems to be highly related to historical trends within the field of physical anthropology itself. Consequently it was the rising interest in the discipline of craniology that gave directional incentives. Collecting began in the 19th century, and the first material to be addressed by contemporary physical anthropologists was henceforward always cranial (Spencer 1997). This explains why the first systematic study of suture closure trends was initiated in the 1860s (Baker 1984; Masset 1989). Likewise, dental wear research commenced within the latter half of the 19th century (Rose and Ungar 1998). Gradually anthropologists began to shift from collecting skulls to the acquisition of complete skeletons and consequently some of the most famous anatomy collections were established worldwide (see Usher, Chapter 3, this volume). The availability of these documented cadaver series gave new impetus to innovative research aims and a growing number of questions relating to age and sex estimation were thereby answered. While the recognition of age-related patterns in pubic metamorphosis may antedate the 1800s (McKern 1956), the first comprehensive study was not published until the third decade of the following century (Meindl and Lovejoy 1985).

Only after the advent of forensic osteology were new research avenues successively explored, not merely in terms of possible traits but even more so in terms of methodology. Notwithstanding a growing insight that the search for an all-encompassing, single age indicator might be elusive, innovative techniques are often welcomed as the long-awaited solution to a time-old problem. For example, a biochemical method based on aspartic acid racemization (AAR) that can be employed on teeth, and also on bone and soft tissues, has been hailed as the method of choice when it comes to providing simple, cost-effective and accurate results (Ritz-Timme *et al.* 2000). However, inconsistencies between different laboratories, due to different protocols, must be resolved (Waite *et al.* 1999). Likewise, interpersonal heterogeneity (Ohtani 1997) and general restriction of the method to adult individuals must be considered. But the most problematic issue centers on the fact that the preservation of the skeleton is a severely limiting factor. Chemical alteration of the proteins infringes greatly on the accuracy of older samples (Carolan *et al.* 1997). Thus only a few investigations were able to successfully apply this technique to cases with longer postmortem intervals (Ogino *et al.* 1985).

When it comes to the exploration of the true nature of the aging process,

Table 4.1. *Primary, secondary, and tertiary criteria of age markers (after Spirduso 1995)*

Primary criteria	Strong correlation between biological feature and age
	Age indicator is not altered by pathological events
	Age-related alteration is not secondary to metabolic or nutritional changes
	Sequential and unambiguously identifiable aging pattern
	Continuous remodeling throughout lifespan
Secondary criteria	Wide applicability
	Generalization across species
Tertiary criteria	Reliable changes within a short time interval as compared with total lifespan

for any given indicator to be of unequivocal value, certain prerequisites need to be fulfilled. In reference to the norms applied in identifying gerontological biomarkers (Spirduso 1995), a robust skeletal age indicator should likewise satisfy several fundamental criteria (see Table 4.1). Extending these norms to skeletal age estimators, it is quite apparent that a single age marker cannot fulfill these criteria. The human aging process is far too complex. The sequential passage of time of any given estimator is a function not only of age but also of a multitude of confounding factors. Currently, very effective interventions into the aging process have been documented for many vertebrate species, including humans (Arking 1998). It must be concluded, then, that all markers employed in skeletal age assessment are inherently flawed.

Issues of validity and reliability

Despite unequivocal endeavors to attain improved age estimates in both the archaeological and the forensic context, none of the methodological approaches available to date presents itself without inherent pitfalls (Table 4.2). Virtually every bone of the human skeleton may be aged via an array of techniques. The choice of procedure is therefore guided mostly by the circumstances of sample preservation and the laboratory equipment and resources at hand.

Blind evaluations between various techniques have yielded somewhat contradictory results (Masters and Zimmerman 1978; Aiello and Molleson 1993; Dudar *et al.* 1993; Turban-Just and Grupe 1995; Ericksen 1998; Kvaal and During 1999). Since most of these studies were based on

Table 4.2. *Comparison of age estimation techniques (for a more detailed review of these methods, refer to İşcan and Loth (1989), Pfeiffer et al. (1995), Stout (1998), Pasquier et al. (1999)*

Methods	Pro	Con
Macroscopic		
1. Morphology	No special equipment	No measure of objectivity
	Cost-effective and fast	Interobserver error bias?
	In situ determination	
	Sample integrity preserved	
	No bone selectivity	
2. Quantification by numerical imagery	Simple preparation of specimen	Specialized equipment required
3. Radiography	Invaluable in developmental biology	Specialized training necessary
	Living reference samples for comparison	X-ray standards are not transferable
	Integrity of sample preserved	Technical problems (film)
	Complements gross morphology	
Microscopic		
1. Histology/ histomorphometry	Invaluable information about health and disease	Requires exceptional preservation
		Specialized equipment
		Need for strict standardization of parameters
		Methods limited to certain bones
		Sampling error due to intraskeletal variation
		Elaborate preparation of thin sections
		Not all factors of osteon creation and remodeling are understood
2. Aspartic acid racemization	Exceptional results	Diagenetic factors
		Elaborate preparation and analysis

undocumented samples, the observed discrepancies cannot be validated. In cases where the true age-at-death of the specimen was known, histological methods seem to fare slightly, but not appreciably, better than traditional morphological standards (Aiello and Molleson 1993). However, not all microscopic techniques may be equally suitable for all sexes and age groups (Pratte and Pfeiffer 1999).

Regrettably, very few attempts have been outwardly directed at developing common standards, adequate calibration, or evaluation procedures. Yet efforts to establish reliability and validity standards are necessary to guarantee the quality estimates so important for forensic as well as paleodemographic inquiries.

Reliability

Issues of reliability encompass observer error, phenotypic expression, quasi-continuity, age and sex dimorphism, asymmetry, intertrait correlation, causation factors, and heritability (Saunders 1989). The most important class of reliability estimates focuses on the problem of observer error. Morphological assessment, in particular, has been repeatedly accused of being prone to both inter- and intra-observer interference, although microscopic methods of age determination are likewise at risk (Lynnerup *et al.* 1998). As osteomorphognostic methods are usually based on discrete, highly descriptive traits it is stipulated that these traits – despite photographic standards or casts – easily lend themselves to subjective interpretations. Consequentially, the ability of a researcher to properly identify and diagnose a given morphological trait is crucial to the method's overall predictive potential. Some techniques, indeed, seem to be highly biased by observer error (Suchey 1979; Lovejoy *et al.* 1985b). However, the majority of researchers report a negligible interobserver error (İşcan *et al.* 1986a,b; Charles *et al.* 1986; Galera *et al.* 1995). Apparently, several measures, such as narrow category scales (Galera *et al.* 1995) and seriation of the sample (Bedford *et al.* 1993), successfully counteract interobserver bias. Likewise, the relative experience of the investigator may also be a contributing factor (Baccino *et al.* 1999).

Validity

Issues of validity focus on the predictive values of given age indicators. The accuracy of any given assessment hinges on a strong correlation between the biological feature and age. A low correlation coefficient thus runs a considerable risk of error to both the individual estimate as well as the entire sample's death structure. This holds true for single- as well as multiple-trait methods (Table 4.3).

Table 4.3. *Coefficients of correlation between age indicators and age at death (Bocquet-Appel and Masset 1982; Katz and Suchey 1985; Lovejoy et al. 1985a; Meindl and Lovejoy 1985; Meindel et al. 1985; Kemkes-Grottenthaler 1996b)*

Indicator	Females	Males	Both sexes[a]
Endocranial sutures (Acsádi and Nemeskéri)	0.35	0.51	
Humerus (Acsádi and Nemeskéri)	0.34	0.44	
Femur (Acsádi and Nemeskéri)	0.58	0.56	
Pubic symphysis (Acsádi and Nemeskéri)	0.49	0.47	
Pubic symphysis (McKern and Stewart)[1]		0.72	
Pubic symphysis (McKern and Stewart)[2]	0.68	0.37	0.36
Pubic symphysis (Todd)[1]		0.85	
Pubic symphysis (Todd)[2]	0.64	0.57	0.57
Auricular surface (Meindl *et al.*)			0.72
Multifactorial Summary Age (Lovejoy *et al.*)	0.79	0.90	0.85
Dental wear (Lovejoy)			0.70
Ectocranial sutures (Meindl and Lovejoy)[3]			0.57 (L); 0.50 (V)
Ectocranial suture (Meindl and Lovejoy)[4]	0.34	0.59	0.56

References: (1) Katz and Suchey 1985; (2) Meindl *et al.* 1985; (3) Meindl and Lovejoy 1985; (4) Kemkes-Grottenthaler 1996b.
[a]L, lateral–anterior sutures; V, vault sutures.

Whereas Bocquet-Appel and Masset (1982) stipulated that a correlation coefficient of less than 0.9 is unable to yield accurate assessments, Lovejoy and colleagues (1985a) asserted that a factor of 0.7 is indeed sufficient. At first glance, this may seem nothing more than a purely academic dispute; however, the practical consequences for paleodemography would be genuinely devastating. The figures listed in Table 4.3 readily demonstrate that accepting a lowered threshold of 0.7 would make a majority of the most widely used age markers unfit for paleodemographic inquiries. However, in cases of correlation coefficients as low as 0.6, it has been suggested that iterative techniques might compensate for weak estimators (Bocquet-Appel and Masset 1996).

Yet, from a statistical point of view, there are several fundamental problems associated with the use of correlation coefficients. For one thing, the traits typically used in age assessment are discrete. Furthermore, the relationship between the assigned phase and corresponding age span is usually highly nonlinear, as can be deduced from the fact that these phases often overlap and represent intervals of variable length. Lastly, the prediction of age-at-death depends on the mortality schedule of the target sample (see Müller *et al.* 2001; Hoppa and Vaupel, Chapter 1, this volume). To circumvent these shortcomings, while still providing some measure of the strength of a given technique, scatterplots of predicted versus actual ages should become an integral part of the validation process. In addition to providing a statistically sound alternative to the computation of correlation coefficients, this procedure might be used to detect nonlinearities and can be coupled with measures of association between predicted and actual values.

Phases or components? The case of the pubic symphysis

The English anatomist T. W. Todd was the first to describe the progressive morphological metamorphosis of the pubic symphysis within the framework of a proper age assessment technique. What makes Todd's opus such a remarkable and valuable resource is the fact that he based his system on a collection of fully documented specimens. His 10-phase system[1] of modal standards initially incorporated sex- and population-specific trends (Todd 1920, 1921a–c, 1923, 1930); however, none of these differences proved to be sufficiently distinct to preclude using the classic "white male" standards for all specimens. Todd's pubic aging standards focus on five main features of the symphyseal face: surface, ventral border (or "rampart"), dorsal border (or "plateau"), superior and inferior extremity. In addition, several subsidiary traits such as "ridging", "billowing", or "ossific nodules" may be distinguished. Todd's phase system is still widely used today, along with several subsequent refinements (Brooks 1955; Hoppe 1969; Hanihara and Suzuki 1978; Meindl *et al.* 1985; Suchey *et al.* 1986; Zhang *et al.* 1989; Garmus 1990). These modifications were directed mainly at narrowing or expanding the age limits set by Todd, as well as condensing the original 10-phase scheme.

Although modal systems have repeatedly proved themselves to be successful age estimators, several apparent weaknesses of Todd's system gave rise to a scoring method that is based on single components rather than combined sets of features (McKern 1956; McKern and Stewart 1957). Three components, which had also been previously identified by Todd, were isolated: the dorsal plateau, the ventral rampart, and the symphyseal rim. Each of these three is further divided into five chronological stages. The resultant score, ranging in value from 0 to 15, is then used to derive at

---

[1] Interestingly, Todd later added other patterns of metamorphosis to his pubic aging standards, which he named "anthropoid strain" (Todd 1923). These may be taken as morphological changes alternative to the more commonly found patterns.

Table 4.4. *Phase methods versus component techniques*

	Phases	Components
Pro	Easy to use due to cases, photographic standards etc.	Each component is easily evaluated
		Scoring eliminates observer bias
	Simple evaluation of results	Better suited for assessing variability
Con	Static system, that does not make allowances for variability	More time consuming
	Highly descriptive	
	Prone to observer bias	
	If specimen does not depict modal stage, method is limited	

an age from the appropriate tables. These provide the mean, standard deviation, and observed age range for each increment of the score. Due to the fact that there is a developmental sequence within the three components, only 21 formulas have been documented, as compared with the total number of possible combinations of 125 (İşcan 1979).

Gilbert and McKern (1973) subsequently established a separate set of pubic standards for females. However, the standard deviations initially provided were miscalculated and needed revision (Snow 1983). Snow altered the procedure and implemented a set of simple linear and polynomial equations that also simplified the evaluation.

Diligent comparisons of both techniques (Table 4.4) have found that the original phase method established by Todd, as well as the subsequent improvements proposed by other researchers, proved to be superior to the alternative component approach (Hanihara and Suzuki 1978; Suchey 1979; Meindl *et al.* 1985; Klepinger *et al.* 1992). So far, this gap between the two approaches has been interpreted on purely methodological grounds. However, attention should also focus on the neurobiological basis of object recognition, which consists of three steps: feature extraction, solving correspondence problems, and comparison with reference. Thus the modal phase approach might, by its very nature, be the more adapt way of age attribution.

From single- to multiple-trait techniques

Each bone is merely a single aspect of the whole skeleton and by its very nature varies in its structure, function, and ultimately its aging pattern. In order to minimize errors introduced by aberrant individual indicators, the combined analytical approach is desirable, whenever complete individuals are available for analysis. Comprehensive approaches to age determination have proved to be consistently superior to individual ones (Baccino *et al.* 1999).

The Gustafson method

The Swedish stomatologist G. Gustafson (1950, 1955) was the first to combine several age estimators. His method encompasses six variables that are determined in a longitudinally sectioned tooth: attrition, periodontosis, secondary dentin, cementum apposition, root resorption and root transparency.[2] Each criterion is ranked individually and allotted 0 to 3 points. The point-values are then entered into a formula and the sum of points by means of a standard curve gives the estimated age.

While the original publication described an error of estimation of ± 3.6 years, several subsequent re-evaluations demonstrated that the margin of error was much broader than had been initially proposed (Nalbandian and Sognnaes 1960; Elsner 1961). A substantial reworking of the original data by Maples and Rice (1979) finally corrected Gustafson's regression statistics and found the error to be ± 7.09 years, nearly double that claimed in the original publication. It is generally assumed today that the true error may be approximated to ± 8 years (Lucy and Pollard 1995).

The ongoing debate about the correct error margin is due largely to the fact that the statistical methods of regression analysis originally employed by Gustafson had insufficient data (Lucy *et al.* 1996). Moreover, the misapplication of statistical methods is also responsible for an obvious regression toward the mean (Solheim and Sundnes 1980). Endless alterations have been stipulated (Rösing and Kvaal 1998) and the method is still being modified and elaborated.

Complex method

Ever since the complex method was recommended by a joint group of leading international anthropologists in 1980 (NN 1980), it has subsequently become the most popular basis for morphological age estimation in Europe. Basing their model on that of Gustafson, Acsádi and Nemeskéri

---

[2] Several other dental methods that rely on a combined approach to dental aging are described by Kilian and Vlček (1989) and Xu *et al.* (1992).

(1970) devised their method after it became apparent that the cranial sutures provided merely rough estimates of biological age. Their approach therefore co-utilizes structural changes in the spongy tissue of humerus and femur, and the metamorphosis of the pubic symphysis. All four age indicators are averaged, giving equal weight to each region.

It is on the grounds of the averaging procedure, however, that the validity of this approach was subsequently questioned (Lovejoy *et al.* 1977; Meindl *et al.* 1985; Lovejoy *et al.* 1985a; Brooks and Suchey 1990). Factually, the symphyseal face is given a slightly dominant role, since its gross estimate will determine the limits of the ranges of the remaining age markers. Nevertheless, evidence has come to light that this method results in an obvious overaging effect in younger individuals (Brooks and Suchey 1990; Kemkes-Grottenthaler 1996a). Moreover, Molleson and Cox (1993) ascertained a bidirectional systematic error of constant overaging of individuals under 40 years and underaging of individuals of over 70 year, thus largely contributing to the well-known phenomenon of "attraction of the middle".

Multifactorial summary age

Contrary to the complex method, the multifactorial summary age (MSA) ideally can incorporate as many indicators as are available (Lovejoy *et al.* 1985a). The original study encompassed five indicators (auricular surface, pubic symphysis, dental wear, ectocranial sutures, and proximal femur). However, the analysis can also be run employing fewer age indicators or even additional standards, as long as the sample is seriated according to each method (Bedford *et al.* 1993). More recently Kunos *et al.* (1999) have shown that the incorporation of the first rib age indicator can successfully strengthen the quality of the summary method.

All age indicators are independently applied to the entire population sample and then processed to generate a population matrix. This matrix is then subjected to principal components analysis (PCA), where the first factor is assumed to represent true chronological age. The PCA provides weights for each indicator according to its general reliability for the particular sample in question. The final age of any individual is the weighted average of all chosen indicators. Application of this method indicates that it produces an estimated age distribution that is (statistically) indistinguishable from the real. However, this does not imply that each individual age estimate is accurate.

Table 4.5. *Comparison of four currently utilized multitrait methods*

	Gustafson's method	Complex method	Summary age	Transition analysis
Sample preparation	Longitudinal sections of teeth	Minimal	Seriation	None
Number of age indicators	6	4	Variable	3
Anatomical regions	Attrition Periodontosis Secondary dentin Cementum apposition Root resorption Root transparency	Sutures Humerus Femur Pubis	Variable	Pubis Auricular surface Sutures
Evaluation	Regression analysis	Tables	Principal components analysis	Likelihood estimation

Transition analysis method

This multifactorial age assessment method remains as yet unpublished (Milner and Boldsen 1999; see Boldsen *et al.*, Chapter 5, in this volume), although the technique itself has been utilized in various archaeological endeavors (Usher *et al.* 2000). The scoring system involves a detailed skeletal age coding format incorporating various aspects of the pubic symphysis, the auricular surface, and cranial suture closure. Two stage designations are possible. This technique permits likelihood of death estimates occurring at different ages for each character (confidence intervals) and thus is useful in both the archaeological as well as the forensic context.

This abridged rebuttal of polysymptomatic approaches (see Table 4.5) documents that while the first multifactorial methods were still based on the idea that each bone equally reliably reflects age-at-death, the introduction of weighted combinations of several bones has yielded superior results. However, due to the plasticity of human aging, future strategies will have to go beyond multiregional assessment and will have to incorporate multi-methodological concepts as well. Preliminary tests have already shown encouraging results in terms of accuracy, although many methodological issues still need to be resolved (Thomas *et al.* 2000).

Future research perspectives

Whether attention is focused on devising innovative approaches to age assessment or recalibrating existing techniques, researchers have always been preoccupied with stipulating aging norms that are universally applicable. Paradoxically, gerontologists believe in the basic axiom that aging is a highly individual phenomenon (Bryant and Pearson 1994). Therefore, applying the growing evidence from gerontology to questions of skeletal age estimation, the key to a comprehensive understanding of age-related changes may lie ultimately in the exploration of intra- and interpersonal as well as population variation.

Intra-individual differences

Intra-individual differences are nowhere better represented than in the conceptual framework of biological age. The extent to which within-subject variability is stable throughout the lifespan differs mainly with the function measured (Spirduso 1995). The problem of within-subject variability has been rarely addressed and, if so, almost exclusively within the context of microscopic age determination. Consequently, Stout (1989, 1998) distinguished between spatial variance, incoherence, and temporal variance. Some morphological evidence is available, but unfortunately the observed trends could not be conclusively verified in the underlying archaeological sample (Kemkes-Grottenthaler 1993). One interesting aspect of intra-individual variation that has come to light, however, centers on the phenomenon of a markedly asymmetrical age progression of bilateral age markers. This has been documented in ectocranial suture closure, where left-sided sutures showed a retarded tendency toward fusion (Kemkes-Grottenthaler 1996b) and also in the auricular surface method (Moore-Jansen and Jantz 1986).

Interpersonal differences – young versus old individuals

It is a well-documented fact that age markers become more progressively inefficient with advancing senescence (Angel 1984). The gap between estimated and chronological age inadvertently widens as a consequence of the aging process itself. Due to the fact that the developmental phase is predominantly characterized by definite and predictive sequences of change, age estimation within younger age groups remains relatively straightforward. However, once maturity is reached, more variable and less distinct changes take place. In addition, the last stretch of the human lifespan is characterized by degenerative changes. The failure to diagnostically isolate older individuals may have led to a systematic bias of constant underestimation (Molleson and Cox 1993; Aykroyd *et al.* 1997). It is therefore of the utmost importance to extend the range of efficacy to include older individuals, in order to verify whether the nonexistence of older individuals in prehistoric settings is a true reflection of past life histories or merely an artifact (see Aykroyd *et al.* 1997; Ericksen 1998).

Interpersonal differences – sexual dimorphism

Overall, the assessment of female age seems to be less accurate (Hanihara 1952; Brooks 1955; Jackes 1985; Molleson and Cox 1993). This phenomenon has been attributed primarily to differences between the reproductive roles of males and females, especially as it pertains to pubic metamorphosis. Consequently, the apparent divergence in female pubic morphology has been attributed to child-bearing. However, whenever parity is actually included in the analysis, variation in the mean stage by age between low-birth and high-birth females appears to be insignificant (Hoppa 2000). This demonstrates that the observed sexual dimorphism is not so much a function of extrinsic factors, but rather an indication of genuine sex-specific trends in age progression. Evidence from cranial suture closure documents this phenomenon as well. Differential sex-specific correlation coefficients (0.59 for males versus 0.34 for females (Kemkes-Grottenthaler 1996b)) indicate that females show a significant number of open sutures until a later age (Hershkovitz *et al.* 1997). This is also apparent in the maxillary suture closure trends (Mann *et al.* 1991). Not taking the female disposition toward delayed obliteration into consideration will inevitably lead to a distinct underestimation of female age-at-death. Thus the skewed mortality profiles observed in many archaeological samples may simply rest on a methodological artifact (Kemkes-Grottenthaler 1996a).

Interpopulation differences – horizontal considerations

The horizontal transfer of age assessment criteria derived from one population to a given target sample is implicitly based on the assumption that these two samples carry the same biological aging characteristics. Although many findings in the field of aging studies suggest that intergroup differences are not intrinsic, but to great extent attributable to socio-economic and cultural factors (Arking 1998), several characteristics of bone aging such as bone mineral density, bone aging scores (OSS) or joint degeneration are clearly subject to ethnic variation (for a review, see Plato *et al.* 1994). However, it needs to be stressed that it is not population differences per se but certain geoclimatic factors which trigger initial bone changes in sensitive individuals. Two key agents, temperature and humidity, have been identified. Both directly affect the level of thermoregulation and thus indirectly the metabolic rate (Belkin *et al.* 1998). Although the evidence of biologically induced differences in the aging mechanism may be scant, numerous studies indicate interpopulation differences (see among others Todd 1920, 1921a–c; Biggerstaff 1977; Zhang 1982; İşcan *et al.* 1987; Katz and Suchey 1989).

Interpopulation differences – vertical considerations

A fundamental axiom of paleodemography stipulates that growth rates and mechanisms of aging established for modern humans can be readily applied to extinct populations, a premise referred to as "uniformitarianism" (Howell 1976). However, bone is an extremely dynamic tissue that is constantly being remodeled owing to its responsiveness to a multiplicity of environmental, genetic, metabolic, nutritional, hormonal, or mechanical stimuli. Longevity thus fits the definition of a phenotype, i.e., a property of an organism produced by the interaction between the organism's genetic potential and its environment (Arking 1998). Although only a few studies have indicated possible diachronic trends (Bocquet-Appel and Masset 1982; Owings Webb and Suchey 1985; Simon 1987), the unequivocal transfer of age assessment standards from modern reference populations to archaeological samples needs to be scrutinized critically.

The general assumption that it is merely the progression of morphological manifestations of the aging process that decides whether a technique is suitable for cross-temporal use (Loth and İşcan 1994) must be energetically challenged. In determining the validity of age assessments, two terms have proved useful, "inaccuracy" and "bias". The concept of "bias" is especially relevant in this context, as bias alludes to the fact that a certain age marker may have a directional error (Lovejoy *et al.* 1985a). As the exact progression rate remains unknown, differences in the velocity of such changes would inadvertently introduce systematic under- or over-estimation trends.

The reference sample

In their critical rebuttal of paleodemographic analysis, Bocquet-Appel and Masset (1982) were able to demonstrate impressive reference sample artifacts. It is their contention that the overwhelming majority of skeletal assemblages rarely fulfill the criteria of an adequate test sample. As a result, the target sample's distribution merely mimics the reference sample. One feasible approach to circumvent this dilemma presents itself in the use of reference samples that have been subject to similar age-modulating factors. However, these are, by their very nature, rarely documented, and do not fulfill the criterion of a uniform age distribution. The other solution rests on the idea of employing standardized reference samples. As such collections are still extremely limited (see Usher, Chapter 3, this volume), much effort needs to focus on the construction and design of such samples according to a set of recognized standards.

Conclusions

Paleodemographic research is always based on taphonomically altered material. Decomposition artifacts can, if undetected, add a directional bias toward overestimation by mimicking more mature stages of age progression (Eidam *et al.* 1990). Furthermore, archaeological samples always represent a distorted portion of the once-living population and, to this end, sociocultural selectivity must be taken into consideration when one is making inferences about historical population structures. Consequently, much attention has to focus on the phenomenon of sampling bias. Lastly, some errors are statistical rather than biocultural in nature. The mathematical approaches employed for paleodemographic reconstruction therefore need to be re-evaluated as well.

One of the most basic problems of eliciting vital statistics from skeletal biomarkers centers on the question of the reliability and validity of the estimators employed. This holds especially true for the estimation of adult age-at-death. Due to the unbridgeable phenomenon of age plasticity, the quest for the perfect aging standard remains futile. However, shifting the research focus from symptomology to causality might prove to present itself as a veritable research alternative. Sex and population heterogeneity need to be addressed more thoroughly, and intra-individual variation taken into consideration. Moreover, to successfully overcome the weaknesses of osteological age markers, genuinely polysymptomatic age assessment criteria need to be devised that incorporate multiregional as well as multimethodological techniques.

References

Acsádi G and Nemeskéri J (1970) *History of human life span and mortality.* Budapest: Akadémiai Kiadó.

Aiello LC and Molleson T (1993) Are microscopic ageing techniques more accurate than macroscopic ageing techniques? *Journal of Archaeological Science* **20**, 689–704.

Angel JL (1984) Variation in estimating age at death of skeletons. *Collegium Anthropologicum* 8, 163–168.

Arking R (1998) *Biology of aging. Observations and principles.* Sunderland, MA: Sinauer Associates Inc.

Aykroyd RG, Lucy D, Pollard AM, and Solheim T (1997) Technical note: regression analysis in adult age estimation. *American Journal of Physical Anthropology* **104**, 259–265.

Baccino E, Ubelaker, DH, Hayek LA, and Zerilli A (1999) Evaluation of seven methods of estimating age at death from mature human skeletal remains. *Journal of Forensic Science* **44**, 931–936.

Baker RK (1984) The relationship of cranial suture closure and age analyzed in a modern multi-racial sample of males and females. M.A. thesis, California State University, Fullerton, CA.

Bedford ME, Russell KF, Lovejoy CO, Meindl RS, Simpson SW, and Stuart-Macadam PL (1993) Test of the multifactorial aging method using skeletons with known ages-at-death from the Grant collection. *American Journal of Physical Anthropology* **91**, 287–297.

Belkin V, Livshits G, Otremski I, and Kobyliansky E (1998) Aging bone score and climatic factors. *American Journal of Physical Anthropology* **106**, 349–359.

Biggerstaff RH (1977) Craniofacial characteristics as determinants of age, sex and race in forensic dentistry. *Dental Clinics of North America* **21**, 85–97.

Bocquet-Appel JP and Masset C (1982) Farewell to paleodemography. *Journal of Human Evolution* **11**, 321–333.

Bocquet-Appel JP and Masset C (1996) Paleodemography: expectancy and false hope. *American Journal of Physical Anthropology* **99**, 571–583.

Brooks ST (1955) Skeletal age at death. The reliability of cranial and pubic age indicators. *American Journal of Physical Anthropology* **13**, 567–597.

Brooks ST and Suchey JM (1990) Skeletal age determination based on the os pubis: a comparison of the Acsádi–Nemeskéri and Suchey–Brooks methods. *Human Biology* **5**, 227–238.

Bryant LJ and Pearson JD (1994) Modeling the variability in longitudinal patterns of aging. In DE Crews and RM Garruto (eds.): *Biological anthropology and aging. Perspectives on human variation over the life span.* New York: Oxford University Press, pp. 373–393.

Carolan VA, Gardner ML, Lucy D, and Pollard AM (1997) Some considerations regarding the use of amino acid racemization in human dentine as an indicator of age at death. *Journal of Forensic Science* **42**, 10–16.

Charles DK, Condon K, Cheverud JM, and Buikstra JE (1986) Cementum annulation and age determination in *Homo sapiens*. I. Tooth variability and observer error. *American Journal of Physical Anthropology* **71**, 311–320.

Dudar JC, Pfeiffer S, and Saunders SR (1993) Evaluation of morphological and histological adult skeletal age-at-death estimation techniques using ribs. *Journal of Forensic Science* **38**, 677–685.

Eidam J, Urban R, and Tröger HD (1990) Two conspicuous findings in human tabular bones following longer exposure time. *Beiträge der Gerichtlichen Medizin* **48**, 443–453.

Elsner J (1961) Altersbestimmungen an Zähnen. Ph.D. thesis, Humboldt University, Berlin.

Ericksen MF (1998) Comparison of two methods of estimating age at death in a Chilean preceramic population. *International Journal of Osteoarchaeology* **7**, 65–70.

Galera V, Ubelaker DH, and Hayek LC (1995) Interobserver error in macroscopic methods of estimating age at death from the human skeleton. *International Journal of Anthropology* **10**, 229–239.

Garmus AK (1990) Determination of individual age by morphologic characteristics of pubic joint. *Sudebno-Meditsinskaia Ekspertiza* **33**, 22–24.

Gilbert BM and McKern TW (1973) A method for aging the female os pubis. *American Journal of Physical Anthropology* **38**, 31–38.

Gustafson G (1950) Age determinations on teeth. *Journal of the American Dental Association* **41**, 45–54.

Gustafson G (1955) Altersbestimmungen an Zähnen. *Deutsche Zahnärztliche Zeitschrift* **10**, 1763–1768.

Hanihara K (1952) Age changes in the male Japanese pubic bone. *Journal of the Anthropological Society of Nippon* **62**, 245–260.

Hanihara K and Suzuki T (1978) Estimation of age from the pubic symphysis by means of multiple regression analysis. *American Journal of Physical Anthropology* **48**, 233–240.

Henschen F (1966) *Der menschliche Schädel in der Kulturgeschichte*. Berlin, Heidelberg, New York: Springer-Verlag.

Hershkovitz I, Latimer B, Dutour O, Jellema LM, Wish-Baratz S, Rothschild C, and Rothschild BM (1997) Why do we fail in aging the skull from the sagittal suture? *American Journal of Physical Anthropology* **103**, 393–399.

Hoppa RD (2000) Population variation in osteological aging criteria: an example from the pubic symphysis. *American Journal of Physical Anthropology* **111**, 185–191.

Hoppe H (1969) Altersbestimmung nach dem Relief der Symphysenfläche des Schambeines. Ph.D. thesis, University of Freiburg im Breisgau.

Howell N (1976) The population of the Dobe area !Kung. In RB Lee and I DeVere (eds.): *Kalahari hunter–gatherers*. Cambridge, MA: Harvard University Press, pp. 137–151.

İşcan MY (1979) Review of forensic anthropology. *Medical Anthropology Newsletter* **10**, 18.

İşcan MY (1989) Assessment of age at death in the human skeleton. In MY İşcan (ed.): *Age markers in the human skeleton.* Springfield, MA: C. C. Thomas, pp. 5–18.

İşcan MY and Loth SR (1989) Osteological manifestations of age in the adult. In İşcan MY and KAR Kennedy (eds.): *Reconstruction of life from the skeleton.* New York: Alan R. Liss, pp. 23–40.

İşcan MY, Loth SR, and Wright RK (1986a) Determination of age from the sternal rib in white males: a test of the phase method. *Journal of Forensic Science* **31**, 122–132.

İşcan MY, Loth SR, and Wright RK (1986b) Determination of age from the sternal rib in white females: a test of the phase method. *Journal of Forensic Science* 31, 990–999.

İşcan MY, Loth SR, and Wright RK (1987) Racial variation in the sternal extremity of the rib and its effect on age determination. *Journal of Forensic Science* **32**, 452–466.

Jackes MK (1985) Pubic symphysis age distributions. *American Journal of Physical Anthropology* **68**, 281–299.

Katz D and Suchey JM (1985) Age determination of the male os pubis. *American Journal of Physical Anthropology* **69**, 427–435.

Katz D and Suchey JM (1989) Race differences in the pubic symphyseal aging patterns of the male. *American Journal of Physical Anthropology* **80**, 167–172.

Kemkes-Grottenthaler A (1993) Kritischer Vergleich osteomorphognostischer Verfahren zur Lebensalterbestimmung Erwachsener. Ph.D. thesis, University of Mainz.

Kemkes-Grottenthaler A (1996a) Critical evaluation of osteomorphognostic methods to estimate adult age at death: a test of the "complex method". *Homo* **46**, 280–292.

Kemkes-Grottenthaler A (1996b) Sterbealterbestimmung anhand des ektokranialen Nahtverschlusses: Eine Evaluierung der Meindl–Lovejoy-Methode. *Rechtsmedizin* **6**, 177–184.

Kilian J and Vlček E (1989) Age determination from teeth in the adult. In MY İşcan (ed.): *Age markers in the human skeleton.* Springfield, IL: C. C. Thomas, pp. 255–275.

Klepinger LL, Katz D, Micozzi MS, and Carroll L (1992) Evaluation of cast methods for estimating age from the os pubis. *Journal of Forensic Science* **37**, 736–770.

Kunos CA, Simpson SW, Russell KF, and Hershkovitz I (1999) First rib metamorphosis: its possible utility for human age-at-death estimation. *American Journal of Physical Anthropology* **110**, 202–323.

Kvaal SI and During EM (1999) A dental study comparing age estimation of the human remains from the Swedish warship Vasa. *International Journal of Osteoarchaeology* **9**, 170–181.

Loth SR and İşcan MY (1994) Morphological indicators of skeletal aging: implications for paleodemography and paleogerontology. In DE Crews and RM

Garruto (eds.): *Biological anthropology and aging.* Perspectives on human variation over the life span. Oxford: Oxford University Press, pp. 394–425.

Lovejoy CO, Meindl RS, Pryzbeck TR, Barton TS, Heiple KG, and Kotting D (1977) Paleodemography of the Libben site, Ottawa County, Ohio. *Science* **198**, 291–293.

Lovejoy CO, Meindl RS, Mensforth RP, and Barton TJ (1985a) Multifactorial age determination of skeletal age at death: a method and blind tests of its accuracy. *American Journal of Physical Anthropology* **68**, 1–14.

Lovejoy CO, Meindl RS, Pryzbeck TR, and Mensforth RP (1985b) Chronological metamorphosis of the auricular surface of the ilium: a new method for the determination of adult skeletal age at death. *American Journal of Physical Anthropology* **68**, 15–28.

Lucy D and Pollard AM (1995) Further comments on the estimation of error associated with the Gustafson dental age estimation method. *Journal of Forensic Science* **40**, 222–227.

Lucy D, Aykroyd RG, Pollard AM, and Solheim T (1996) A Bayesian approach to adult human age estimation from dental observations by Johanson's age changes. *Journal of Forensic Science* **41**, 189–194.

Lynnerup N, Thomsen JL, and Frohlich B (1998) Intra- and inter-observer variation in histological criteria used in age at death determination based on femoral cortical bone. *Forensic Science International* **91**, 219–230.

Mann RW, Jantz RL, Bass WM, and Willey PS (1991) Maxillary suture obliteration: a visual method for estimating skeletal age. *Journal of Forensic Science* **36**, 781–791.

Maples WR and Rice PM (1979) Some difficulties in the Gustafson dental age estimations. *Journal of Forensic Science* **24**, 168–172.

Masset C (1989) Age estimation on the basis of cranial sutures. In MY İşcan (ed.): *Age markers in the human skeleton.* Springfield, IL: C. C. Thomas, pp. 71–103.

Masters PM and Zimmerman MR (1978) Age determination of an Alaskan mummy: morphologic and biochemical correlation. *Science* **201**, 811–812.

McKern TW (1956) The symphyseal formula: a new method for determining age from pubic symphyses. *American Journal of Physical Anthropology* **14**, 388.

McKern TW and Stewart TD (1957) *Skeletal age changes in young American males. Analyzed from the skeletal standpoint of age identification.* Technical report EP-45; Natick, MA: US Army Quartermaster Research and Development Center.

Meindl RS and Lovejoy CO (1985) Ectocranial suture closure: a revised method for the determination of skeletal age at death based on the lateral-anterior sutures. *American Journal of Physical Anthropology* **68**, 57–66.

Meindl RS, Lovejoy CO, Mensforth RP, and Walker RA (1985) A revised method of age determination using the os pubis, with a review and tests of accuracy of other current methods of pubic symphyseal aging. *American Journal of Physical Anthropology* **68**, 29–45.

Milner GR and Boldsen J (1999) Skeletal age coding format. Danish Medieval Project, unpublished manuscript.

Molleson T and Cox (1993) *The Spitalfields Project*. Vol. 2. CBA Research Report 86.

Moore-Jansen PH and Jantz RL (1986) *A computerized skeletal data bank for forensic anthropology*. Knoxville, TN: Department of Anthropology, University of Tennessee.

Müller HG, Love B, and Hoppa R (2001) A semiparametric method for estimating demographic profiles from age indicator data. *American Journal of Physical Anthropology*, in press.

Nalbandian J and Sognnaes RF (1960) Structural changes in human teeth. In NW Shock (ed.): *Aging*. Washington, DC: American Association for the Advancement of Science, pp. 367–382.

NN (1980) Recommendations for age and sex diagnoses of skeletons. *Journal of Human Evolution* 9, 517–549.

Ogino T, Ogino H, and Nagy B (1985) Application of aspartic acid racemization to forensic odontology: post mortem designation of age at death. *Forensic Science International* 29, 259–267.

Ohtani S (1997) Different racemization ratios in dentin from different locations within a tooth. *Growth Development and Aging* 61, 93–99.

Owings Webb PA and Suchey JM (1985) Epiphyseal union of the anterior iliac crest and medial clavicle in a modern multiracial sample of American males and females. *American Journal of Physical Anthropology* 68, 457–466.

Pasquier E, de Saint Martin Pernot L, Burdin V, Mounayer C, Le Rest C, Colin D, Mottier D, Roux C, and Baccino E (1999) Determination of age at death: assessment of an algorithm of age prediction using numerical three-dimensional CT data from pubic bones. *American Journal of Physical Anthropology* 108, 261–268.

Pfeiffer H, Mörnstad H, and Teivens A (1995) Estimation of chronologic age using the aspartic acid racemization method. II. On human cortical bone. *International Journal of Legal Medicine* 108, 24–26.

Plato CC, Fox KM, and Tobin JD (1994) Skeletal changes in human aging. In DE Crews and RM Garruto (eds.): *Biological anthropology and aging. Perspectives on human variation over the life span*. Oxford: Oxford University Press, pp. 272–300.

Pratte DG and Pfeiffer S (1999) Histological age estimation of a cadaveral sample of diverse origins. *Journal of the Canadian Society of Forensic Science* 32, 155–167.

Ritz-Timme S, Cattaneo C, Collins MJ, Waite ER, Schutz HW, Kaatsch HJ, and Borrman HI (2000) Age estimation: the state of art in relation to the specific demands of forensic practice. *International Journal of Legal Medicine* 113, 129–136.

Rose JC and Ungar PS (1998) Gross dental wear and dental microwear in historical perspective. In KW Alt, FW Rösing and M Teschler-Nicola (eds.): *Dental anthropology. Fundamentals, limits, and prospects*. Wien, New York: Springer-Verlag, pp. 349–386.

Rösing FW and Kvaal SI (1998) Dental age in adults – a review of estimation methods. In KW Alt, FW Rösing, and M Teschler-Nicola (eds.): *Dental anthropology. Fundamentals, limits, and prospects.* Wien, New York: Springer-Verlag, pp. 443–468.

Saunders SR (1989) Nonmetric skeletal variation. In MY İşcan and KAR Kennedy (eds.): *Reconstruction of life from the skeleton.* New York: Wiley-Liss, pp. 95–108.

Simon C (1987) Evolution de la synostose des sutures crâniennes dans quelque populations anciennes. In H Duday and C Masset (eds.): *Anthropologie physique et archéologique. Méthodes d'étude des sépultures.* Paris: CNRS, pp. 239–244.

Snow CC (1983) Equations for estimating age at death from the pubic symphysis: a modification of the McKern–Stewart method. *Journal of Forensic Science* **28**, 864–870.

Solheim T and Sundnes PK (1980) Dental age estimation of Norwegian adults – a comparison of different methods. *Forensic Science International* **16**, 7–17.

Spencer F (ed.) (1997) *History of physical anthropology. An encyclopedia.* New York, London: Garland Publishing.

Spirduso WW (1995) *Physical dimensions of aging.* Champaign, CT: Human Kinetics.

St Hoyme LE and İşcan MY (1989) Determination of sex and race: accuracy and assumptions. In MY İşcan and KAR Kennedy (eds.): *Reconstruction of life from the skeleton.* New York: Wiley-Liss, pp. 53–93.

Stout SD (1989) The use of cortical bone histology to estimate age at death. In MY İşcan (ed.): *Age markers in the human skeleton.* Springfield, IL: C. C. Thomas, pp. 195–207.

Stout SD (1998) The application of histological techniques for age at death determination. In KJ Reichs (ed.): *Forensic osteology. Advances in the identification of human remains.* Springfield, IL: C. C. Thomas, pp. 237–252.

Suchey JM (1979) Problems in the aging of females using the os pubis. *American Journal of Physical Anthropology* **51**, 467–470.

Suchey JM, Wiseley DV, and Katz D (1986) Evaluation of the Todd and McKern–Stewart methods for aging the male os pubis. In KJ Reichs (ed.): *Forensic osteology. Advances in the identification of human remains.* Springfield, IL: C. C. Thomas, pp. 33–67.

Thomas CD, Stein MS, Feik SA, Ward JD, and Clement JG (2000) Determination of age at death using combined morphology and histology of the femur. *Journal of Anatomy,* **196**, 463–471.

Todd TW (1920) Age changes in the pubic bones. I. The male white pubis. *American Journal of Physical Anthropology* **3**, 285–334.

Todd TW (1921a) Age changes in the pubic bones. II. The pubis of the male Negro–white hybrid. III. The pubis of the white female. IV. The pubis of the female Negro–white hybrid. *American Journal of Physical Anthropology* **4**, 4–70.

Todd TW (1921b) Age changes in the pubic bones. V. Mammalian pubic bone metamorphosis. *American Journal of Physical Anthropology* **4**, 333–406.

Todd TW (1921c) Age changes in the pubic bones. VI. The interpretation of variations in the symphyseal area. *American Journal of Physical Anthropology* **4**, 407–424.

Todd TW (1923) Age changes in the pubic bones. VII. The anthropoid strain in human pubic symphysis of the third decade. *Journal of Anatomy* **57**, 274–294.

Todd TW (1930) Age changes in the pubic bones. VII. Roentgenographic differentiation. *American Journal of Physical Anthropology* **14**, 255–271.

Turban-Just S and Grupe G (1995) Post-mortem-Rekonstruktion von Stoffwechselraten mittels Histomorphometrie bodengelagerter menschlicher Knochenkompakta. *Anthropologischer Anzeiger* **53**, 1–25.

Usher BM, Boldsen JL, and Holman D (2000) Age estimation at Tirup cemetery: an application of the transition analysis method. *American Journal of Physical Anthropology* **30**, 307.

Waite ER, Collins MJ, Ritz-Timme S, Schutz HW, Cattaneo C, and Borrman HI (1999) A review of the methodological aspects of aspartic acid racemization analysis for use in forensic science. *Forensic Science International* **103**, 113–124.

Xu X, Philipsen HP, Jablonski NG, Pang KM, and Jiazhen Z (1992) Age estimation from the structure of adult teeth: a review of the literature. *Forensic Science International* **54**, 93–128.

Zhang Z (1982) A preliminary study of estimation of age by morphological changes in the symphysis pubis. *Acta Anthropologica Sinica* **1**, 132–136.

Zhang Z, Wu X, and Li X (1989) Estimation of pubic age among Chinese Han people by means of multiple stepwise progressive analysis. *Nippon Hoigaku Zasshi* **43**, 416–419.

5 Transition analysis:
a new method for estimating age from skeletons

JESPER L. BOLDSEN, GEORGE R. MILNER,

LYLE W. KONIGSBERG, AND JAMES W. WOOD

Introduction

Estimating the ages of skeletons is an essential part of any osteologist's job, regardless of whether the skeletons come from forensic or archaeological contexts. The ages of juvenile skeletons can usually be estimated with minimal bias and an acceptable range of error, although even this endeavor is not entirely free from problems. But the situation is far worse when one is dealing with the skeletons of adults. Here a number of serious osteological and statistical problems plague the process of estimating an individual's age-at-death (see Bocquet-Appel and Masset 1982; Boldsen 1988; Masset 1989; Jackes 1992, 2000; Konigsberg and Frankenberg 1992, 1994; Milner *et al.* 2000). Among these difficulties is the tendency of age estimates to mimic the structure of the known-age reference samples used as standards of calibration (a problem often called "age mimicry") and an inability to estimate the ages of older skeletons (those greater than about 50 years of age).

The Rostock protocol outlined in the present volume represents a step toward a solution of these problems. In particular, the strategy of estimating the entire age-at-death distribution $f(a)$ *before* trying to estimate the age of any individual skeleton is an important, if at first somewhat counter-intuitive, innovation. However, the strategy has one serious practical shortcoming: the target population has to be large enough to provide good estimates of $f(a)$. Many archaeological skeletal samples examined by paleodemographers are simply too few in number to proceed in this manner. The protocol is completely inapplicable to the "samples" of single skeletons typically encountered by forensic scientists. How can we estimate the age of an individual skeleton when that skeleton is the only one we have to work with?

In this chapter, we outline a new method of age estimation that is applicable to small samples, including individual skeletons. The need to find a compromise between a method that is ideal from a mathematical perspective and one that can be applied to small samples has done much to motivate the development of this method. Our general approach to the problem of age estimation can be applied equally well to the skeletons of young people, but we have chosen to focus here on adults because the limitations of current age estimation methods are much greater for them than for juveniles.

New ways of estimating age are no better than the skeletal information upon which they are based. And here we encounter a further problem. Existing methods of scoring age-related changes in the skeleton are generally inadequate for the needs of more sophisticated statistical approaches to age estimation. Thus the problems we address in this chapter are both statistical and osteological in nature. To tackle one while ignoring the other serves no practical purpose, regardless of how interesting the exercise might be in theory.

The method presented here can be used with any skeletal trait that can be arranged into an invariant series of senescent stages. While the precise timing of transition from one stage to the next will presumably vary among individuals, the direction of the sequence can be regarded as essentially fixed because osteological structures often age in a regular manner. Elsewhere we have used the term "transition analysis" to refer to this kind of estimation procedure (Boldsen 1997; Milner *et al.* 1997; Boldsen *et al.* 1998) because the results allow us to make inferences about the timing of transitions from one stage to the next (see below).

After developing the basic estimation procedure, we apply it to data on the pubic symphysis, the iliac portion of the sacroiliac joint, and several cranial sutures in a sample of known-age skeletons from the Terry Collection at the Smithsonian Institution. Each of the three anatomical complexes is broken down into several separate components (or suture segments), and new scoring procedures are developed for the pubic symphysis and sacroiliac joint. Age-related changes in the pubic symphysis are regarded by many osteologists as providing the best means of establishing age-at-death in adult skeletons (e.g., McKern and Stewart 1957; Buikstra and Ubelaker 1994). Recently, it has been demonstrated that the iliac auricular surface also provides useful information on age-at-death (Lovejoy *et al.* 1985a). It has long been recognized that cranial sutures first close and then become obliterated with advancing age, but for the past 50 years or more they have been considered of questionable value in estimating age (Brooks 1955; McKern and Stewart 1957; İşcan and Loth 1989; Buikstra and Ubelaker 1994). We include sutures in our analyses because isolated crania are often found in forensic and archaeological work, and we must do something with them. Here we follow Meindl and Lovejoy (1985) in saying that, if used properly, cranial sutures still provide some information about age-at-death.

Problems of adult age estimation

Juveniles display numerous developmental traits that change with age in a sufficiently regular way to permit estimation of their ages at death with minimal error, either systematic or random. But senescent changes in bone are degenerative rather than developmental. By their very nature, they are likely to be more variable among individuals and across populations. Estimates of age-at-death based on senescent changes are, therefore, always likely to involve a considerable degree of error, which can be reduced but not eliminated. The common practice of lumping skeletons together into an open-ended terminal age interval, such as 50+ years, is an honest admission of this problem. Many, but not all, of the characteristics traditionally used by osteologists to estimate the ages of adult (*ca.* 20+ years) skeletons fall into the senescent category.[1]

There are at least four basic analytical difficulties in adult age estimation, all of which become more critical in older skeletons. First, what is the best way to represent the unavoidable (and often quite large) uncertainty involved in adult age estimation? Second, how can we avoid age mimicry, the contamination of our estimates by the age composition of the reference sample? Third, since different morphological traits may not provide independent information on age, how can we best combine multiple skeletal indicators of age? Fourth, how can anatomical features be scored in a way that most effectively captures any morphological variation that is informative about age?

Faced with the first of these problem, osteologists generally use discrete age intervals, often of constant width, to capture at least some of the imprecision inherent in estimating skeletal age-at-death. Constant age intervals, however, involve an assumption that all individual age estimates have the same degree of error. But just as no osteologist believes that an exact age can be assigned to any particular skeleton, no one would claim that all skeletons that appear to be roughly the same age can be assigned with equal confidence to a single age interval. Every skeleton has its own degree of error or precision, depending upon its own particular suite of

---

[1] An obvious exception pertinent to this paper is early change in the pubic symphysis, especially the outgrowth of bone that makes up the ventral margin, which osteologists often call the ventral rampart.

traits and quality of preservation. What is needed is not a point estimate of age or even a fixed age interval, but rather the whole probability density function $\Pr(a|c_j)$ calculated separately for each skeleton and for every value of a. $\Pr(a|c_j)$ is the probability that a skeleton died at age a given that it has characteristics c_j, where c_j is the set of skeletal traits observed in the j-th skeleton in our sample. If we wish to estimate a confidence interval around a point estimate of age for the j-th skeleton, it should be based directly on the density function $\Pr(a|c_j)$ or something closely related to it.

Twenty years ago, Bocquet-Appel and Masset (1982) showed that most traditional aging methods produce estimates for the target sample of archaeological skeletons that are biased in the direction of the composition of the known-age reference sample used as a standard of calibration. For example, the Korean War dead used by McKern and Stewart (1957) understandably have a much younger average adult age than do "natural" mortality samples, and age estimates using them as a reference sample often appear very young on average. This "age mimicry" bias can create the illusion that adult mortality rates in the target sample were extraordinarily high and accelerated more rapidly than is true of any historically well-attested human population.

Masset (1989) has provided one of the clearest explanations of how this problem arises. The relationship between age and skeletal trait in a reference sample is typically examined by applying some form of regression analysis (using the term in the broadest possible sense). But in doing such an analysis, we need to decide whether to regress c_j on a or a on c_j, since the two regression lines will usually be different. If we regress a on c_j, we obtain an estimate of a for each value of c_j, which is exactly what we want. Unfortunately, these estimates turn out to be sensitive to the age composition of the reference sample. If, for example, the reference sample contains many 20-year-olds but few 50-year-olds, then $\Pr(20|c_j)$ will almost certainly be greater than $\Pr(50|c_j)$ even if trait complex c_j is more typical of *living* 50-year-olds than of people in their 20s. Any prehistoric or forensic skeleton aged in this way will appear to be more like a 20-year-old than a 50-year-old, purely because of the reference sample's age distribution.

But what if we regress c_j on a? Then we obtain results that are much less sensitive to the composition of the reference sample, but we end up with estimates of $\Pr(c_j|a)$ rather than $\Pr(a|c_j)$. In other words, we can get good estimates of the probability that we do not want, but only poor estimates of the probability that we do want.

Konigsberg and Frankenberg (1992) have shown how to solve this problem in principle, and Love and Müller (Chapter 9, this volume) have developed a way to solve it in practice. It is best to start with estimates of

$\Pr(c_j|a)$ – which Love and Müller call "weight functions" – since these can be obtained without bias from a good reference sample. (Love and Müller also provide a promising nonparametric method for estimating the weight functions; Chapter 9, this volume.) Only after $\Pr(c_j|a)$ has been estimated should $\Pr(a|c_j)$ be derived secondarily from the regression results. The correct value of $\Pr(a|c_j)$ can be obtained from our estimates of $\Pr(c_j|a)$ using Bayes' theorem, which states that:

$$\Pr(a|c_j) = \frac{\Pr(c_j|a)f(a)}{\displaystyle\int_0^\infty \Pr(c_j|x)f(x)\mathrm{d}x}, \tag{5.1}$$

where $f(a)$ is the age-at-death distribution of the ancient population that we are trying to analyze – i.e., the probability that a randomly selected dead individual from that population is exactly age a. In Bayesian analysis, $f(a)$ would be called the prior distribution of ages at death, since information on it must come prior to estimation of $\Pr(a|c_j)$. As Love and Müller show in their contribution to this volume (Chapter 9), it is possible to estimate a parametric model of $f(a)$ by maximum likelihood using the estimated weight functions and the marginal distribution of skeletal traits in the target sample – if, that is, the target sample is large enough to provide a good estimate of $f(a)$. Alternatively, we can base our estimate of $f(a)$ on information independent of the target sample of skeletons, if such information is available.

As outlined in the Rostock Manifesto (see Hoppa and Vaupel, Chapter 1, this volume), Bayesian inversion (equation 5.1) is applied only *after* $f(a)$ has been estimated for the sample as a whole. Thus any individual age estimate is, in effect, a secondary by-product of the aggregate-level analysis. We agree, in principle, that this is the right way to estimate an individual skeleton's age-at-death. But the right way may not always be the most *useful* way, simply because target samples in archaeological and forensic research will often be too small to support the estimation of $f(a)$. Although at this stage it is difficult to be precise about how many skeletons are needed, the Rostock protocol almost certainly requires samples larger than those found in most forensic or archaeological situations. So a method is needed that is applicable to the kinds of small samples (including single skeletons) that are typical of much osteological research.

In this chapter we develop such a method based on either a uniform prior distribution or documentary information on $f(a)$ that is independent of our skeletal material. In the case of a uniform prior, the $f(\cdot)$ values cancel in equation (5.1), as first noted by Konigsberg and Frankenberg (1994). Their suggestion of using a uniform prior was criticized by Di Bacco *et al.*

(1999), who noted that it places disproportionate weight on extremely old, and highly unlikely, ages-at-death. While we agree with this critique, in our experience the empirical weight functions dominate most informative priors for age-at-death. In other words, the age information contained in a skeleton (and in the weight functions) is much greater than the age information that comes from knowing that it was randomly sampled from a particular adult mortality profile. Good practice or bad, there is ample precedent for using uniform priors in the calibration literature (Brown 1993; Konigsberg *et al.* 1998).

Use of a uniform prior seems particularly appropriate in paleodemographic research, where any assumption about an informative prior can create a tautological circle. (The only way to avoid such circularity is to use a very general parametric model of mortality as advocated by Wood *et al.*, Chapter 7, this volume.) In certain cases, however, we may have independent information on the prior – independent, that is, of the skeletal sample we are trying to age – and proper use of that information will almost always give us better estimates than if we had assumed a uniform prior. For example, if we are trying to age a skeleton from western Europe dated to the 17th century, we may be able to estimate $f(a)$ from parish burial records. In forensic work, informative priors might be constructed from information on the ages of homicide victims in the general population. Whenever it is possible to use an *appropriate* informative prior, we should do so, because our estimates using equation (5.1) will then be entirely free from age mimicry.

It is also important to find an appropriate way to combine information from different skeletal indicators of age, as osteologists have recognized for a long time (Acsádi and Nemeskéri 1970; Workshop of European Anthropologists 1980; Lovejoy *et al.* 1985a; İşcan and Loth 1989). The problem here is that multiple age indicators can be correlated with each other, so the information they contain is not independent. One approach to this problem is the recent suggestion that the correlation matrix among traits can be estimated from a reference sample by a stochastic expectation-maximization (SEM) algorithm and used to condition traits properly (Konigsberg and Holman 1999). Unfortunately, for m traits this approach requires us to estimate $\frac{1}{2}m(m-1)$ correlations for each transition, which in turn demands an enormous reference sample. The dimensionality of the problem can be reduced considerably by adopting the latent trait approach of Holman *et al.* (Chapter 10, this volume). In the work presented here, we simplify things even further by assuming that any correlation among traits is purely attributable to age, so that the traits would be independent if they could be conditioned on age (Boldsen 1997; for similar assumptions, see Roche *et al.* 1988; Lucy and Pollard 1995). This assumption of "conditional independence" may work well for many senescent changes in the skeleton. At least one standard theory for the evolution of senescence – the so-called mutation accumulation mechanism (Rose 1991:72–78) – suggests that it *should* work well. But we would never argue that it accurately reflects the biology of all skeletal traits, especially developmental traits in juveniles. When the assumption is incorrect, our method still provides asymptotically unbiased point estimates, but the confidence intervals associated with them appear narrower than they really are (Boldsen *et al.* 1998). In what follows, we develop an ad hoc correction for this bias.

The final problem, which is strictly osteological in nature, has to do with how one should classify morphological features that are potentially informative about age. Our approach to scoring age-related variation follows the logic of McKern and Stewart (1957), who broke the pubic symphysis down into three separate components, each of which was coded as a series of unidirectional stages (also see Gilbert and McKern 1973).

This approach captures the changes that occur in complex biological structures much better than classificatory schemes that rely on the appearance of these anatomical structures in their entirety (see e.g., Todd 1920, 1921; Brooks and Suchey 1990). Because senescent changes in morphology do not occur in lockstep – and there is no conceivable biological reason why they should do so – it is typically difficult to classify adult skeletons unambiguously. That is to say, it is often difficult to shoehorn a complex anatomical structure, such as the sacroiliac joint, into one particular developmental stage. One solution to this problem is to use categories that encompass considerable morphological variation, but then potentially valuable information on age is lost. It is for these reasons that we follow the lead of McKern and Stewart (1957). Indeed, we take their approach a step further by scoring the pubic symphysis in terms of five, not three, components. This same approach has been adopted in dealing with the iliac portion of the sacroiliac joint. Previous work with this joint has focused on its appearance in its entirety (Lovejoy *et al.* 1985b). Sutures have long been described in terms of separate segments, so in scoring them we have not departed from traditional practice.

Materials and methods

Skeletal sample

The skeletons used in this study are from the Smithsonian Institution's Terry Collection, one of the few large collections of purportedly known-

Table 5.1. *Race, sex, and age composition of the reference sample*

| Age (years) | Black | | White | | |
	Female	Male	Female	Male	Total
<20	0	1	0	2	3
20–24	7	7	1	2	17
25–29	7	9	2	5	23
30–34	2	5	4	6	17
35–39	3	3	4	4	14
40–44	2	3	2	1	8
45–49	4	2	3	3	12
50–54	1	3	2	3	9
55–59	2	3	3	2	10
60–64	2	1	2	2	7
65–69	3	3	3	3	12
70–74	4	1	3	2	10
75–79	3	3	4	3	13
80–84	2	3	3	3	11
85–89	2	3	3	1	9
90–94	1	1	1	0	3
95–99	5	1	0	0	6
>99	2	0	0	0	2
Total	52	52	40	42	186

age skeletons in the USA (St Hoyme and İşcan 1989).[2] They are from people who died somewhere between the 1920s and 1960s in St Louis, Missouri.

Skeletons were selected on the basis of age, sex, and race (as indicated by documentation that accompanies the collection), as well as skeletal completeness. The four sex and race groups were broken down by age, and skeletons were chosen randomly from the collection. The objective was to obtain a sample of skeletons spread across all of adulthood for the sex and race groups. Individuals who were less than 40 years old at the time of death were oversampled because some of the morphological changes of interest take place rapidly during early adulthood. Since we were interested in age-related morphological change in both the cranium and the pelvis, skeletal completeness was of concern only when one of them was missing or badly damaged. The reference sample consisted of 186 individuals: 52 from black females, 52 from black males, 40 from white females, and 42 from white males (Table 5.1). As is immediately apparent, the age-at-death

[2] The ages provided in the Terry Collection documentation are not necessarily the true ages of these individuals, but the overwhelming majority are likely to be approximately correct.

distribution of the reference sample does not resemble anything that would be observed in a "natural" population.

An additional 84 skeletons from the same collection were used in a validation study of the age estimation method (24 black females, 24 black males, 18 white females, and 18 white males). They were selected randomly from the skeletons that were not part of the reference sample, and they were examined three years after the initial work.

Osteological measures

The features used in our study were derived from previous descriptions of bony changes in the pelvis and cranium, as well as our experience with several thousand prehistoric and historical skeletons. In all, there are five characteristics for the pubic symphysis and nine for the iliac portion of the sacroiliac joint, as well as five suture segments. Archaeological skeletons from North America and Denmark were used when defining the characteristics of the pubic symphysis and all but one of the sacroiliac joint features. The exception – widely distributed, tightly packed, and uniformly low exostoses across the ilium posterior to the auricular surface, which we regard as an "old age" trait (posterior iliac exostoses) – was only noticed when we were handling the many skeletons from elderly people in the Terry Collection. There would have been few such individuals in the archaeological samples used when the skeletal traits were initially defined.

Brief descriptions of age-related changes in the morphology of the various anatomical units are provided in Appendix 5.1. Many of the terms used are immediately recognizable as being derived from earlier work, especially that of McKern and Stewart (1957) and Lovejoy *et al.* (1985b). We have intentionally used these terms to make our classification of skeletal traits easier to understand by researchers who are familiar with existing age estimation methods.

Estimation procedure

Transition analysis for a single trait

We first consider the simplest case, in which data for only one skeletal trait are available (e.g., the pubic symphysis considered as a single unit, as in the Todd or Suchey–Brooks approaches). We assume that the developmental trajectory for the trait can be broken down into an invariant sequence of *s* distinct, nonoverlapping stages, and that morphological change is strictly unidirectional with respect to those stages. In other words, an individual can only move from state i to $i + 1$, never in the opposite direction, and never directly from i to $i + 2$ or higher. For simplicity, we first assume that we are dealing with a skeletal trait that has only two stages. In this case y_j, the skeletal trait in the j-th individual, has only two states that we will score as 0 and 1. We assume we have access to a known-age reference sample of n skeletons.

The probability that a skeleton is in stage 1 (as opposed to stage 0) is a binomial random variable whose one parameter is assumed to be a function of age. If we have joint data from the reference sample on each skeleton's trait and age at death – which we assume to be known without error – we can use a generalized linear model (McCullagh and Nelder 1989):

$$\Pr(y_j = 1 | a_j) = \Lambda(\alpha + \beta a_j), \tag{5.2}$$

where a_j is the age at death of the j-th skeleton in the reference sample and α and β are parameters to be estimated from the reference sample. The symbol $\Lambda(\cdot)$ represents what is known as the inverse of the link function in a generalized linear model (see Johnson and Albert 1999: equation 3.4 and surrounding discussion). We use the logit link, $\exp(\cdot)/(1 + \exp(\cdot))$ in this chapter.[3] This type of analysis is referred to as a "transition analysis" because the intercept and slope in equation (5.2) can be converted to the mean and standard deviation for a logistic distribution of the age at the transition from stage 0 to stage 1. Specifically, the mean is α/β and the standard deviation is $3^{-1/2}\pi/\beta$. Under the model in equation (5.2), the likelihood function for estimating α and β is:

$$L(\alpha, \beta) = \frac{\prod_{j=1}^{n} \exp[(\alpha + \beta a_j)y_j]}{\prod_{j=1}^{n} [1 + \exp(\alpha + \beta a_j)]} \tag{5.3}$$

(Cox 1970:19). Maximum likelihood estimates of α and β can be obtained using one of many readily available statistical packages, including the proprietary program GLIM (Francis *et al.* 1994) or the glm function within the freely available statistical package "R".

For a skeletal trait with more than two stages, equation (5.2) can be applied as a binary contrast between those individuals who have made a particular transition and those who have not. This model is called a

---

[3] In Chapter 11, Konigsberg and Herrmann use the probit link.

cumulative logit or proportional odds model (McCullagh 1980) and can be written as:

$$\Pr(y_j \geq i|a_j) = \Lambda(\alpha_i + \beta a_j). \tag{5.4}$$

This model has a slope common to all the transitions, but intercepts that differ. In the transition analysis paradigm, this means that the average age at which individuals make transitions differs by stage (e.g., the average age at the transition from stage 0 to 1 is lower than the average age at the transition from stage 1 to 2), but the standard deviations are the same for all transitions. This is an unattractive by-product of the proportional odds model. Everything we know about developmental biology indicates that the standard deviations of age-to-transition increase with increasing stages.

As an alternative to the proportional odds model, we can use what is known in the statistical literature as a "continuation ratio model" (Fienberg 1977:86; Agresti 1990:319; Lindsey 1995a:98, 1995b:59; Long 1997:146) or in survival analysis as a "discrete time proportional hazards model" (see McCullagh 1980:140). In the continuation ratio model we fit a series of binary logistic models as:

$$\Pr(y_j \geq i|y_j \geq i - 1, a_j) = \Lambda(\alpha_i + \beta_i a_j), \tag{5.5}$$

where the successive conditioning means that we form subsamples that contain only those skeletons in stage $i - 1$ or greater. We assume that there are s stages, so that the last stage is numbered $s - 1$ (because we began counting stages at zero). Consequently, the first logistic regression contrasts individuals in stage 1 or higher against individuals in stage 0 or higher (i.e., all individuals), the second contrasts individuals in stage 2 or higher against those in stage 1 or higher (thus excluding individuals in stage 0), and the last regression contrasts individuals in stage $s - 1$ with those in $s - 1$ and $s - 2$ (to the exclusion of all stages less than $s - 2$). The conditioning in equation (5.5) can be removed by forming the product

$$\Pr(y_j \geq i|a_j) = \prod_{k=1}^{i} \Lambda(\alpha_k + \beta_k a_j). \tag{5.6}$$

The probability of being in *exact* stage i at any given age at death is then:

$$\Pr(y_j = i|a_j) = \Pr(y_j \geq i|a_j) - \Pr(y_j \geq i + 1|a_j), \tag{5.7}$$

which makes cross-overs impossible (Long 1997).

Equations (5.5) to (5.7) specify what is usually referred to as a "forward" continuation ratio model, but we can also write a "backward" continuation ratio model by replacing equation (5.5) with

$$\Pr(y_j = i \mid y_j \leq i, a_j) = \Lambda(\alpha_i + \beta_i a_j). \tag{5.8}$$

Equation (5.7) then becomes

$$\Pr(y_j = i \mid a_j) = \Pr(y_j = i \mid y_j \leq i, a_j) \prod_{k=i+1}^{s-1} [1 - \Pr(y_j = k \mid y_j \leq k, a_j)]. \tag{5.9}$$

Equation (5.9) is quite similar to equation 5.24 of Powers and Xie (2000:163), which they present in a discussion of discrete-time hazard models (showing that continuation ratio and discrete-time hazard models are alternative ways of viewing the same process).

The continuation ratio logit can be fit by explicitly forming each of the subsamples and applying a logistic regression, or more expeditiously using Frank Harrell's "cr.setup" and "lrm" in S+ or "cr.setup" and "glm" in "R".[4] One of the best computing environments for applying the continuation ratio model is the US Environmental Protection Agency's (2000) "CatReg" script for S+. In addition to fitting the continuation ratio model (referred to as an "unrestricted conditional odds model" in CatReg) with a logit, probit, or complementary log–log link function (McCullagh and Nelder 1989), CatReg also includes the unrestricted cumulative model used by Konigsberg and Herrmann (Chapter 10, this volume), and it can test whether the speed of transition varies between phases (using the parallel.test command after fitting an unrestricted model). The CatReg package for S+ fits the "backward" continuation ratio model, in contrast to the forward model (equations (5.5) to (5.7)) that we use here. Unfortunately, the "forward" and "backward" continuation ratio models usually give different probabilities of being in a particular stage at a given age. For example, we have fit both models to Suchey's data on 737 male pubic symphyses, and find in the "forward" model that the probability of being in the initial stage at exact age 20 years is 0.776 while in the "backward" model the probability is 0.675. Greenland (1994:1668) has previously noted this problem with the continuation ratio model, writing that the method is "not invariant under reversal of the outcome codes unless Y is binary". He also noted that the method "is not invariant under collapsing of categories", a problem that does not carry over to the proportional odds (cumulative logit) or unrestricted cumulative probit that Konigsberg and Herrmann use in Chapter 11.

Since equations (5.7) and (5.9) refer to a single age and behave as proper probability functions at that age, they are uninfluenced by the distribution of the reference sample at other ages – except in the indirect sense that the age distribution may influence how well we can estimate α_i and β_i. Thus,

---

[4] See http://heswebl.med.virginia.edu/biostat/s/Design.html

our estimate of $\Pr(y_j = i | a_j)$ is robust to the biasing effects of the reference sample's age distribution.

If we assume a uniform prior distribution for age between birth and the highest age attained by anyone in the target population, we can find the probability density function for age conditional on the skeleton being in the i-th stage of the indicator:

$$f(a | y_j = i) = \frac{\Pr(y_j = i | a)}{\displaystyle\int_0^{\infty} \Pr(y_j = i | x) dx}. \qquad (5.10)$$

This posterior density for age yields a maximum likelihood estimator, which in the calibration literature would be called a classical calibration estimate (Konigsberg *et al.* 1998) or more properly a "controlled" calibration estimate (Brown 1993). Equation (5.10) can be used to write the individual likelihood for age-at-death conditional on the observed skeletal stage. In equation (5.10) the denominator is a constant of proportionality that can be ignored in the likelihood function, so that the final likelihood is simply

$$L(a | y_j = i) \propto \Pr(y_j = i | a). \qquad (5.11)$$

The value of a that maximizes this function is the maximum likelihood estimate of the skeleton's age-at-death. Note, however, that we ultimately want the full density function provided by equation (5.10), not just a point estimate of age.

Transition analysis for multiple traits

The presentation thus far has concerned transitions among stages defined by a single skeletal trait, and such an approach is arguably not the best way to handle the morphological variation that actually occurs in a skeleton. Imagine that we have observations on a total of m traits from a single anatomical complex – for example, the pubic symphysis, the iliac part of the sacroiliac joint, or the cranial sutures – each of which is subdivided into a series of stages (the number of which may vary from one trait to another). If entry into stages for one trait were conditionally independent of all the other traits – i.e., if the trait stages were uncorrelated once the age effect is removed – a combined likelihood function could be formed by multiplying the stage likelihoods for each trait. Under the assumption of conditional independence, the likelihood for m traits is

$$L(a|\mathbf{y}_j = \mathbf{i}) = \prod_{k=1}^{m} L(a|y_{jk} = i_k). \tag{5.12}$$

As before, the value of a that maximizes equation (5.12) is regarded as the best point estimate of age-at-death. We will refer to this value of a as $\hat{a}$.

Approximate confidence intervals

It is comparatively easy to compute confidence intervals for multivariate normal data, including intervals that correct for the lack of independence among measures. Unfortunately, categorical data such as staging scores do not readily lend themselves to such analysis. We can, however, find an approximate confidence interval by exploiting the fact that -2 times the natural logarithm of the likelihood ratio is asymptotically distributed as a χ^2 random variable (Cox and Hinkley 1974). For the j-th skeleton in the reference sample, we form a "Z score" defined jointly by the two points

$$Z_j = \pm \sqrt{|2\ln[L(a|\mathbf{y}_j = \mathbf{i})/L(\hat{a}|\mathbf{y}_j = \mathbf{i})]|}. \tag{5.13}$$

If the traits are indeed conditionally independent once the effect of age has been partialled out, then $Z \sim N(0, 1)$. If the traits are not conditionally independent, the mean should still remain 0 but the variance will be greater than 1. Assuming conditional independence, we can compute a $(1 - \alpha)$th % confidence interval for the j-th age estimate by finding the range of α values that satisfy:

$$-2\ln[L(a|\mathbf{y}_j = \mathbf{i})/L(\hat{a}|\mathbf{y}_j = \mathbf{i})] \leq \chi^2_{(1-\alpha)}. \tag{5.14}$$

In this expression, $\chi^2_{(1-\alpha)}$ is the value at the $(1 - \alpha)$-th percentile of a chi-square distribution with one degree of freedom. If the traits are not conditionally independent, this confidence interval can be corrected by replacing $L(a|\mathbf{y}_j = \mathbf{i})/L(\hat{a}|\mathbf{y}_j = \mathbf{i})$ in equation (5.14) with $[L(a|\mathbf{y}_j = \mathbf{i})/L(\hat{a}|\mathbf{y}_j = \mathbf{i})]^{1/\mathrm{var}(Z)}$, where var(Z) is the estimated variance of the full set of Z scores. This correction is an exponential version of the standard formula for transforming a variable so that it has a variance of 1.

The likelihood-based confidence region given in equation (5.14) has been used by Brown and Sundberg (1987) in the general multivariate calibration setting. In their article they consider a number of possible contexts, including estimation of a confidence region for one variable (such as age) from multiple continuous indicators. They show that the confidence region for a single case will increase as an "inconsistency diagnostic" increases. Their inconsistency diagnostic is a measure of how discrepant the indicators are in their prediction of (in our case) age. More accurately, in our situation, the inconsistency diagnostic is a quadratic form based on the deviation of the observed indicators from their predicted values at the "classical calibration" estimate of age. This quadratic form is written in the inverse of the residual variance–covariance matrix among indicators (i.e., the inverse of the variance–covariance matrix among indicators after regression on age). As we have assumed conditional independence, the residual variance–covariance matrix must be diagonal. This being the case, the confidence interval given in equation (5.14) is unaffected by increasing discrepancies in skeletal indicators. This is an undesirable side-effect of assuming conditional independence if there is in fact dependence among skeletal indicators after accounting for the effect of age.

A test of internal consistency

When dealing with multivariate trait data, certain combinations of traits are extremely unlikely to occur at any age. For example, we would not expect to observe any combination of the highest and lowest scores for any two components of the pubic symphysis in the same individual – a fact explicitly recognized by McKern and Stewart (1957). If such a combination were in fact observed, it might indicate the mixing of skeletal elements from different individuals or an error on the part of the observer. Using the value of the untransformed likelihood function from equation (5.12), it is possible to define a test statistic δ_j that evaluates the consistency of the trait scores for the j-th skeleton in the sample as:

$$\delta_j = -2\ln[\mathrm{L}(\hat{a}|\mathbf{y}_j = \mathbf{i})]. \tag{5.15}$$

Under the assumptions of conditional independence and internal consistency, the values of δ_j should follow a χ^2 distribution with degrees of freedom equal to the number of traits minus 1. This test will usually be conservative; the test statistic δ_j is likely to be biased downward when conditional independence does not hold – i.e., when skeletal traits remain positively correlated once the effects of age have been partialled out.

Using an "external" f(a)

Many of the practical problems in applying Bayes' theorem (equation (5.1)) occur because we do not have any information on $f(a)$ apart from that contained in the bones themselves. Sometimes, however, we have ancillary information – for example, on the target sample's historical or archaeological context – that allows us to select suitable $f(a)$ values that are independent of the bones. We have relevant information on the distribution of age-at-death from many parts of the modern world and for some places in the past that can serve as general models for our archaeological populations. For example, here we use an age-at-death distribution from 17th century Danish rural parish records to provide estimates of $f(a)$ in equation (5.1) (Johansen 1998). For forensic purposes, one could use national homicide data, such as the 1996 figures for the USA that are incorporated into the transition analysis computer program (Peters *et al.* 1998).

Computer program

A computer program for all the analyses outlined here is currently available at: www.sdu.dk/tvf/Demcenter/transitionanalysis.html

Results

Transition analysis for a single trait

The dorsal margin of the pubic symphysis in black males from the Terry Collection is used as an example of single-trait analysis. Figures 5.1–5.3 show the empirical relationship between morphological stage and reported age, the transition probabilities $\Pr(y_j \geq i | y_j \geq i - 1, a_j)$, and the stage probabilities $\Pr(y_j = i | a_j)$. The actual distribution by age of individuals in each of the dorsal margin stages is shown in Figure 5.1. Similar information was collected for each part of the pubic symphysis, sacroiliac joint, and cranial sutures used in the transition analysis. These data are used to generate transition curves that show the passage from one stage to the next (Figure 5.2). In Figure 5.3, the transition curves have been subtracted from each other. The likelihood curves thereby produced aid in a simple visual understanding of what happens to the various dorsal margin stages throughout adulthood. The best point estimate of age for this single trait is the peak of the curve. A 95% confidence interval for the point estimate can be obtained by excluding the upper and lower 2.5% tails of the distribution.

All three of these figures – from raw data to likelihood curves – show that the dorsal margin trait is strongly age progressive. Useful age information can be derived from these data by transition analysis. As expected

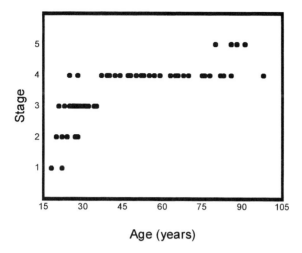

Figure 5.1. The relationship between the dorsal margin of the pubic symphysis and reported age using bones from black males from the Terry Collection.

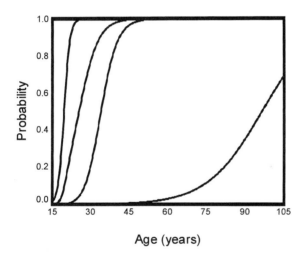

Figure 5.2. Estimated curves showing the age-specific probabilities of making the transition from one stage to the next, based on the Terry Collection data in Figure 5.1.

from the original data (Figure 5.1), the likelihood curves get broader later in life (Figure 5.3). The relative widths of these curves plainly show the well-known error associated with estimating the ages of old people. The dorsal margin goes through rapid transitions early in adulthood, and then it reaches a point where little or no morphological change occurs. Thus our

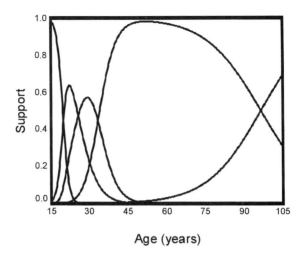

Figure 5.3. Likelihood curves showing the proportions of individuals in the several stages at each age as calculated from the transition curves shown in Figure 5.2.

results conform to what is known about the aging process and to practical osteological experience.

This example is not particularly realistic because only rarely will only one part of a single anatomical structure be available. It would most commonly happen with a skull fragment because the suture segments of interest are, comparatively speaking, widely separated from one another. The quality of age estimates obtained by combining information on all components of each of the three anatomical units was evaluated by calculating correlation coefficients between estimated age ($\hat{a}$) and reported age (a). The correlation coefficients for each of the three complexes were reasonable high: 0.86 for the pubic symphysis, 0.82 for the iliac part of the sacroiliac joint, and 0.66 for the cranial sutures. The combination of all three complexes, 0.88, is only slightly higher than the value for pubic symphysis alone. These results are what osteologists would expect: the pubic symphysis works best, and the cranial sutures worst. The pubic symphysis is essentially as informative as all three parts of the skeleton combined. But it is not practical to limit ourselves to the pubic symphysis because it is the most likely part of the skeleton to be damaged postmortem.

Once we move from a single-trait to multiple-trait analysis, the assumption that the different features of each of the three complexes are conditionally independent of each other becomes critically important. It is necessary, therefore, to examine this assumption carefully. It should be emphasized that the structure of correlations among scores in different components of each of the three complexes is, strictly speaking, a property of the reference sample and cannot be studied apart from that particular sample. But the underlying assumption of an invariant biological relationship between age and c_j means that the partial correlations remain constant among all samples. The correction used here to compute approximate confidence intervals is obviously only a first step toward solving the problem of a lack of conditional independence among scores. It is encouraging, however, that the point estimates of age-at-death derived from the Terry Collection reference sample do in fact appear to be conditionally independent. This means there is no strong indication of a separate factor that acts on the aging of all three anatomical units in the same way. We have not, however, examined the correlations among characters within complexes after conditioning on age. We would expect, for example, that correlations in the closure times of neighboring sutures might be high even after partialling out the effect of age.

Age estimates (and their confidence intervals) tend to vary from one skeleton to the next because the particular suite of observable traits is usually different. That is to say, each skeleton has its own set of morphological characteristics, a fact that transition analysis deals with effectively. It is interesting, however, that age estimates are often different for blacks versus whites and for men versus women, even when identical combinations of morphological traits are involved. There are a number of possible reasons for such discrepancies – most obviously, differences in genetic background or lifetime experiences of the various samples. In general the effect of changing race or sex in transition analysis estimates is much greater for a single component, such as the dorsal margin, than on the aggregate level where all components from the pelvis and skull are combined. Nonetheless, the discrepancies across races and sexes highlight the need to identify an appropriate reference sample.

As discussed above, use of a uniform prior age distribution poses a problem. We have used such a distribution here in the absence of other information about the age structure of the population that produced the skeletons. The effects of its use were explored using an age-at-death distribution derived from 17th century rural Danish parish records (Johansen 1998). In general, the largest differences associated with the use of this informative prior rather than a uniform distribution occur at older ages, where the uniform prior produces estimates that are too high. Figure 5.4 illustrates the effect of using an appropriate $f(a)$ distribution instead of a uniform one for a 17th century Danish skeleton of known age. Laurits Ebbesen was a Danish nobleman who died in 1637 and was buried in

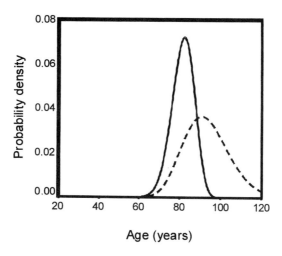

Figure 5.4. Estimated likelihood curves for Laurits Ebbesen, a Danish nobleman who died in 1637 at age 87 years. Estimates are shown for a uniform prior distribution (dashed line) and one generated from 17th century Danish rural parish records (solid line).

Århus Cathedral. His skeleton was removed from its crypt for two days during the restoration of the church in 1998, making it possible to score the bones according to the characteristics listed in Appendix 5.1. Figure 5.4 illustrates the moderating effect of using an informative $f(a)$ schedule when trying to estimate the age of a very old individual such as Herre Ebbesen. But it should be noted that Ebbesen's known age of 87 (in fact, 87 years, 3 weeks, and 5 days) falls within the 95% confidence intervals for both the informative $f(a)$ *and* the uniform age-at-death distribution.

Depending on the mix of skeletal characteristics, the use of an informative $f(a)$ distribution in place of a uniform one does not always have such a noticeable effect. For example, Figure 5.5 shows transition analysis results for an archaeological skeleton of unknown age from medieval Denmark. In this case, the point estimate of age was moved less than 1 year with the use of the informative $f(a)$ distribution, and the 95% confidence intervals are essentially identical. In this particular case, discrepancies between the two sets of estimates would be of no concern in either archaeological or forensic applications.

To determine whether the age distributions of skeletal samples mimic those of reference samples, we examined an additional 84 skeletons randomly selected from that part of the Terry Collection not used in the reference sample. Their ages were estimated using the uniform prior age distribution, and point estimates of age were taken from the peaks of the

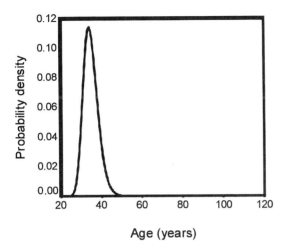

Age (years)

Figure 5.5. Estimated likelihood curves for an adult of unknown age from medieval Denmark. The age estimates using a uniform age distribution and one from 17th century Denmark are so similar that they cannot both be distinguished in this figure because they are almost completely superimposed on one another.

resulting likelihood curves. Figure 5.6 shows the distribution of known ages in the reference sample and the validation study (target) sample, along with the ages estimated by transition analysis for the validation sample. All four sex and race groups are combined in this figure. The target and estimated age distributions are similar to one another, and the latter bears no obvious relation to the reference sample, which is weighted toward younger ages. Thus age mimicry does not appear to be a problem for transition analysis.

In all these analyses, it is important to keep in mind that we are not really interested in point estimates of age-at-death, no matter how they were obtained. Instead, we want the *probability* that death occurred at each possible age, not just the single age when it was *most likely* to have occurred. Thus we would argue that the distribution shown in Figure 5.5, for example, is a better representation of an individual skeleton's age at death than is a single point estimate such as "36 years".

Discussion

The transition analysis results for both single and multiple skeletal traits conform to what osteologists would expect: age ranges for skeletons from old people are broader than for those of young ones. More importantly,

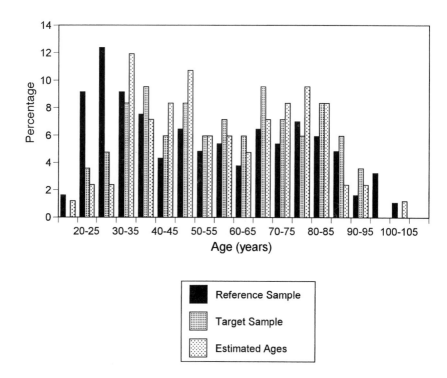

Figure 5.6. Distribution of reported ages for the reference sample and the validation study (target) sample, and of estimated ages for the validation sample. The 84 age estimates for the four sex and race groups are combined.

they make sense in terms of what happens at the pubic symphysis, the anatomical feature used most often in this chapter. Here some of the initial bony changes that are scored, especially the formation of the ventral rampart, are developmental in nature. Later changes in the pubic symphysis are essentially degenerative. It can be expected that such senescent changes would show considerable interindividual variation in their timing, and that is precisely what happens.

The last stage of the dorsal margin of the pubic symphysis – breakdown of the dorsal rim – turns out to be of special interest (Figures 5.1–5.3). It is one of two "old age" traits coded in this study, the other being widely and thickly distributed exostoses posterior to the iliac auricular surface where ligaments attach during life. Not all of the elderly have the dorsal margin breakdown of the symphyseal face, which can be seen from the transition curves. That is true of the posterior exostoses on the ilium as well. But the people whose skeletons do have these traits were old, particularly if dorsal rim breakdown is accompanied by thickly distributed bony projections on the posterior part of the ilium. There are likely to be other skeletal indicators of advanced age that can enhance our ability to estimate the ages-at-death of elderly people. Until now, however, there has been little reason to look for them.

An important point should not be missed when looking at the broad likelihood curves late in life, such as those shown for Laurits Ebbesen (Figure 5.4). Transition analysis can be used to estimate the ages-at-death of old people, something that has long resisted the efforts of osteologists. Osteologists usually know when they are looking at a skeleton from an old person, but they cannot say with any assurance just how old that person might have been at the time of death. This age estimation method not only provides a likely age range, but also shows the uncertainty inherent in estimating the ages of old people. It is now possible to deal with a part of the mortality distribution that was once beyond the reach of paleodemographers. We are no longer forced to use an open-ended terminal interval such as 50 + years.

The close agreement between estimated and known ages in the Århus case are due in part to the use of a nonuniform prior age distribution, one derived from 17th century Danish records. But even with a uniform prior and an abundance of error-prone estimates of the age of old individuals, the reported and estimated age distributions looked roughly similar in the validation study (Figure 5.6). At the very least, a better match has been produced than has been possible with previous age estimation methods, particularly when one considers that much of the validation sample consisted of skeletons of individuals who are usually lumped into a category such as 50 + years. There is, however, one very old individual in the estimated age distribution, a result of the use of the uniform prior distribution.

The quality of age estimates can be improved only by including multiple indicators of age. Thus it is better to use the various components of the pubic symphysis instead of any single part of it alone, such as the dorsal margin. In fact, our approach – specifically the ability to combine information from multiple skeletal indicators of age – should serve as incentive for osteologists to continue the search for the considerable amount of age-related morphological variation that surely exists in skeletons. There is a real need to do this work because the subjective opinion of experienced osteologists can perform as well as, if not better than, age estimation techniques based on single anatomical units, such as the pubic symphysis (judging by our Terry Collection experience).

The problem we face in dealing with such traits is that the information content of these changes in normal bony structure is low. Many are basically presence or absence features, such as rounded instead of sharp borders of the femoral fovea (the former is the younger condition). But if these parts of the skeleton can be combined in some sort of rigorous manner, such as in transition analysis, then age estimates will certainly improve. In fact, we feel they will improve by a considerable amount considering our experience with subjective estimates of age based on the overall appearance of entire skeletons. It remains for osteologists to examine what they look at when they make subjective estimates of age, see how these traits are distributed in a known-age sample (preferably the same Terry Collection skeletons), and incorporate them as standard features of the transition analysis computer program.

It is also essential to conduct further validation studies. Preferably this work will be done on known-age samples as dissimilar to the Terry Collection as possible. After all, it would be useful to know whether this method is applicable to skeletal samples other than the indigents who died during the early to mid 20th century in the USA. Our work to date with a few archaeological specimens of known or suspected age suggests that it is indeed useful.

Acknowledgments

This work was supported by the Danish Research Council of the Humanities, the American–Scandinavian Foundation, and by an RGSO grant from the College of Liberal Arts at the Pennsylvania State University. We are grateful to David Hunt for making arrangements for us to examine the Terry Collection skeletons; his knowledge of the collection helped us immeasurably. Bethany Usher entered data into a computer file. Detailed comments and suggestions were provided by Darryl Holman. We also profited from discussions with other participants at the Rostock meetings on paleodemographic age estimation, and we thank the Max Planck Institute for Demographic Research in Rostock – particularly its director Jim Vaupel – for providing this opportunity for meeting and developing some of the ideas presented here.

Appendix 5.1

Brief descriptions of the stages used in the transition analysis program are provided below. It is occasionally difficult or impossible to distinguish between two sequential stages in a particular bony feature. This problem can arise because a bone is modified through a pathological process or damaged after death. Pathological features should be treated as missing data because they do not correspond to the defined stages. When bones are simply damaged, the features that are observable should be recorded if possible, even when two-stage designations must be used (e.g., stages 2 and 3). By doing so, one makes use of the information that still exists in combined scores. It will be immediately apparent that there is no substitute for experience when classifying anatomical features. Like anything else that relies on good judgment, researchers should know what they are doing before using this age estimation method.

Pubic symphysis

The pubic symphysis is scored for age-related morphological changes in five separate components. Many of the terms used here are derived from earlier work with the pubic symphysis, especially that of McKern and Stewart (1957).

Symphyseal relief

1. *Sharp billows*: At least half of the entire symphyseal face is covered with sharply crested billows. These billows consist of distinct ridges separated by deep furrows, and they extend completely across the symphyseal face. The low parts of furrows cut deeply into the ventral and dorsal margins of the symphyseal face. In some specimens, great vertical relief is accompanied by rounded, not sharp, crests on billows. Symphyseal faces are scored as having *Sharp Billowing* if the distance between the high and low points of adjacent ridges and furrows is 3 mm or more. This stage has only been noted in bones from teenagers, especially young ones.
2. *Soft, deep billows*: At least half of the symphyseal face, typically the dorsal demiface, is covered with softly crested to flat billows separated by deep furrows. There is no obvious filling of furrows with bone.
3. *Soft, shallow billows*: Much of the symphyseal surface, typically the dorsal demiface, is covered by shallow, but clearly visible and discrete, billows. Remnants of the ridge-and-furrow system are clearly visible. The billows extend most, or sometimes all, of the way across the face.
4. *Residual billows*: Billows blend into one another, and they form an important element of the surface, but they are much less pronounced than in the previous categories. The subtle billows do not fulfill the criteria for the previous categories. Two or more billows that conform to the residual category must be present. They typically extend only part way across the symphyseal face, usually no more than one-half the width of the face.
5. *Flat*: Over one-half of the symphyseal face is flat or slightly recessed. It sometimes presents a pebbly appearance because of the presence of numerous small, flat, pillows of bone. The rest of the symphysis does not indicate a billow score (i.e., no more than one discrete billow is present).

6. *Irregular*: Over one-half of the symphyseal surface is markedly irregular because of pitting, which is sometimes deep, often accompanied by small, sharp exostoses scattered thickly across the face. Occasionally the entire surface of what is otherwise a flat face is covered by the small knobs of bone (here pitting is largely absent). None of the criteria used to define earlier symphyseal stages is fulfilled.

Symphyseal texture

1. *Smooth*: Most, or all, of the dorsal demiface is covered by fine-grained or smooth bone.
2. *Coarse*: More than one-third of the dorsal demiface consists of coarse-textured bone.
3. *Microporosity*: More than one-third of the dorsal demiface is covered by bone that has a porous appearance. The overall impression is of numerous, closely packed, pin-pricks.
4. *Macroporosity*: More than one-third of the dorsal demiface is marred by generally closely spaced, deep pits, which are 0.5 mm or more in diameter. They collectively give the face an irregular, porous appearance.

Superior apex

1. *No protuberance*: The surface of the cranial end of the symphyseal face displays deep to shallow billowing. There is no evidence of a raised bony protuberance.
2. *Early protuberance*: A distinct knob of bone is present in the cranial end of the symphyseal face. This rounded bony protuberance is clearly differentiated from the immediately adjacent symphyseal face (i.e., the symphyseal face and the ventral beveled area, which is often present).
3. *Late protuberance*: The cranial end of the symphyseal face immediately anterior to the midline is raised somewhat above the rest of the articulation surface. The margins of the protuberance are poorly defined, creating a raised area that is more completely integrated with the remainder of the symphyseal face than in the previous category. The raised area should not be confused with a narrow elevated rim defining the cranial end of the symphyseal face. In some specimens the cranial part of the face may be more or less isolated by breakdown pitting, but these faces should not be coded as belonging to the *Late protuberance* stage. That is to say, a raised area of bone must be visible on a rather smooth symphyseal face.
4. *Integrated*: There is no raised area of bone on the cranial end of the symphyseal face. The symphyseal face is flat and it has a smooth or pitted appearance. The area where the protuberance was located is fully integrated with the rest of the symphyseal face.

Ventral symphyseal margin

1. *Serrated*: The ventral edge of the pubic symphysis is irregular because of an uninterrupted extension of the ridges and furrows typical of pronounced billowing.

2. *Beveled*: There is a distinct flattening (or loss) of billows in the ventral portion of the pubic symphysis. The beveling generally begins in the superior part of the ventral demiface. It must extend over one-third or more of the ventral margin to be scored as present.

3. *Rampart formation*: The ventral rampart refers to a distinct outgrowth of bone defining the ventral margin of the symphyseal face. In this stage the bony rampart is incomplete, it does not extend along the entire ventral edge, and usually some ridges and furrows on the symphyseal face can be followed uninterrupted to the ventral edge of the symphysis. Often the remnants of billows can be seen dipping below the partially formed ventral rampart, which looks like a roll of gum laid across a shallowly furrowed surface. An incomplete ventral rampart often extends inferiorly from the bony protuberance defining the cranial end of the face. An incomplete ventral rampart can also extend superiorly from the caudal end of the pubic symphysis. In many specimens there is a gap in the middle one-third of the ventral margin where bony ramparts from the ends of the symphysis have not yet met. Specimens in an early formation stage can have one or more bony knobs, which are often located in the middle one-third of the ventral margin. These knobs occur with or without the bony extensions from the cranial and caudal ends of the symphysis. A well-developed bony protuberance at the cranial end of the face that lacks a distinct inferiorly oriented extension of bone (the rampart) should not be coded as *Rampart formation*; i.e., the cranially located knob is not alone sufficient to score the ventral rampart as being present.

4. *Rampart completion I*: The ventral rampart is complete. There is, however, a shallow sulcus that extends for much of the length of the ventral surface of the pubis immediately lateral to the ventral edge of the symphyseal face. This groove is a residual feature related to rampart extension over the original symphyseal surface. Occasionally there is a gap in the ventral rampart, usually in the superior half of the ventral margin; the ventral rampart, however, is otherwise completely formed. The flat pubic symphyseal surface, which extends uninterrupted from its dorsal to ventral margins, contrasts with the typically furrowed *Rampart formation* stage.

5. *Rampart completion II*: The ventral rampart is complete. There is no shallow sulcus as described in *Rampart completion I*. Occasionally there is a gap in the ventral rampart, usually in the superior half of the ventral margin; however, the ventral rampart is otherwise completely formed. The flat pubic symphyseal surface, which extends uninterrupted from its dorsal to ventral margins, contrasts with the furrowed appearance of the typical *Rampart formation* stage.

6. *Rim*: There is a narrow bony rim on the ventral rampart that demarcates a generally flat or irregular symphyseal face. The ventral rim can be incomplete or complete, but it must be at least 1 cm long and readily identifiable as a

distinct raised ridge bordering a slightly recessed symphyseal face. The presence of a rim meeting the length criterion is sufficient to score the pubis as being in the *Ventral rim* stage, regardless of the ventral rampart configuration.

7. *Breakdown*: The ventral aspect of the symphyseal face shows signs of breakdown, which takes the form of pitting and an erosion of part of the ventral margin. To be scored as present, the breakdown of the ventral margin must exceed 1 cm (either in one place or when two or more areas of erosion are combined).

Dorsal symphyseal margin

1. *Serrated*: The dorsal edge of the pubic symphysis is irregular because of an uninterrupted extension of the ridges and furrows typical of pronounced billowing.
2. *Flattening incomplete*: There is a well-defined flattened area at least 1 cm long, usually in the superior part of the dorsal demiface, where the articular surface meets the dorsal surface of the pubis. Some residual billowing is present that produces an undulating dorsal edge, which is not as extreme as that found in the *Serrated* category. This undulating edge is typically found along the inferior dorsal margin.
3. *Flattening complete*: There is a complete, or virtually complete, well-defined area of flattening where the symphyseal face meets the dorsal surface of the pubis. Occasionally there will be a small area at the inferior end of the dorsal margin that still retains an undulating appearance.
4. *Rim*: There is a narrow bony rim at least 1 cm long demarcating a generally flat or irregular face. The dorsal rim can be incomplete or complete, but it must be readily identifiable as a raised ridge bordering a slightly recessed symphyseal face. It generally appears first along the superior part of the dorsal margin.
5. *Breakdown*: The dorsal aspect of the symphyseal face shows signs of breakdown, which takes the form of pitting and erosion of the dorsal margin. To be scored as present, the breakdown of the dorsal margin must exceed 1 cm in length (either in one place or when two or more areas of erosion are combined). Antemortem destruction of the dorsal margin attributable to large parity pits that undercut the symphyseal face can occur in females, but it is not considered breakdown, and it often results in this feature being unscorable.

Iliac portion of the sacroiliac joint

Many of the terms used here are derived from the pioneering work of Lovejoy *et al.* (1985b). Different parts of the auricular surface are scored for the same morphological features because bony changes do not necessarily take place simultaneously in all parts of the joint.

Superior and inferior demiface topography

The superior and inferior demifaces are divided by a line extending posteriorly from the most anterior part of the apex to the posterior border of the joint surface.

1. *Undulating*: The surface is slightly undulating, especially in a superior to inferior direction. The rise and fall of the bone surface is often best detected by feel. There is no centrally located area of elevated bone (the *Median elevation*). Surface billows superimposed on the wavy joint surface give it a somewhat hummocky appearance. The superior demiface, especially the most cranial part of it, is typically flatter than the inferior demiface.
2. *Median elevation*: In the middle of the demiface there is a broad raised area where the middle part of the joint is elevated above the rest of the surface. This bony elevation is flanked anteriorly and posteriorly by one or two long low areas. The elevated area takes the form of an elongated ridge, particularly in the inferior demiface, with the long axis paralleling the main orientation of the joint. This ridge need not occupy the entire length of the joint surface.
3. *Flat to irregular*: The surface is essentially flat or recessed, a result of marginal lipping, or it is irregular, a result of a degeneration of the joint or the formation of low pillow-like exostoses. Sometimes the inferior demiface has a slight curve to it so the inferior portion is located somewhat laterally to the superior part, a result of the joint conforming to the general shape of the ilium in this area. In such instances, the articulation surface does not have the softly rounded, wavy appearance of the *Undulating* category.

Superior, apical, and inferior surface morphology

The joint surface is divided into three segments labeled, for convenience, as superior, apical (middle), and inferior. The superior part of the joint extends from the superior end to a point half of the way to the apex of the joint. The apical (middle) portion stretches from that point to the apex and then beyond it for another 1 cm. The inferior part of the joint is the remainder of the joint surface.

1. *Billows over >2/3 of the surface*: Low rounded and typically narrow ridges separated by furrows, which have rounded bases, are clearly identifiable. The ridge surfaces are curved from the depths of the furrows completely across their crests. Most or all of the billowing is oriented roughly anterior to posterior, and individual furrows sometimes run across much, or all, of the face. The billowing covers most (> 2/3) of the auricular surface (i.e., it is a dominant element of the surface).
2. *Billows over 1/3 to 2/3 of the surface*: About one-half of the surface is covered by billows.
3. *Billows over <1/3 of the surface*: Billows are a noticeable, but minor, component of the joint surface. The rest of the surface is flat or bumpy.

4. *Flat*: The auricular surface is flat.
5. *Bumps*: Most, or all, of the auricular surface is covered by low, rounded areas of raised bone, much like little irregular pillows. Part of the surface may be flat, but over half of it is bumpy.

Inferior surface texture

This part of the joint surface is 1 cm long, as measured in a superior to inferior direction. Its lowermost point is a line defined by the margin of the greater sciatic notch on either side of the sacroiliac joint.

1. *Smooth*: Most or all of the bone comprising the auricular surface exhibits a smooth to slightly granular appearance.
2. *Microporosity*: At least one-half of the surface has a porous appearance with the apertures being less than 0.5 mm in diameter. The surface appears to be covered with numerous closely spaced pinpricks.
3. *Macroporosity*: At least one-half of the surface is porous, and most or all of the apertures exceed 0.5 mm in diameter.

Superior and inferior posterior iliac exostoses

The two areas examined are located on the medial surface of the posterior ilium where ligaments attach during life. The superior area is superior to the sacroiliac joint surface; i.e., to a line that passes from the anterior superior iliac spine to the most superior point of the joint surface (the superior angle), and on through the posterior part of the ilium. The inferior area is located inferior to that line. It is immediately posterior to the middle of the sacroiliac joint; i.e., it lies behind the most anteriorly projecting part of the joint's posterior margin. Exostoses appear on all but the bones of the youngest adults (with rare exceptions), and they tend to be clustered together to form nicely defined and easily identifiable patches of rough bone.

1. *Smooth*: The iliac surface is flat to slightly raised, but the surface is smooth. That is to say, it shows no evidence of round to sharp bony elevations. At most there are a few isolated and very small exostoses.
2. *Rounded exostoses*: Definite but low exostoses with rounded crests dominate the scoring areas.
3. *Pointed exostoses*: Sharply pointed but still low exostoses dominate the scoring areas.
4. *Jagged exostoses*: The scoring areas have a jagged appearance because of the presence of high round to sharp exostoses.
5. *Touching exostoses*: There is a pronounced outgrowth of bone with a relatively flat top, which is usually roughly oval, where the raised part of the ilium meets the sacrum.
6. *Fused*: The ilium and sacrum are fused together.

Posterior iliac exostoses

The area that is examined is the medial side of the ilium bordered posteriorly by the iliac crest, anteriorly by the sacroiliac auricular surface, superiorly by a slightly raised area often surmounted by exostoses (superior posterior iliac exostoses), and inferiorly by a similarly raised area also typically covered by exostoses (inferior posterior iliac exostoses). As opposed to the areas where the superior and posterior iliac exostoses are located, the part of the ilium of interest here is much less likely to have enough bony projections to be counted as present (i.e., rounded or pointed).

1. *Smooth*: The area posterior to the sacroiliac joint is smooth, except for the two areas coded as the superior and inferior posterior iliac exostoses. Surfaces interrupted by isolated projections of bone, either rounded or sharp, are still considered as smooth. Such exostoses typically occur on all but the youngest adults, yet much of the original smooth iliac surface is retained.
2. *Rounded exostoses*: Low, rounded, bony projections cover the entire bone surface posterior to the sacroiliac joint, except for a *ca.* 1 cm band of smooth bone immediately adjacent to the posterior edge of the joint. The entire surface is rough because little, if any, of the original smooth iliac surface remains. The exostoses are normally lower than the superior and inferior posterior iliac exostoses.
3. *Pointed spicules*: Low, pointed bony projections cover the entire bone surface posterior to the sacroiliac joint, except for a *ca.* 1 cm band of smooth bone immediately adjacent to the posterior edge of the joint. The entire surface is rough because little, if any, of the original smooth iliac surface remains. The exostoses are normally lower than the superior and inferior posterior iliac exostoses.

Cranial suture closure

Ectocranial suture closure, not endocranial suture closure, is scored for the coronal, sagittal, and lambdoidal sutures because of problems with seeing into the interiors of dirty archaeological crania. The names for the suture segments conform to those in common use. Because it is difficult to identify the *Juxtaposed* category for the interpalatine suture, it is not scored.

Coronal pterica, sagittal obelica, lambdoidal asterica, zygomaticomaxillary, interpalatine (median palatine, posterior portion)

1. *Open*: The suture is visible along its entire length, and there is a noticeable gap between the bones.
2. *Juxtaposed*: The suture is visible along its entire length, but the suture is narrow

because the bones are tightly juxtaposed. If bony bridges are present they are rare and very small (< 1 mm), sometimes with a trace of the original suture still evident.
3. *Partially obliterated*: The suture is partially obscured. There is no trace of the original suture in the bony bridges.
4. *Punctuated*: Only remnants of the suture are present. These remnants appear as scattered small points or grooves, each no more than 2 mm long.
5. *Obliterated*: There is no evidence of a suture.

References

Acsádi G and Nemeskéri J (1970) *History of human life span and mortality.* Budapest: Akadémiai Kiadó.

Agresti A (1990) *Categorical data analysis.* New York, NY: John Wiley & Sons.

Bocquet-Appel JP and Masset C (1982) Farewell to paleodemography. *Journal of Human Evolution* **12**, 321–333.

Boldsen JL (1988) Two methods for reconstruction of the empirical mortality profile. *Human Evolution* **3**, 335–342.

Boldsen JL (1997) Transition analysis: a method for unbiased age estimation from skeletal traits (abstract). *American Journal of Physical Anthropology, Supplement* **24**, 76.

Boldsen JL, Milner GR, and Usher BM (1998) The quality of osteological age estimation based on transition analysis: the effect of lack of conditional independence. Presented at the annual meeting of the American Anthropological Association, Philadelphia.

Brooks ST (1955) Skeletal age at death: the reliability of cranial and pubic age indicators. *American Journal of Physical Anthropology* **13**, 567–597.

Brooks S and Suchey JM (1990) Skeletal age determination based on the os pubis: a comparison of the Acsádi–Nemeskéri and Suchey–Brooks methods. *Human Evolution,* **5**, 227–238.

Brown PJ (1993) *Measurement, regression, and calibration.* New York: Oxford University Press.

Brown PJ and Sundberg R (1987) Confidence and conflict in multivariate calibration. *Journal of the Royal Statistical Society* **49**, 46–57.

Buikstra JE and Ubelaker DH (1994) *Standards for data collection from human skeletal remains.* Research Series 44. Fayetteville: Arkansas Archeological Survey.

Cox DR (1970) *Analysis of binary data.* London: Chapman & Hall.

Cox DR and Hinkley DV (1974) *Theoretical statistics.* London: Chapman & Hall.

Di Bacco M, Ardito V, and Pacciani E (1999) Age-at-death diagnosis and age-at-death distribution estimate: two different problems with many aspects in common. *International Journal of Anthropology* **14**, 161–169.

Fienberg SE (1977) *The analysis of cross-classified categorical data.* Cambridge, MA: MIT Press.

Francis B, Green M, and Payme C (1994) *The GLIM system, release 4 manual.* Oxford: Clarendon Press.

Gilbert BM and McKern TW (1973) A method for aging the female *os pubis. American Journal of Physical Anthropology* **38**, 31–38.

Greenland S (1994) Alternative models for ordinal logistic regression. *Statistics in Medicine* **13**, 1665–1677.

İşcan MY and Loth SR (1989) Osteological manifestations of age in the adult. In MY İşcan and KAR Kennedy (eds.): *Reconstruction of life from the skeleton.* New York: Alan R. Liss, pp. 23–40.

Jackes M (1992) Paleodemography: problems and techniques. In SR Saunders and MA Katzenberg (eds.): *Skeletal biology of past peoples: research methods.* New York: Wiley-Liss, pp. 189–224.

Jackes M (2000) Building the bases for paleodemographic analysis: adult age estimation. In MA Katzenberg and SR Saunders (eds.): *Biological anthropology of the human skeleton.* New York: Wiley-Liss, pp. 417–466.

Johansen HC (1998) *Four early Danish parish registers.* Research Report 6. Odense: Danish Center for Demographic Research.

Johnson VE and Albert JH (1999) *Ordinal data modeling.* New York: Springer-Verlag.

Konigsberg LW and Frankenberg SR (1992) Estimation of age structure in anthropological demography. *American Journal of Physical Anthropology* **89**, 235–256.

Konigsberg LW and Frankenberg SR (1994) Paleodemography: "Not quite dead". *Evolutionary Anthropology* **3**, 92–105.

Konigsberg LW, Hens SM, Jantz LM, and Jungers WL (1998) Stature estimation and calibration: Bayesian and maximum likelihood prespectives in physical anthropology. *Yearbook of Physical Anthropology* **41**, 65–92.

Konigsberg LW and Holman D (1999) Estimation of age at death from dental emergence and its implications for studies of prehistoric somatic growth. In RD Hoppa and CM FitzGerald (eds.): *Human growth in the past: studies from bones and teeth.* Cambridge: Cambridge University Press, pp. 264–289.

Lindsey JK (1995a) *Modelling frequency and count data.* New York: Oxford University Press.

Lindsey JK (1995b) *Introductory statistics: a modelling approach.* New York: Oxford University Press.

Long JS (1997) *Regression models for categorical and limited dependent variables.* Thousand Oaks, CA: Sage.

Lovejoy CO, Meindl RS, Mensforth RP, and Barton TJ (1985a) Multifactorial determination of skeletal age at death: a method and blind tests of its accuracy. *American Journal of Physical Anthropology,* **68**, 1–14.

Lovejoy CO, Meindl RS, Pryzbeck TR, and Mensforth RP (1985b) Chronological metamorphosis of the auricular surface of the ilium: a new method for the determination of adult skeletal age at death. *American Journal of Physical Anthropology* **68**, 15–28.

Lucy D and Pollard AM (1995) Further comments on the estimation of error associated with the Gustafson dental age estimation method. *Journal of Forensic Science* **40**, 222–227.

Masset C (1989) Age estimation based on cranial sutures. In MS İşcan (ed.): *Age markers in the human skeleton.* Springfield, IL: C. C. Thomas, pp. 71–103.

McCullagh P (1980) Regression models for ordinal data. *Journal of the Royal Statistical Society,* Series B **42,** 109–142.

McCullagh P and Nelder JA (1989) *Generalized linear models,* 2nd edn. New York: Chapman & Hall.

McKern TW and Stewart TD (1957) *Skeletal age changes in young American males.* Technical Report EP-45. Natick, MA: US Army Quartermaster Research and Development Center.

Meindl RS and Lovejoy CO (1985) Ectocranial suture closure: a revised method for the determination of skeletal age at death based on the lateral-anterior sutures. *American Journal of Physical Anthropology* **68,** 57–66.

Milner GR, Boldsen JL, and Usher BM (1997) Age-at-death determination using revised scoring procedures for age-progressive skeletal traits (abstract). *American Journal of Physical Anthropology, Supplement* **24,** 170.

Milner GR, Wood JW, and Boldsen JL (2000) Paleodemography. In MA Katzenberg and SR Saunders (eds.): *Biological anthropology of the human skeleton.* New York: Wiley-Liss, pp. 467–497.

Peters KD, Kochanek KD, and Murphy SL (1998) Deaths: final data for 1996. *National Vital Statistics Reports* **47,** 9.

Powers DA and Xie Y (2000) *Statistical methods for categorical data analysis.* New York: Academic Press.

Roche AF, Chumlea WC, and Thissen D (1988) *Assessing the skeletal maturity of the hand–wrist: Fels method.* Springfield, IL: C. C. Thomas.

Rose MR (1991) *Evolutionary biology of aging.* Oxford: Oxford University Press.

St Hoyme LE and İşcan MY (1989) Determination of sex and race: accuracy and assumptions. In MY İşcan and KAR Kennedy (eds.): *Reconstruction of Life from the Skeleton.* New York: Alan R. Liss, pp. 53–93.

Todd TW (1920) Age changes in the pubic bone. I. *American Journal of Physical Anthropology* **3,** 285–334.

Todd TW (1921) Age changes in the pubic bone. II, III, IV. *American Journal of Physical Anthropology* **4,** 1–70.

US Environmental Protection Agency (2000) CatReg Software Documentation. National Center for Environmental Assessment Report EPA/600/R-98/053F. Research Triangle Part, NC: Office of Research and Development. (web site: http://www.epa.gov/ncea/catreg.htm)

Workshop of European Anthropologists (1980) Recommendations for age and sex diagnoses of skeletons. *Journal of Human Evolution* **9,** 517–549.

6 Age estimation by tooth cementum annulation:

perspectives of a new validation study

URSULA WITTWER-BACKOFEN AND HELENE BUBA

Introduction

Discussions during the Rostock paleodemography workshops have shown two areas that clearly suffer from severe problems in transforming a skeletal sample into an historical population. First, more effort was needed to establish a reliable mortality pattern for skeletal samples. Second, although the Rostock Manifesto concentrated on the modeling of individual age and sex data, discussions frequently criticized the basic data, especially the insufficiently large age ranges in individual age estimations obtained from established morphological age estimation techniques. The group therefore drew attention to the search for methods that are able to determine age with higher accuracy.

Owing to recent significant improvements, a promising method for age estimation is the evaluation of tooth cementum annulation (TCA). The proposed procedure reduces time-consuming, and therefore costly, preparation steps, so that larger samples can be observed with less expense. If a few simple guidelines are followed, the method may be among the best and most reliable of those used for age estimation of skeletal samples.

To validate this method for frequent use, a standard protocol and use of confidence intervals are required, and these may be established by studying a known-age reference sample. The aim of this chapter is to introduce the concept and the methodological bases of an ongoing validation study, as well as the preliminary results.

Morphological age estimation methods versus tooth cementum annulation

Almost all established methods for age estimation in the skeleton suffer from severe problems (see Kemkes-Grottenthaler, Chapter 4, this volume).

In historical skeletons only *biological* age changes can be observed. The reliability of an age determination method depends on the correlation between biological and chronological age. With greater age, individual variability of age-dependent changes in the skeleton increases. Thus, the skeletons of older adults in particular are influenced by methodological problems.

Only very few age-known historical skeletal samples exist. Owing to their ecological, cultural, and chronological heterogeneity they are not suitable for age validation studies (see Usher, Chapter 3, this volume). Chronological variability of biological–chronological age correlations can be calculated in only a few exceptional cases. Acceleration or delay of biological aging processes during time cannot be detected. Another problem is that the deterioration of historical skeletons due to burial rites, soil conditions, excavation, etc. limits the application of age estimation methods. Reference populations are usually insufficient representations of the age structure in skeletal samples, and often do not cover the necessary age groups properly. So, an age determination method that is independent of these continuous and nonquantified aging parameters is badly needed.

TCA promises a substantial improvement in age estimation for adult skeletons as it relies on observation of the annual incremental lines in the tooth cementum. These are not a continuously varying trait, as is, for example, the age change in the surface of the pubic symphysis. They show clearly distinct quantitative histological features, each probably corresponding to one year of life, and thus they stand for a quasi-chronological age.

Development of tooth cementum annulation age estimation

The TCA method for individual age determination has already been established for age estimation among wildlife biologists for decades (Laws 1952; Mitchell 1963; Geiger 1993). The annual apposition of cementum has been established for more than 50 mammalian species (Grue and Jensen 1979), following the detection of a seasonal rhythm of cementum apposition. Since the initial investigations, there have been numerous studies, including some on nonhuman primates (Wada *et al.* 1978; Stott *et al.* 1980; Yoneda 1982; Kay *et al.* 1984), especially chimpanzees (Cipriano 1999). Up to 1979, age determination methods in human teeth had included the width of the tooth cementum layer (Gustafson 1950, 1955; Azaz *et al.* 1974; Philipsen and Jablonski 1992). In the early 1980s the first study of three human teeth showed that TCA was applicable to humans as well (Stott *et al.* 1982). Improved sample sizes in follow-up studies added preliminary recommendations for the practical aspects of the method (Charles *et al.* 1986; Condon *et al.* 1986). But contradictory results concerning the use of specific tooth types (canines versus premolars), the origin of a suitable sample (fresh extractions versus forensic cases), as well as conflicting recommendations of methodology confused potential users (Lipsinic *et al.* 1986; Jackes 1992). In addition, the procedure was rejected as being time consuming and cost intensive. Previously, studies were limited to freshly extracted teeth and teeth from forensic cases, but Großkopf (1989, 1990) was one of the first to test TCA for application in historical teeth and cremations of unknown age. The age of historical skeletons was estimated by morphological methods. Großkopf's results, limited by the small sample size of five cremated teeth in addition to 66 historical teeth, showed that there was a general possibility of establishing the method for age estimation. She concluded that the apposition of incremental lines seems to be very stable, and not influenced by functional processes, the structure of the teeth, nutrition, or other conditions of a specific ecosystem.

A subsequent study tested the hypothesis that severe periodontal disease might influence the process of cementum annulation by reducing or even arresting the annual apposition process (Großkopf *et al.* 1996), but no influence was found in a small sample of 15 teeth from 10 individuals. A more recent study contradicts these results, observing that the degree of periodontal disease correlates with the number of missing lines in an age-known sample (Kagerer and Grupe 2001).

Apart from using Pearson's correlation coefficients, none of these studies developed confidence intervals for age estimation in age-unknown teeth. When compared with all previous studies, the method was recommended for age estimation because of its high correlation between estimated and chronological age (for a review see Buba 1999). An overview of the main indicators from previous studies of TCA in humans is shown in Table 6.1.

All these studies leave unresolved several problems regarding the use of TCA for age estimation. These are:

> The estimation quality is not well known.
> The method is not verified on known-age historical reference samples.
> The method is not verified by comparisons with morphological age estimation methods.
> The influence of periodontal disease on the TCA is not clear.
> It is not clear whether the reasons for more precise estimation in

Table 6.1. *Evaluation of tooth cementum annulation studies for age estimation in humans*

Reference	Aim of the study	n^a	Tooth type[b]	Section[c]	Counting method[d]	Age range[e]	Country	Correlation of age and TCA age[f]	Evaluation
Azaz et al. 1974	Age and thickness of cementum layer	60	c, p	Longitud. sections	–	9–70	Israel	r = 0.872 cervical; r = 0.860 middle root	Incrementum lines not counted
Stott et al. 1982	First application in humans	17	i, c, p, m	100–150	p	57–76	USA	Not calculated	Age 57, TCA 57.5–59.7 Age 67, TCA 63–70 Age 76, TCA 73–78
Naylor et al. 1985	Different techniques	n.m.	n.m.	50, 75, 100	p, m	n.m.	USA	Not calculated	100 µm sections best; best area 15–45% from root tip
Charles et al. 1986	Different techniques, tooth type, intraobserver and interobserver error	71	c, p	80 min 7 demin	p, m	55–86 36–79	USA	n.m.	Demineralized thin sections best, premolars better than canines; interobserver error 5%, intraobserver error 2%
Condon et al. 1986	Application to known-age teeth	80	p	7	p,m ×400	11–70	USA	r = 0.78 all; r = 0.86 healthy teeth	Standard error 4.7–9.7; better estimates for females than for males
Lipsinic et al. 1986	Different techniques	31	p	5	m ×100	11–60	USA	r = 0.85 all; <30 yrs r = 0.93; >30 yrs r = 0.631	Mean age 42.5 yrs; mean TCA age 16.5 yrs
Miller et al. 1988	Application	100	srt	350	p (screen)	9–78	USA	Not calculated	5.7% within 5 years, 85% estimated with > 10 yrs error
Großkopf 1990	Application on historical skeletons and cremations	45 r 66 h 15 c	i, c, p, m	100	m ×562	10–72 recent	Germany	Not calculated	Mean error 3.23 yrs (recent), high correlation between morphological and TCA age for historical and cremated teeth

Study		Number of teeth[a]	Tooth type[b]	Thickness (µm)[c]	Method[d]	Age (yrs)[e]	Country	r[f]	
Solheim 1990	Techniques for measuring cementum layer width, no incremental lines	1000	i, c, p			n.m.	Norway	r = 0.40–0.65	Reduced cementum apposition in higher age; less cementum for females and in cadavers
Jacobshagen 1999	Application to Neolithic teeth	57 + 7r	n.m.	40–60	m × 500	n.m.	Germany	r = 0.88	High accuracy
Stein and Corcoran 1994	Basic quality	52	srt	5–7		27–82	USA	r = 0.93 all; <55 yrs; r = 0.98; >55 yrs; r = 0.85	Despite periodontal diseases and dental caries, good results
Kvaal and Solheim 1995	Test for yearly incremental line apposition	95	c, p	5–7 longitud.	video camera	13–89	Denmark	r = 0.84 counted lines; r = 0.74 calculated lines	Premolars better than canines, periodontal diseases affect results
Großkopf et al. 1996	Periodontal diseases and incremental lines	15	i, p, m	100	m × 200	25–59	Germany	Not calculated	Mean error 1.9–2.6 yrs
Renz et al. 1997	Ultrastructure of incremental lines	n.m.	n.m.	100 1–2	m, CLSM, TEM, EDX	n.m.	Germany	n.m.	Confusing results: "So the intrastructural nature of the incremental lines is still an open Question"
This study	Method validation	500	srt	70–80	p m × 400 screen	12–96	Germany	r = 0.94 (preliminary)	Ongoing study

[a] Number of all teeth included in the study; r, recent; h, historical; c, cremated teeth; n.m., not mentioned.

[b] i, incisor; c, canines; p, premolars; m, molars; srt, single root teeth.

[c] Thickness of tooth root cross-sections: if not mentioned separately, all measurements in µm; min, mineralized teeth; demin, demineralized teeth.

[d] Methods of counting the incremental lines; p, photos; m, bright-field light microscope; × 100, magnification; CLSM, confocal laser scanning microscopy; TEM, transmission electron microscopy; EDX, electron-dispersive X-radiation.

[e] L, age range in years of all teeth included in the study; n.m., not mentioned.

[f] r, Pearson correlation coefficient; n.m., not mentioned.

younger ages, in comparison with older subsamples, lie in methodological problems or functional variabilities in line formation.
It is not clear why age estimation should be better in females than
males, as reported from a few studies.

Biological basis of tooth cementum annulation

The biological basis for cementum apposition in teeth is far from being
elucidated. The tooth cementum, which surrounds the dentin, extends from
the neck of the tooth, where it represents a small layer, to the apex of the
root, up to 0.5 mm thick (Alt and Türp 1997).

The basis of the method came from the observation that the continuous
change in functioning teeth throughout life includes phasic cementum
apposition, which shows a regular yearly increment in cementum lines
(Klevezal 1970). It has been observed that dark zones of cementum apposition with high density, called incremental lines, alternate with light zones of
accelerated cementum apposition (Klevezal and Kleinenberg 1967; Morris
1972; Saar 1991). These layers have different optical properties, which may
be detected under a bright-field light microscope. They are assumed to be
added once yearly.

Seasonal climatic changes, as well as nutritional alterations, have been
suggested as possible reasons for the apposition of cementum in the light
and dark zones. In addition ecological conditions, such as temperature,
light, humidity, altitude, pollution, or nutrition are supposed to be responsible for the varying width and density of the incremental lines (Grue and
Jensen 1979), as has been demonstrated in a case study by Cipriano (1999).
In captured chimpanzees in Europe and the USA, she was able to trace
back specific intensive line patterns to an extremely cold winter in the areas
where their zoos were located.

It was argued that this observation in previously wild animals reflected
a natural metabolic rhythm in mammals all over the world (Grue and
Jensen 1979). Seasonal changes in cementum annulation are connected
with the metabolism of parathyroid hormone and vitamin D, the former
being responsible for the regulation of calcium and phosphate levels in the
blood, and interacting with vitamin D, which regulates the resorption of
calcium. Thus both hormones and vitamins may interact in a circannual
rhythm via a complex mechanism of ecological and physicochemical "syn-
chronizers" (Halberg *et al.* 1983).

Cementum apposition has been observed not only in wild animals but
also in humans. Even in highly industrialized populations, where seasonal
alterations in climate and nutrition are minimized, cementum annulation is

still observed. Thus it is argued that cementum annulation, to a certain degree, is genetically ordered, but can be modified by external conditions (Grue and Jensen 1979). The occasional presence of the "doubling" phenomenon, where exactly twice as many incremental lines are present as are predicted (Stein and Corcoran 1994; Jacobshagen 1999), as well as the fact that incremental lines are produced also in impacted teeth (see below) (Nitzan *et al.* 1986), supports this hypothesis.

The year of eruption of the tooth is when the first incremental line is formed. Incremental lines have been observed even in deciduous teeth (Verderber 1996). This phenomenon led to the suggestion that either the mechanical use of the tooth in occlusion or the growth of the root to two-thirds of its maximum length is an initiating factor for cementum apposition (Kvaal and Solheim 1995). The use of the tooth, however, was not necessarily connected with the presence of cementum annulation, as has been demonstrated in impacted teeth where the same phenomenon occurs but without mechanical stress.

As cementogenesis involves calcification of the root surrounding the periodontal ligament, which contains growth factors and drives the metabolism of neighboring tissues, both the tooth and the periodontium have to be regarded as an interactive system for cementum annulation (Schumacher *et al.* 1990).

Currently, interactions between the tooth cementum and the surrounding tissues are far from being well understood. In particular, the influence of periodontal disease is contradictory and has been described as having no influence (Großkopf *et al.* 1996) to inflicting severe disturbance on the cementum annulation process (Kagerer and Grupe 2001). Even an intravital stop in cementum apposition has been proposed for severe periodontal disease where the reduction of the alveolar attachment tissue causes it to fall below a minimum amount (Kagerer and Grupe 2001).

In summary, many questions remain to be solved before the mechanisms of tooth cementum annulation and its influencing factors are known. At the moment, we do not know much more than that the method is very useful for age estimation, nor do we know why.

The concept of the current validation study

Improvements in the TCA method have enabled the investigation of larger samples than was possible previously. Therefore we set out to do a validation study. For this purpose, we use a large sample of known-age teeth.

The fundamental significance of earlier studies of TCA was to show the suitability of the method for age estimation in humans. They also demonstrated its advantage over other methods of age estimation, although on more of a descriptive than a statistical level, and this led to its acceptance for age evaluation in forensics (Stott *et al.* 1982).

However, sample sizes in these studies were too small to establish significant statistical parameters, especially when the data were subdivided according to age group, sex, periodontal disease, ethnic group, etc. The main focus of the current study was therefore the age range estimations within given confidence intervals of a reference sample. This has led to a recommendation that the TCA method be applied to age estimation in unknown skeletal samples – a requirement for the acceptance of TCA measurement as a valid method for age estimation.

The results of the current study could be extended to several other aspects of historical anthropology. Individual age estimation will be improved by smaller confidence intervals, thus estimating individual ages with high probability in smaller age ranges. This is especially useful for older age groups, for which all other morphological methods fail. Additionally, the quality of age estimation is strongly dependent on the state of preservation of the skeletal remains. Chemical or mechanical processes in the soil, specific burial rites, excavation methods, etc. may create a wide range of states of preservation, from a more or less complete skeleton to very few small fragments. Teeth, especially the enamel crown, as the hardest tissue in the human body, are significantly better preserved than the bones of the skeleton. This applies to the tooth root as well, if preserved in the alveolus embedded in the jaws. Application of the TCA method on historical teeth, however, showed that some teeth were not suitable for the technique. In these cases, the cementum was not preserved or did not emerge as incremental lines.

This limitation aside, recent observations on large Bronze Age and Medieval samples (Wittwer-Backofen 1998, 2000) more often revealed specimens with preserved teeth than ones with skeletal fragments, the latter being necessary for age estimations based on morphological traits. For these skeletons the TCA method improved age estimation significantly, so that the proportion of those individuals that were not suitable for estimation of age within the whole adult age range was reduced.

Individual age estimations have strong effects on the reconstruction of the overall population mortality pattern (M. Luy *et al.*, unpublished data), and hence influence significantly the quality of paleodemographic parameters. Until now, in paleodemographic analyses the oldest age group has been subjective and varied significantly between 70 and 90 years in most cases.

If the chronological age of the oldest old in a historical population can be estimated nearly exactly, the highest age group can be determined. This will allow us to get an idea of what the maximum lifespan could have been within the population under study. Certainly, we will not claim to find the Bronze Age or Medieval Methuselah, but we might be able to separate historical populations by their proportion of higher age classes. This is a significant marker for paleodemographic calculations, as completely different mortality parameters result from different definitions of the highest age group. If the highest age groups are defined without any substantial idea of the real highest age groups, this may be a source of fundamental error in paleodemography.

A population's mean lifespan can be regarded as an indicator of ecological stress factors, and, thus, allows conclusions to be drawn as to the adaptation of the human population to its ecological conditions, a primary focus in the field of prehistoric anthropology.

Thus, in the current validation study, as a first step we concentrated on the calculation of confidence intervals useable as a standard in the practice of age estimation in the skeleton.

We focused on the following questions:

> What methods produce the best results, and are time efficient and cost effective?
> How can reproducible estimates by image analysis techniques be established?
> How can images be enhanced to improve results?
> How many observers are necessary to produce reliable results?
> How many counts are necessary to produce reliable results?
> Does periodontal reduction influence the TCA and, if so, to what extent? Can we calculate missing incremental lines by the amount of periodontal reduction?
> Does tooth type affect TCA age estimation? Do all teeth produce the same quality of results?
> Is there intra-individual variability between different teeth?
> How can confidence intervals be calculated properly?

The sample in the validation study

The first validation step of the study was based on around 500 known-age teeth from fresh extractions that were collected from several dentists and clinics in Germany during January and July 2000. Besides the date of birth of the individual and extraction date of the tooth, further information concerning sex, ethnic group, and the medical reason for the tooth extraction were collected. The teeth cover an age range of individuals from 12 to 96 years, around 85% of whom are older than 35 years. Both sexes are represented, two-thirds being males.

For more than 100 patients, teeth from multiple extractions are available. In these cases, loss of two or three teeth was most common, but even up to 10 teeth from a single person, extracted for prosthetic reasons, are included in the study. This allows the study of intra-individual correlations.

It may be argued that the validity of the method is limited because around 90% of all teeth in the sample were extracted as a result of medical intervention related to periodontal disease or dental caries. However, the method is planned for application to historical teeth, whose owners suffered from similar symptoms and also at younger ages, so that this issue is relevant to the whole lifespan. Thus the validation study can infer the amount of uncertainty due to periodontal disease and can express this in the confidence intervals for age estimation in unknown teeth. Quantifying the influence of periodontal diseases on TCA is therefore a major aspect of the study.

Methods

The method of incremental line preparation is not standardized. The choice of one of the various methods of preparation, staining, and microscopic technique may influence the result. The wide variety of the reliability of TCA for age estimation may be at least partly based on different methods of preparation and documentation. With the proposed methodology we are able to reduce time-consuming parts of the procedure without information loss.

Directly after extraction, the teeth were stored in 70% (v/v) alcohol. To quantify the degree of periodontal reduction, we stained whole teeth in order to make the periodontal margin at the time of extraction visible. Each tooth was stained for three to four minutes with 1% (v/v) Fuchsin water solution at room temperature.[1] This resulted in the soft tissue cytoplasts appearing blue to violet in color. The teeth were then rinsed in distilled water to remove excess stain.

The distance between the enamel margin and the stained periodontal line was measured with a microcaliper[2] at the labial, buccal, mesial, and distal surfaces of the tooth (Figure 6.1). Until maceration, the teeth were

---

[1] Protocol after Professor Kocher, Centre for Odontology and Parodontology, University of Greifswald, Germany.   [2] Measuring precision 0.05 mm.

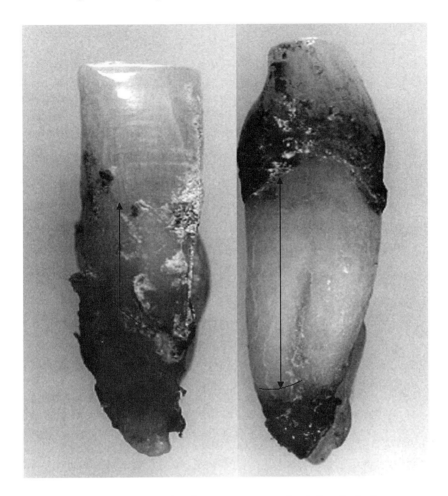

Figure 6.1. Stained teeth and measurement area of periodontal reduction.

fixed in a 10% (v/v) formalin solution. To remove the periodontal ligament and to improve the stability of the acrylic sockets, the teeth were leached in an alkaline solution of washing powder, pH 9.0, for five days at 45 °C. The solution was changed twice during this procedure to improve enzymic activities of proteases and lipases.

Since decalcification did not improve the microscopic contrast in a small subsample, we omitted this time-consuming procedure and continued to work with mineralized teeth.

No embedding of the fresh teeth was necessary, only an acrylic socket

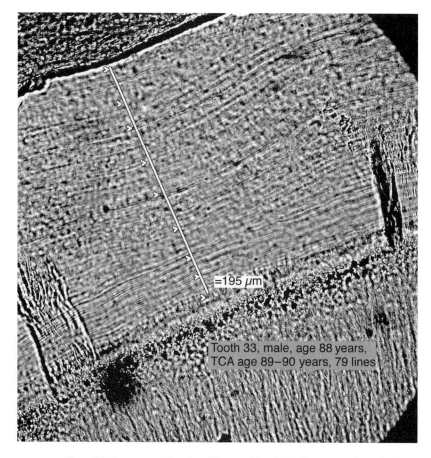

Figure 6.2. Incremental lines in a 88-year-old male, 79 lines counted, tooth 33, bright-field microscopy, × 400 (white marker set every 10 lines, 9 lines for the last, starting at the margin of the cemento-dentin margin at the bottom).

was needed to hold each tooth during the cutting procedure in the adapter of the saw. We use a saw microtome[3] with a precision diamond wafering blade. Around one-third of the root tip was removed with the first cut. Three consecutive 70–80 μm thick cross-sections were cut from each tooth root with low speed,[4] followed by a dehydration process in 70%, 96%, and absolute alcohol,[5] cleaning in Xylene, and mounting using Microkit. Stain-

---

[3] Leitz saw microtome 1600.   [4] 20–30 rotations per second.
[5] 2 min in 70% alcohol, 30 s in 96% alcohol, 30 s in absolute alcohol.

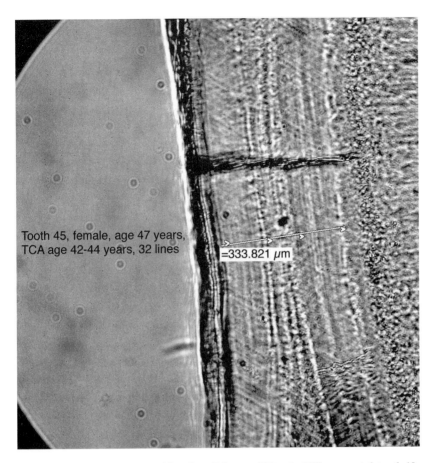

Tooth 45, female, age 47 years,
TCA age 42-44 years, 32 lines

=333.821 μm

Figure 6.3. Incremental lines in a 43.5-year-old female, 32 lines counted, tooth 45, bright-field microscopy, × 400, digital camera imaging, graphic software applied (white marker set every 10 lines, 2 lines more after the last, starting at the margin of the cemento-dentin margin at the right).

ing of the sections did not improve the detection of the incremental lines, and was therefore omitted.

The sections were evaluated under bright-field microscopy with a magnification of 400–500 times. The number of dark lines were counted in the variable region of dark and light lines between the cemento-dentin junction and the periodontal ligament (Figures 6.2 and 6.3). In the three sections of each tooth, the observers counted three suitable regions after having looked at the whole area surrounding the root cross-section. Each of the three observers counted the same teeth three times in randomly assorted order, so that 27 incremental line counts for each tooth were available.

None of the observers had knowledge about the exact age of the teeth. After registration, the teeth were given anonymous numbers, independently of the observers. The observers were trained with a set of 10 teeth of given age, and another control set of 10 teeth of known, but not given, age until consistent results were obtained.

During the first phase the sections were counted directly under the microscope, a tiring procedure under the bright-field light, which may lead to significant counting errors. During that phase, photographs were taken of the sections.[6] Counting from these photos did not prove as accurate as the direct microscopic counting, where the microscope focus was used to reveal additional smaller lines that were not clearly visible in the photograph. According to our experience, photographs without any image enhancement are unsuitable for counting.

Significant improvement will be reached through digital scanning or digital photography, which directly connects the computer with the microscope. Digital image equipment available today is vastly superior to earlier apparatus and, as a result, can provide images of better quality to traditional film cameras, without the need for film and photographic processing, while allowing for real-time imaging. Most importantly, graphic enhancement procedures can be applied to the images. This part of the methodological study is not yet finished, but up to now has revealed promising results, which improve the counting procedure and permit further investigation of interobserver variability.

Preliminary results

As the current study is ongoing, only preliminary results are presented. These are limited to a small subsample of 42 single-root teeth, which up to now have been counted by two observers. Owing to this limited sample size, sophisticated statistical test methods are not applicable. However, showing the basic correlation of exact age and TCA age estimation is the goal of this chapter.

Mean age of the subsample is 50.9 years with a range of 17 to 81 years, the teeth having been obtained from 23 female and 19 male patients. Calculated age estimations are based on the maximum of three counts by each observer, remembering that counting errors may occur by incremen-

---

[6] With microscopic photoadapter tubes, Rolleiflex 3003 and Ilford FP4 film.

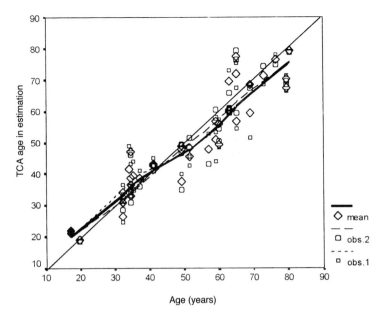

Figure 6.4. Scatterplot of true age and age estimation by cementum annulation. Lowess regression of a 50 teeth subsample: Lowess-regression lines (3 iterations with 50% of the values) for two observer counts (broken lines) and overall means (solid bold line). The solid line shows the expected regression in 100% fitting.

tal lines being missed rather than inclusion of nonexistent, additional lines. Age estimation is based on the counted incremental lines added since the eruption age according to an established worldwide variability (Schumacher *et al.* 1990). Periodontal diseases (21 reported cases) are evident in the subsample.

Results of TCA age estimation are given in Table 6.2. It presents the mean age of the estimations for two observers separately as well as a mean value over both observers. Pearson's correlation coefficients approach 0.94 for the total subsample. All correlation coefficients are statistically significant, almost all of them with less than 1% estimated error.

Figure 6.4 shows the single estimates versus the exact age in years for both observers as well as for the mean estimates. From the Lowess regression line with 50% of the counts for model adaptation it is seen that there is a slight overestimation for younger ages up to 40 years and an underestimation for ages above 40 years. Also, the error estimation shows a higher mean difference of 5.8 years between reported and estimated ages in the higher age group (> 50 years of age), whereas the mean error in the

Table 6.2. *Preliminary results of cementum annulation age estimation compared with known ages (subsample)*

			Observer 1			Observer 2			Mean		
	n	Exact age	Age range	Mean age	r	Mean error	Mean age	r	Mean error	Mean age	r	Mean error
Total sample	42	50.9	17–81	50.2	0.91**	4.7	48.9	0.95**	4.4	49.0	0.94**	4.6
Females	23	54.1	32–80	53.7	0.90**	6.2	51.7	0.94**	4.6	51.8	0.93**	5.3
Males	19	47.1	17–73	46.0	0.92**	5.1	45.8	0.95**	3.1	45.9	0.96**	3.8
Age <50 years	20	33.3	17–49	37.2	0.81***	4.7	34.2	0.86**	2.7	34.5	0.85***	3.5
Age >50 years	22	66.9	52–80	62.1	0.78***	6.6	63.6	0.77***	5.1	62.3	0.81**	5.8
Incisors + canines	31	51.5	20–80	49.4	0.93**	5.5	49.8	0.94**	4.8	50.6	0.94**	5.0
Premolars	11	49.4	17–81	52.7	0.76*	6.2	46.1	0.99**	1.3	50.1	0.95**	3.6

**p < 0.01, *p < 0.05.

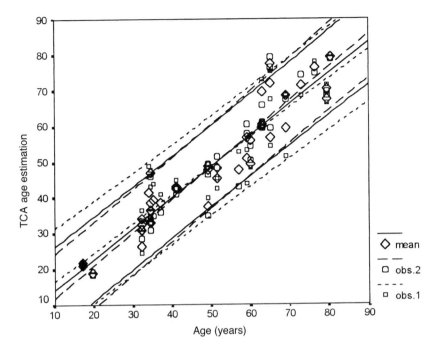

Figure 6.5. Age and age estimation by cementum annulation, 95% confidence intervals of a 50 teeth subsample for two observer counts (broken lines) and overall means (solid lines).

younger age group (<50 years) is only 3.5 years (Table 6.2). Linear regression estimates of mean age for both observers produces a slope of 0.94 and a y-axis intercept of 0.12. Considering the small size of the sample, the model adjustment is extremely good, as it does not differ significantly from the linear regression model fit.

Under the assumption of linear regression the calculated 95% confidence intervals are still quite large, which is mostly an effect of the small sample size (Figure 6.5). As the fit is better for younger ages, the confidence intervals in these cases are unnecessarily wide.

Sex differences did not prove the same as in other studies. Here the fit for males was slightly better than for females, but the age structure of both sexes favored younger male individuals. This may have affected the observed sex disparities.

Because of the practical limitations due to root bifurcation, and the high intratooth variability of cementum apposition found in previous studies, multiple-root teeth proved to be unsuitable for age estimation by TCA. Hence the current study concentrates on single-root teeth exclusively.

Basically, we have demonstrated that all single-root teeth are suitable for the TCA method. In particular, incisors were excluded in previous studies, but here they proved to deliver good results. Separation of two different classes of tooth type – one of them all incisors and canines, the other one all premolars – gave partially different results, especially when compared between the two observers. This issue is being further explored in the final large sample.

Perspectives

The methodologies described here for making tooth incremental lines visible in mineralized sections of 70–80 μm lead to significant savings in time. The technique of visualizing the microscopic images on a computer monitor and the use of image enhancement procedures and line marking is also a second major advance, namely that of equalizing observer countings and thus gaining reproducible count. Discrepancies can be discussed in real time by specifying the area containing the lines under scrutiny. This will lead to specific recommendations for an optimal counting procedure.

With these preconditions, we can give the basis for the recommendation of confidence intervals for the TCA age estimation method. Out of a large sample of more than 500 teeth, the first preliminary results of a small 10% subsample demonstrated the validity of the method. Even this subsample has already shown much better age estimations than have morphological or other histological methods for age estimation (Jackes 1992; Stout 1992; see also Kemkes-Grottenthaler, Chapter 4, this volume). As a result, the detection of a wider age range in historical populations may be expected, if we succeed in encouraging anthropologists in the use of TCA age estimation, although it is more cost intensive and time consuming than other methods (but not nearly as much as was anticipated with the first methodological studies several years ago).

One major objective is the detection of a realistic amount of older individuals in historical skeletal populations and, thus, contributing to the history of human aging by establishing a more reliable age structure. In this context the relation of sex-specific mortality patterns will come to the forefront again, since available datasets in historical demography and anthropology have been proved to be full of errors (Wittwer-Backofen 1991).

Despite the results presented from the current study, as discussed above, a number of questions still remain to be solved. Following discussions in the Rostock workshops on paleodemography, there are very likely to be improvements in age estimates with the TCA method. Workshop discussions closed with agreement on a three-step procedure to establish TCA age estimation as a major aging method:

1. The current validation study on recent age-known teeth shall establish confidence intervals for the individual age estimation by TCA.
2. The second step shall be an evaluation of the TCA method in an age-known historical reference sample in order to evaluate the TCA method against the expression of morphological traits of aging.
3. The third step shall be the application of TCA to a historical sample and the testing of the applicability of the suggested methodology, resulting in a comparison of mortality profiles calculated on the basis of the TCA age estimation with those based on morphological age estimations.

Despite the promise that the TCA method shows for more accurate age estimations, it will not be able to replace other morphological or histological methods for several reasons. First, we should be careful to extract as much information as possible from the skeleton, which is an important historical source. It reflects a multitude of reactions to various ecological conditions to which the former living individual was exposed. Our task, as anthropologists, is to extract these markers from the bones and to contribute to an ecologically orientated interpretation of human population development and adaptation. In this context it is essential that we apply all methods to deliver the best estimates for the remains of each individual, be it a single tooth, a few fragmented long bones, or more or less complete skeletons. In most cases, teeth survive skeletal decomposition or selective burial rites, but in many others, due to intravitam or postmortem tooth loss, alternative methods become necessary. Preliminary age range estimates by morphological methods avoid the misinterpretation of doubling cases by TCA age estimation and help to reveal such instances.

Thus, at the present state of research, we have outlined an approach to add to the established methods for age estimation; one which may lead to more accurate individual age estimations than was possible up to now.

Acknowledgments

This research was supported by the Max Planck Institute for Demographic Research, Rostock.

References

Alt K W and Türp JC (eds.) (1997) *Die Evolution der Zähne: Phylogenie–Ontogenie – Variation.* Berlin, Chicago, London: Quintessenz.

Azaz B, Ulmansky M, Moshev R, and Sela J (1974) Correlation between age and thickness of cementum in impacted teeth. *Oral Surgery* **28**, 691–694.

Buba H (1999) *Experimentelle Untersuchungen zur Anwendbarkeit der Methode der annuellen Zementringauflagerung bei menschlichen Zähnen.* Giessen: Wissenschaftliche Hausarbeit, Universität Giessen.

Charles K D, Condon K, Cheverud JM, and Buikstra JE (1986) Cementum annulation and age determination in *Homo sapiens*. I. Tooth variability and observer error. *American Journal of Physical Anthropology* **71**, 311–320.

Cipriano A (1999) Stress markers in tooth cementum annulation in non-human primates. Presentation on the workshop of the section for prehistoric anthropology and palaeanthropology. Göttingen, October 1999.

Condon K, Charles K D, Cheverud JM, and Buikstra JE (1986) Cementum annulation and age determination in Homo sapiens. II. Estimates and accuracy. *American Journal of Physical Anthropology* **71**, 321–330.

Geiger G (1993) *Vergleich verschiedener Methoden der Altersbeurteilung anhand von Zähnen und anderen morphologischen Merkmalen mit dem Lebensalter vorwiegend altersmarkierter Wildtiere der Ordnungen Artiodactyla und Carnivora.* Giessen: Habilitationsschrift Giessen.

Großkopf B (1989) Incremental lines in prehistoric cremated teeth. A technical note. *Zeitschrift für Morphologie und Anthropologie* **77**, 309–311.

Großkopf B (1990) Individualaltersbestimmung mit Hilfe von Zuwachsringen im Zement bodengelagerter menschlicher Zähne. *Zeitschrift für Rechtsmedizin* **103**, 351–259.

Großkopf B, Denden JM, and Krüger W (1996) Untersuchungen zur Zementapposition bei Paradontitis marginalis profunda. *Deutsche Zahnärztliche Zeitschrift* **51**, 295–297.

Grue H and Jensen B (1979) Review of the formation of incremental lines in tooth cementum of terrestrial mammals. *Danish Journal of Game Biology* **11**, 1–48.

Gustafson, G. (1950) Age determinatin of teeth. *Journal of the American Dental Association* **41**, 45–54.

Gustafson, G. (1955) Altersbestimmung an Zähnen. *Deutsche Zahnärztliche Zeitschrift* **25**, 1763–1768.

Halberg F, Lagoguey M, and Reinberg A (1983) Human circannual rhythms over a broad spectrum of physiological processes. *International Journal of Chronobiology* **8**, 225–268.

Jackes M (1992) Paleodemography: problems and techniques. In SR Saunders and A Katzenberg (eds.): *Skeletal biology of past peoples: research methods.* New York: John Wiley and Sons Inc., pp. 189–224.

Jacobshagen B (1999) Präzisierte Altersschätzungen nach dem Zementzonenverfahren anhand der Zähne einer mittelneolithischen Skelettpopulation aus Trebur, Kreis Gross-Gerau. Vergleich mit den Ergebnissen der kombinierten

Methode. In H. Spatz (ed.): *Das mittelneolithische Gräberfeld von Trebur, Kreis Gross-Gerau. Materialien zur Vor- und Frühgeschichte von Hessen* **19**, 333–348.

Kagerer P and Grupe G (2001) Age-at-death diagnosis and determination of life-history parameters by incremental lines in human dental cementum as an identification aid. *Forensic Science International* **118**, 75–82.

Kay RF, Rasmussen DT, and Beard KC (1984) Cementum annulus counts provide a means for age determination in *Macaca mulatta* (Primates, Anthropoidea). *Folia Primatologica* **42**, 85–95.

Klevezal GA (1970) A retrospective evaluation of the individual features of mammal growth based on the structure of dentine and bone layers. *Soviet Journal of Development Biology: A Translation of Ontogenez* **1**, 261–268.

Klevezal GA and Kleinenberg SE (1967) *Age determination of mammals from annual layers in teeth and bones*, translated from Russian by J. Salkind 1969. Springfield, VA: US Department of Commerce.

Kvaal SI and Solheim T (1995) Incremental lines in human dental cementum in relation to age. *European Journal of Oral Sciences* **103**, 225–230.

Laws RM (1952) A new method of age determination for mammals. *Nature* **169**, 972–973.

Lipsinic FE, Paunovich E, Houston DG, and Robison SF (1986) Correlation of age and incremental lines in the cementum of human teeth. *Journal of Forensic Sciences* **31**, 982–989.

Miller CS, Dove SB, and Cottone JA (1988) Failure of use of cemental annulations in teeth to determine the age of humans. *Journal of Forensic Sciences* **33**, 137–143.

Mitchell B (1963) Determination of age in Scottish red deer from growth layers in dental cement. *Nature* **198**, 350–351.

Morris P (1972) A review of mammalian age determination methods. *Mammal Reviews* **2**, 69–104.

Naylor JW, Miller GW, Stokes GN, and Stott GG (1985) Cementum annulation enhancement: a technique for age determination in man. *American Journal of Physical Anthropology* **68**, 197–200.

Nitzan DW, Michaeli Y, Weinreb M and Azaz B (1986) The effect of aging on tooth morphology: a study on impacted teeth. *Oral Surgery* **61**, 54–60.

Philipsen HP and Jablonski NG (1992) Age estimation from the structure of adult human teeth: review from the literature. *Forensic Sciences International* **54**, 23–28.

Renz H, Schaefer V, Duschner H, and Radlinski RJ (1997) Incremental lines in root cementum of human teeth: an approach to their ultrastructural nature by microscopy. *Advances in Dental Research* **11**, 472–474.

Saar M (1991) Altersabhängige Veränderungen am Schädel und an den Zähnen des Rehes, Capreolus capreolus (Linné, 1758). Eine Untersuchung an altersmarkierten Tieren. Dissertation, Universität Giessen.

Schumacher GH, Schmidt H, Böring H, and Richter W (1990) *Anatomie und Biochemie der Zähne*, 4th revised edition. Stuttgart, New York: Gustav Fischer Verlag.

Solheim T (1990) Dental cementum apposition as an indicator of age. *Scandinavian*

Journal of Dental Research **98**, 510–519.

Stein TJ and Corcoran JF (1994) Pararadicular cementum deposition as a criterion for age determination in human beings. *Oral Surgery, Oral Medicine and Oral Pathology* **77**, 266–270.

Stott GG, Sis RF, and Levy BM (1980) Cemental annulation as an age criterion in the common marmoset (*Callithrix jacchus*). *Journal of Medical Primatology* **9**, 274–285.

Stott GG, Sis RF, and Levy BM (1982) Cemental annulation as an age criterion in forensic dentistry. *Journal of Dental Research* **61**, 814–817.

Stout SD (1992) Methods of determining age at death using bone microstructure. In SR Saunders and A Katzenberg (eds.): *Skeletal biology of past peoples: research methods.* New York: John Wiley and Sons Inc., pp. 21–35.

Verderber M (1996) Anwendbarkeit des Zementzonenverfahrens bei Milchzähnen im Vergleich zu anderen Zahnaltersbestimmungen bei Kindern. Diplomarbeit, Universität Giessen.

Wada K, Ohtaishi N, and Hachiya N (1978) Determination of age in the Japanese monkey from growth layers in the dental cementum. *Primates* **19**, 775–784.

Wittwer-Backofen U (1991) Nekropole und Siedlung, Möglichkeiten und Grenzen der Rekonstruktion prähistorischer Bevölkerungsstrukturen. *Mitteilungen der Berliner Gesellschaft für Anthropologie, Ethnologie und Urgeschichte* **12**, 31–37.

Wittwer-Backofen U (1998) Morbidität und Mortalität. Anthropologische Bearbeitung der Skelettfunde. In G Stanzl *et al.*: *St. Kastor in Koblenz, Ausgrabungen und Bauuntersuchungen 1985–1990.* Denkmalpflege in Rheinland-Pfalz, Forschungsberichte, vol. 3, pp. 276–338.

Wittwer-Backofen U (2000) Demircihüyük-Sariket, anthropologische Bevölkerungsrekonstruktion. In J Seeker *et al.*: *Die Bronzezeitliche Nekropole von Demircihüyük-Sariket.* Istanbuler Forschungen, vol. 44, pp. 239–299.

Yoneda M (1982) Growth layers in dental cementum of *Saguinus* monkeys in South America. *Primates* **23**, 460–464.

7 Mortality models for paleodemography

JAMES W. WOOD, DARRYL J. HOLMAN,
KATHLEEN A. O'CONNOR, AND REBECCA J. FERRELL

Introduction

Population scientists concerned with long-term trends in human mortality ought to be interested in skeletal samples from extinct communities. Such samples are, in principle, the only possible source of information for most pre-industrial populations lacking written records – by far the most common kind of human community that has ever existed. Samples of skeletons provide two broad classes of information of potential interest to demographers and other population specialists: frequency counts of bony lesions that may reveal something about pathological processes active in the population, and data on ages-at-death from which age patterns of mortality may be inferred. Of these, the latter class of information has generally been deemed to be the less problematic. It has been assumed that skeletal age-at-death can be estimated well enough, albeit with some inevitable degree of error, to support a few crude but revealing statistics such as mean age-at-death, life expectancies, and age-specific mortality rates. And so for decades it has been considered perfectly acceptable to use skeletal data to compute "life tables", the traditional demographic tool for investigating age patterns of mortality. All that is needed, in this view, are a few simple modifications of standard life table techniques, modifications that were laid down 30 years ago by Acsádi and Nemeskéri (1970:60–65).

Over the years, paleodemographers have computed innumerable life tables, and they continue to do so to this day (for a few examples, see Green et al. 1974; Lovejoy et al. 1977; Greene et al. 1986; Lanphear 1989; Mensforth 1990; Benedictow 1996:36–41; Alesan et al. 1999). But the life table approach, so long the mainstay of paleodemographic mortality analysis, is open to criticism on several grounds (Sattenspiel and Harpending 1983; Konigsberg and Frankenberg 1992, 1994; Milner et al. 2000). First, paleodemographic studies do not produce the kinds of data needed to compute life table mortality rates using standard methods – specifically, the numbers of deaths among people at each (known) age and the number of

129

person-years of exposure to the risk of death at that age during some well-defined reference period. Instead, paleodemographers have been forced to work with fuzzily defined, error-prone distributions of purported ages-at-death, which can, under restrictive circumstances, be used to generate life tables – if, that is, one is willing to use methods whose statistical properties are poorly characterized.

Second, the life table approach assumes that the target population being studied was "stationary" in the technical demographic sense of the term. That is to say, it assumes that the population was closed to migration and had an intrinsic rate of increase equal to zero, age-specific schedules of fertility and mortality that were unchanging over time, and an equilibrium age distribution induced by those age-specific birth and death rates (Lotka 1922). Only in this special (and not necessarily realistic) case is the empirical age distribution of skeletons expected to have a simple, straightforward relationship to the cohort age-at-death column in the life table. This problem was recognized by one of the earliest advocates of formal paleodemography life tables (Angel 1969) and has been discussed in several more recent treatments (see e.g., Moore *et al.* 1975; Sattenspiel and Harpending 1983; Johannson and Horowitz 1986; Wood *et al.* 1992b; Konigsberg and Frankenberg 1994).

Third, the use of fixed age intervals in the life table implies that the ages of all skeletons are known within the same margin of error, including those of fragmentary skeletons that exhibit only a few, unreliable indicators of age. Thus the life table approach is unacceptably procrustean: it tries to force the complicated error structure of paleodemographic age estimates into a rigid framework of a few discrete age intervals.

Fourth, and perhaps most seriously, the life table is a wasteful way to use the small samples typical of paleodemographic studies – samples that are often on the order of a few dozen or, at best, a few hundred skeletons. In computing a life table we need to estimate one parameter (an age-specific mortality rate) for each and every age interval in the table, often requiring 10 or more separate parameters to be estimated. Few paleodemographic samples will support a method with such a gargantuan appetite for data.

For the past three decades, paleodemographers have attempted to circumvent some of these problems by using so-called "model" life tables (United Nations 1955, 1956; Coale and Demeny 1966; Weiss 1973). In this approach, the investigator searches through published tabulations of theoretical age-specific mortality patterns to find an age-at-death distribution that appears to mimic the empirical distribution being studied. In theory, this approach allows the assumption of stationarity to be relaxed (Paine 1989). In practice, however, the methods for fitting model life tables have been *ad hoc* and informal, and the results are only good if the published tabulations happen to include a table that corresponds closely to the population under study – something that is inherently untestable.

The Rostock Manifesto (see Hoppa and Vaupel, Chapter 1, this volume) – and the earlier work of Konigsberg and Frankenberg (1992), which anticipates it (see also Konigsberg *et al.* 1997) – represents a major advance in our thinking about how to estimate mortality statistics from skeletal samples. Under the Rostock Manifesto, we never compute a life table – although, as we show below, we can eventually compute something that looks like a life table if we so desire. Indeed, we do not begin by classifying skeletons by age at all, as we would have to do in the life table approach. Instead, we directly estimate the age pattern of death from the total sample of skeletons unclassified by age. Using *c* to indicate a vector of observed skeletal traits that provide information about age-at-death *a*, the probability of observing a particular *c* value – say, c_i – out of the sample as a whole is the marginal density of c_i:

$$\Pr(c_i) = \int_0^\infty \Pr(c_i|a)\Pr(a)\mathrm{d}a. \tag{7.1}$$

Since $\Pr(c_i)$ is the "likelihood" of observing a skeleton with characteristics c_i in our sample, the likelihood function for the entire sample of *n* skeletons is

$$L = \prod_{i=1}^n \Pr(c_i) = \prod_{i=1}^n \int_0^\infty \Pr{}^*(c_i|a)\Pr(a)\mathrm{d}a, \tag{7.2}$$

where the asterisk (*) denotes an empirical estimate from a reference sample of skeletons whose ages-at-death are known (see Usher, Chapter 3, this volume). The function $\Pr(a)$ is the age-at-death distribution in the target sample whose mortality pattern we wish to estimate. It is $\Pr(a)$ that tells us what we want to learn about mortality in the past. And maximization of equation (7.2) provides the basis for maximum likelihood estimates of the $\Pr(a)$ function from the target sample.

If the Rostock Manifesto is to be used in paleodemographic research, we need to find a suitable parametric model for the age-at-death distribution $\Pr(a)$. In other words, we need to boil all the complexities of age-specific mortality down to a single, more-or-less simple set of equations – equations containing constants (known as parameters) whose values we hope to estimate from skeletal data. Although some paleodemographers might balk at the notion of reducing all the manifold variability in human mortality to naked mathematics, the parametric approach actually has a number of virtues for paleodemographic analysis. As we show below, it allows us to correct for the confounding effects of nonstationarity – population growth or decline – on the age-at-death distribution. It also permits us to compare mortality patterns across populations in a straightforward way by examining parameter estimates and their associated standard errors. If we construct our parametric model wisely, it may even reveal something interesting about the biological processes underlying the human mortality curve.

The parametric approach does, however, have one profound limitation: it is only as good as the model chosen for the age-at-death distribution. In this chapter, we review parametric models of human mortality with an eye toward identifying models that may be of use in paleodemographic estimation. A secondary (but important) goal is to find models that facilitate "etiological" ways of thinking about paleodemographic mortality profiles; that is, models that allow for some kind of meaningful biological interpretation and insight. We examine the etiological foundations of current models and develop extensions that provide insights into the mortality processes experienced by past populations. Finally, we discuss some important issues, including heterogeneity in the risk of death, nonstationarity, and the sex differential in mortality, that must be considered in reconstructing the demographic past.

Before we go into the details of the different model specifications, it is worth asking what we are trying to accomplish in paleodemographic mortality analysis. We also need to be honest about what we can *never* accomplish, even with the best skeletal samples imaginable. Mainstream demographers often have the luxuries of huge samples, known ages, and information about specific causes of death (both primary and contributory). They can justify using some very complicated models that at once require such data and take advantage of them (see e.g., Schoen 1975; Manton and Stallard 1988; Nam 1990). As a result, they can examine the fine details of human mortality with comparative ease. Paleodemographers do not have – and never will have – any of these luxuries. Paleodemographic samples will almost always be small and subject to a number of unavoidable taphonomic biases (Gordon and Buikstra 1981; Waldron 1987; Walker *et al.* 1988; Mays 1992). It is unreasonable, therefore, to expect that paleodemographers will ever be able to reconstruct the fine details of any set of mortality rates. At best, we can hope to learn something about the overall level and age pattern of death in the distant past – and perhaps something about the gross differences in material conditions that led to the variation observed. This fact places a limit on the kinds of model worthy of consideration by paleodemographers. In general, simple models that reveal overall patterns are to be preferred over complicated models that purport to tell us about the detailed squiggles and bumps of the age-at-death curve. It is on such simple models that we concentrate here.

What exactly do we need to model?

To implement the Rostock approach, we need to model $\Pr(a)$, the age-at-death distribution of the past population under study. But what exactly is this distribution? And what is its relationship to the underlying age pattern of mortality? Intuitively, it might seem as if the relationship has to be simple. In fact it is complicated, and we need to be clear about it if we are to avoid going wrong.

For simplicity, imagine that we observe all the deaths that occurred in a well-defined population during some specified period of time, and that we know the exact age at which each and every death took place. (Needless to say, we never have it so good in paleodemography; but for the moment we are interested in theory, not reality.) How can we best characterize the age-specific mortality pattern of our ideal population in a formal statistical sense? And how can we model that pattern mathematically? Conceptually, if not computationally, it is simplest to begin with $\mu(a)$, the age-specific mortality rate at exact age a (normally measured in years). If we treat age as a continuously varying quantity – and throughout this chapter we will – then $\mu(a)$ is called the "force of mortality" (Keyfitz 1968:5) and is defined as

$$\mu(a) = \lim_{\Delta a \to 0} \left(\frac{\text{number of deaths at age } [a, a + \Delta a)}{\text{person-years of exposure at age } [a, a + \Delta a)} \right). \tag{7.3}$$

This function defines a rate that is strictly nonnegative. It can be thought of as the continuous-time analog of the central mortality rate, the usual starting point for calculation of the life table. But we cannot compute $\mu(a)$ directly from a paleodemographic age-at-death distribution (even if we know that distribution perfectly), so it behooves us to define some related functions. One of these is the survival function, $S(a)$, derived from the age-specific mortality function as

$$S(a) = e^{-\int_0^a \mu(x) dx}. \tag{7.4}$$

$S(a)$ is the probability that an individual survives from birth to *at least* age a. Since a cannot take on negative values, it follows that $S(0) = 1$. In addition, $S(a)$ is monotonically nonincreasing with a, i.e., it can only go down (or remain the same) as age increases. As $a \to \infty$, $S(a)$ approaches zero. Thus $S(a)$ is analogous to the survivorship column in the life table in all its particulars, save that age is reckoned continuously rather than in discrete intervals.

We now inch our way toward something that starts to look like the paleodemographic age-at-death distribution $\Pr(a)$ – but, in most circumstances, is not equivalent to it. This is the probability density function (PDF) of ages-at-death in a birth cohort of individuals subjected to the mortality function $\mu(a)$ at each age. We will write this PDF as $f_0(a)$. (The reason for the zero subscript will become clear presently.) It can be derived from $S(a)$ as

$$f_0(a) = -\,\mathrm{d}S(a)/\mathrm{d}a. \tag{7.5}$$

If we were dealing with skeletons from a single cohort, $f_0(a)$ would indeed be equivalent to $\Pr(a)$. But such is never the case in paleodemography, and if, by some miracle, it were the case, we would never know it.

According to some basic results from renewal theory (Cox 1962), the hazard, density, and survival functions are related to each other in the following ways:

$$\mu(a) = -\frac{\mathrm{d}\ln S(a)}{\mathrm{d}a} = -\frac{1}{S(a)}\frac{\mathrm{d}S(a)}{\mathrm{d}a} = \frac{f_0(a)}{S(a)}, \tag{7.6}$$

$$S(a) = \int_a^\infty f_0(x)\mathrm{d}x, \tag{7.7}$$

$$f_0(a) = \frac{\mu(a)S(a)}{\displaystyle\int_0^\infty \mu(x)S(x)\mathrm{d}x}. \tag{7.8}$$

The denominator in equation (7.8) rescales $f_0(a)$ so that it behaves like a proper PDF and integrates to 1. These relationships will be useful at several points in the following discussion. Because of these mathematical relationships, once we know one of these three functions, we can immediately determine the other two.

It is important to emphasize the parallels that exist between $\mu(a)$, $S(a)$, and $f_0(a)$, on the one hand, and certain columns in the classic life table on the other. We have already mentioned that $\mu(a)$ is analogous to the life table central mortality rate, and $S(a)$ to the survivorship schedule. Similarly, $f_0(a)$ is analogous to the life table (cohort) distribution of ages-at-death. Other "life-table-like" functions can be derived from $\mu(a)$, $S(a)$, or $f_0(a)$. For example, $\mu(a)$ can be converted into an age-specific probability of death, $q(a)$, during some small subinterval $(a - \frac{1}{2}\Delta a, a + \frac{1}{2}\Delta a)$ around a by solving

$$q(a) = 1 - \exp\left(-\int_{a-\frac{1}{2}\Delta a}^{a+\frac{1}{2}\Delta a} \mu(x)\mathrm{d}x\right). \tag{7.9}$$

For $\mu(a)$ in the interval $[0, \infty)$, this expression constrains $q(a)$ to fall between 0 and 1. Another quantity related to $\mu(a), f_0(a)$, and $S(a)$ is the "life expectancy" $e(a)$, or expected remaining lifetime for an individual alive at age a,

$$e(a) = \frac{\displaystyle\int_a^\infty S(x)\mathrm{d}x}{S(a)}. \tag{7.10}$$

As these last two equations show, $\mu(a), f_0(a)$, or $S(a)$ can be used to derive all the information we would normally hope to learn from an old-fashioned life table without ever requiring us to compute one. Or, rather, they *would* if only we could estimate them.

Which brings us back to the age-at-death distribution $\Pr(a)$ – the nearest we can get theoretically to paleodemographic data on skeletal age-at-death. We have hinted that there is a close (if complicated) relationship between $\Pr(a)$ and $f_0(a)$, and it is now time to make that relationship explicit.

As already noted, $f_0(a)$ is the age-at-death distribution of a single birth cohort exposed to the mortality function $\mu(a)$. As it happens, it is also the expected age-at-death distribution for all the deaths occurring in a stationary population over some delimitable period of time – for example, the time span during which skeletons are deposited in a cemetery (see Appendix 7.1). If we were sure that the population was stationary during the entire period of deposition, we could substitute equation (7.8) into our likelihood function (equation 7.2) and – once we have specified a parametric model for $\mu(a)$ and $S(a)$ – maximize it to obtain parameter estimates. But what if our target population was *not* stationary? What, for example, if it was changing in size, no matter how slowly? Then $f_0(a)$ is not the same as $\Pr(a)$, and we cannot use equation (7.8) in our likelihood. What do we do?

Even if we cannot take it for granted that our target population was stationary, it may still be reasonable to assume that it was "stable". In other words, we may be able to make all the assumptions listed above for the stationary population, except allowing for the possibility of a nonzero growth rate. (Note, by this logic, that the stationary population is simply a special case of the more general stable population.) As decades' worth of demographic analysis has shown, the assumption of stability is much less restrictive than the assumption of stationarity; even when fertility and mortality rates are changing and migration is occurring, most human populations still closely approximate a stable age distribution at any given time (Keyfitz 1968:89–94; Parlett 1970; Bourgeois-Pichat 1971; Coale 1972:117–61). This property, known as "weak ergodicity"

(Lopez 1961:66–68), ensures that stable population models almost always fit well, unless the populations to which they are being fit have been subjected to unusually rapid, cataclysmic change.

In a stable but nonstationary population, the age-at-death distribution is only partly a function of age-specific mortality; it is also influenced by the number of living individuals at risk of death at each age, which is influenced in turn by population growth. More precisely, the number of deaths at age a is proportional to the product of the force of mortality, $\mu(a)$, and the fraction of the total population that is age a, conventionally labeled $c(a)$. In a stationary population, $c(a)$ is proportional to $S(a)$, the probability of surviving from birth to age a, which makes the age-at-death distribution a reflection of mortality alone – but *only* in that special case. In a stable population with a nonzero-growth rate equal to r, the value of $c(a)$ is proportional to $S(a)e^{-ra}$. The quantity e^{-ra} corrects for the fact that the absolute number of newborns entering the population each year is changing as a result of population growth, thus distorting the age distribution that would have been expected under conditions of stationarity. For a positive growth rate, for example, there are more individuals born this year than, say, 10 years ago: if B babies are born this year into a stable population, then $B \times e^{-10r}$ babies must have been born 10 years ago.

This change in the number of individuals entering the population at $a = 0$ means that the number of people dying at each subsequent age must be a function not only of the force of mortality, but of the growth rate as well. The number of people surviving to each age is proportional to $S(a)e^{-ra}$; those survivors are then exposed to the age-specific mortality rate $\mu(a)$. Thus the probability density function for deaths in a stable population with growth rate r is

$$f_r(a) = \frac{\mu(a)S(a)e^{-ra}}{\displaystyle\int_0^\infty \mu(x)S(x)e^{-rx}dx} = \frac{f_0(a)e^{-ra}}{\displaystyle\int_0^\infty f_0(x)e^{-rx}dx}. \tag{7.11}$$

(Compare equation (7.8). It should now be clear why we mark $f_0(a)$ with a subscript zero: it represents $\Pr(a)$ only if the population's growth rate is zero – or in the profoundly unlikely event that we are dealing with a single cohort.) As shown in Appendix 7.1, this same expression applies to all the skeletons accumulated by a stable population over some more or less protracted span of time. In principle, then, we can treat $f_r(a)$ as the $\Pr(a)$ function in our likelihood (equation (7.2)) and estimate r as an additional parameter of the model – if we can assume that the population was stable. If it was *not* stable, at least approximately, we have probably reached the outer limits of what we can ever hope to learn about age-specific mortality from skeletal samples.

This correction for nonstationarity still requires us to specify a parametric model for the age pattern of mortality. In other words, we still need to write down an equation for either $\mu(a), f_0(a)$, or $S(a)$. And we should try hard to choose an equation that is flexible enough to approximate all *known* human mortality distributions in order to be reasonably confident that the model will accommodate the *unknown* mortality distribution that we are trying to reconstruct. At the same time, the model must be sufficiently bounded that growth rates are uniquely identifiable, since identifiability of the growth rate is not guaranteed for some possible parametric models (Holman *et al.* 1997, 1998). So we need the simplest possible model that is still complicated enough to capture most of what we know about human mortality patterns. Which immediately raises the question: what *do* we know about human mortality patterns, including their common features and their range of variation?

What does the human mortality curve look like?

Mortality trends and patterns have been well characterized for many contemporary human populations and some historical ones (mostly European, mostly confined to the past four centuries) (Coale and Demeny 1966; Keyfitz and Flieger 1968, 1990; Preston 1976; Gage 1990). Much less is known about mortality conditions among the types of population typically studied by anthropologists: the small foraging or horticultural societies characteristic of most of human existence. Nonetheless, work to date suggests that the mortality profiles of these populations tend to conform to a generalized human pattern, although often at a level of mortality near the upper end of the range typically observed in national and historical populations (Weiss 1973; Gage 1988). It thus seems meaningful to talk about the "common" age pattern of human mortality.

The basic pattern of the age-specific force of mortality is, in some respects, strikingly similar across a wide range of human populations, whether characterized by high mortality or low (Figure 7.1). The general pattern appears to be one of excess mortality at the youngest ages of the lifespan, with a rapid, monotonic decline to a lifetime low at around 10–15 years of age. This low point is followed by an accelerating rise in mortality at later ages, a rise that appears to be roughly exponential. Because this age pattern of mortality looks rather like the cross-section of an old-fashioned clawfoot bathtub, it is sometimes referred to as the "bathtub

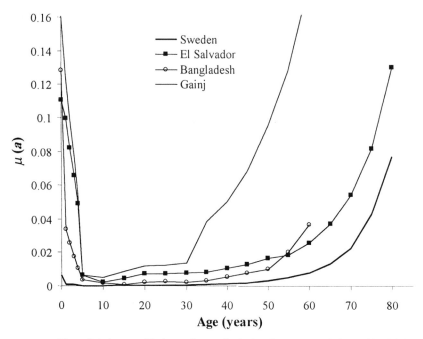

Figure 7.1. Age-specific force of mortality in four human populations with widely differing levels of mortality: Sweden 1985, females (Keyfitz and Flieger 1990); El Salvador 1950, males (Keyfitz and Flieger 1968); Bangladesh 1978, both sexes (Chowdhury *et al.* 1981); Gainj (highland New Guinea) 1970–77, males (Wood 1987b). Note that the Gainj, a small horticultural group, was the only one of the four without regular access to modern medical care at the time of data collection. In addition, the Gainj curve is based on a small sample (< 150 deaths) and therefore appears somewhat more "jagged" than the other examples.

curve". Figure 7.2 shows the survival function and the cohort PDF associated with the bathtub curve.

The principal variations on this common theme that are observed in historical and modern populations include wide differentials in the excess mortality occurring at the youngest and oldest ages and, in some populations, marked differences in the timing of the decline in juvenile mortality or the rise in adult mortality (Coale and Demeny 1966; Keyfitz and Flieger 1968, 1990; Preston 1976). All these phenomena are illustrated in Figure 7.1. These are, we suggest, the minimal kinds of variation we should expect our model to be able to capture.

Types of variation in the age pattern of human mortality that are *less* commonly observed – perhaps because they are of much smaller magnitude and thus require uncommonly good data to show through – include the so-called "accident hump" at late juvenile and early adult ages and an

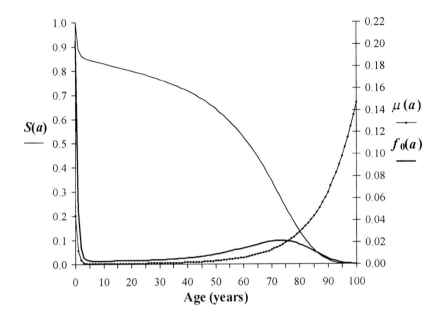

Figure 7.2. Survival, force of mortality, and cohort PDF curves associated with the "typical" human age pattern of mortality.

apparent slowing down of the rate of increase of mortality among the oldest of the old. The accident hump, as Gage and Mode (1993) have noted, is most clearly observed in males from European-derived populations with low mortality (most notably the USA, Canada, and Australia). Luder (1993) has suggested that it also occurs in nonhuman primates, although inadequate data make this claim difficult to evaluate. Even if the accident hump is a widespread phenomenon in human populations, the actual magnitude of the mortality rise associated with it appears to be miniscule, a point rightly emphasized by Gage and Mode (1993).

The deceleration of mortality among the oldest old is sometimes observed in populations for which exceptionally good data on the elderly are available (Horiuchi and Coale 1990; Kannisto 1994; Thatcher *et al.* 1997; Vaupel 1997; Vaupel *et al.* 1998). One possible explanation for this deceleration of mortality at the oldest ages is selective mortality, which might be expected to eliminate all but the least vulnerable individuals by the time the oldest segments of the lifespan are reached (Vaupel *et al.* 1979; Brooks *et al.* 1994; Himes 1994). Recent work on other organisms also highlights the possibility that the deceleration in mortality is real at the individual level, and not just an artifact of selectivity (Carey *et al.* 1992; Fukui *et al.* 1993;

Vaupel *et al.* 1994). From a paleodemographic perspective, these issues seem moot for the simple reason that the deceleration of mortality, whatever its cause, is only observed at ages so advanced (after, say, 90 years of age) that it cannot have been an important feature of mortality in any pre-industrial population.

In our opinion, then, the accident hump and the senescent deceleration in mortality exemplify just the sorts of "bumps and squiggles" in the mortality curve that paleodemographers will never be able to resurrect with any credibility. It would seem sufficiently challenging to try to reconstruct the general shape and level of the bathtub curve.

Ways of modeling mortality

As the previous section suggests, the mortality patterns of human populations can all be regarded as variations on a common, species-wide theme, where both the variations and the commonalities are of interest. The challenge in modeling mortality consists in capturing the underlying "universal" age structure of death while allowing for at least the principal kinds of variation in its detailed realization observed in the real world. Past attempts to model mortality can be classified in several different ways; one way that is especially telling in the present context is to subdivide them into "semi-parametric" (or perhaps "semi-empirical") and "fully parametric" forms. Semi-parametric models start with empirically observed mortality schedules and generalize them, usually by subjecting them to some form of regression analysis. For example, the pioneering work on model life tables, published by the United Nations (1955, 1956), involved regressing estimates of the infant mortality rate on the rest of the age schedule of mortality across 24 different populations. No attempt was made, beyond the regression model itself, to reduce all the empirical complexities to a simple mathematical form. But reduction to a simple mathematical form is precisely what the fully parametric approach seeks to do. In this approach, empirical data are examined rather informally to get a sense of what the age pattern of mortality ought to look like, and then an equation is found that mimics that pattern to some acceptable degree of approximation.

It might be thought that the semi-parametric approach is always preferable because, from its very outset, it hews more closely to real data. But, as we detail in the rest of this chapter, this is far from being the case. Particularly when parametric models are simple and allow some etiological interpretation, they can be much more enlightening about real-world processes affecting mortality.

In the following sections, we discuss one semi-parametric model and several fully parametric ones. The semi-parametric model we have chosen is one of several known as relational models (Zaba 1979, 1981; Heligman and Pollard 1980; Ewbank *et al.* 1983; Aalen 1989), so called because they are all based on statistical relationships among empirical mortality patterns. Relational models, in some respects, represent a compromise between traditional life tables and fully parametric models, hence our description of them as semi-parametric.

Relational models

The development of relational models was originally inspired by a quest to find the minimal number of parameters needed to capture all the variation in the level and shape of the human curve of age-specific mortality. A preliminary solution to this problem was provided by Ledermann and Breas (1959), who performed a factor analysis of estimated age-specific mortality rates from a large number of populations, showing that two latent factors (apart from sex) accounted for more than half of the observed variation in mortality. This result inspired Brass (1971) to develop a two-parameter model of mortality, one that underlies what has come to be called the Brass (or logit) approach to mortality estimation. The Brass model is the prototype for all later relational models (e.g., Zaba 1979; Ewbank *et al.* 1983), and it can be used to exemplify the approach as a whole.

The logic of the Brass system starts with the theoretical survival function $S(a)$. Imagine for the moment that two populations (denoted by the subscripts 1 and 2) differ only in the level of mortality, so that $\mu_1(a) = \kappa\mu_2(a)$ for all a, where κ is a constant. From equation (7.6) it follows that

$$\frac{1}{S_1(a)}\frac{dS_1(a)}{da} = \frac{\kappa}{S_2(a)}\frac{dS_2(a)}{da}.$$ (7.12)

By inspecting a large number of empirical mortality schedules, Brass discovered that the scalar κ relating different schedules is not in fact a constant, but declines toward unity with advancing age. For example, in one extreme comparison $\mu(a)$ was more than 16 times higher in one population than in another in the age interval 1 to 4 years, but dropped to about 1.5 times higher at ages 75 to 79 years (Brass 1971). Brass found that this pattern could be closely approximated by a function of the form

$$\frac{dS_1(a)/da}{S_1(a)(1 - S_1(a))} = \frac{\kappa \, dS_2(a)/da}{S_2(a)(1 - S_2(a))}.$$ (7.13)

Solving for $S_i(a)$,

$$\ln\left(\frac{1 - S_1(a)}{S_1(a)}\right) = \alpha + \beta \ln\left(\frac{1 - S_2(a)}{S_2(a)}\right),$$ (7.14)

where α and β are new constants.

If the number x lies between 0 and 1, then $\ln[x/(1 - x)]$ is known as the "logit transform" of x, often written logit(x). Thus, we can rewrite equation (7.14) as logit$(1 - S_1(a)) = \alpha + \beta$ logit$(1 - S_2(a))$. This equation is the basis of the Brass relational model, and α and β are its two parameters. Roughly speaking, a choice of α sets the overall level of mortality (as reflected in, say, the life expectancy at birth) while β sets the "tilt" of mortality curve 1 compared with curve 2.

Now suppose that "population 2" is a well-studied reference population whose survival schedule has been estimated properly from high-quality data, and "population 1" is some target population whose survival schedule is only poorly known. Then a linear regression of logit $(1 - S(a))$ from the target population on that of the reference population, in the form of equation (7.14), can be used to smooth the target population's mortality curve and fill in any gaps (for technical details see Brass 1975). In this way, information on part of the target population's survival schedule can be used to generate the entire schedule.

In his original article on the subject, Brass (1971) showed that the logit approach is reasonably flexible and provides plausible results when applied to data from a wide variety of national populations. In the same chapter, Brass provided a reference life table that has proven useful in analyses of mortality data from Africa and Asia (see Brass and Coale 1968; Carrier and Hobcraft 1971). It is important to emphasize, however, that neither the logit approach in general nor the Brass reference table in particular has been able to cover all known human mortality patterns, and both may be especially bad for the small, high-mortality populations commonly studied by anthropologists (Wood 1987a). In addition, the form of equation (7.13), and hence (7.14), was not derived from theoretical considerations, but is purely empirical. Nonetheless, relational models provide a simple system for mortality estimation that is flexible enough to warrant more attention by paleodemographers than they have hitherto received.

Fully parametric models

An alternative to model life tables and relational models are parametric models of the age pattern of mortality (Wood *et al.* 1992a). If constructed properly, these models reduce the numerous life table age classes into a small number of biologically meaningful parameters that can all be estimated from data on the target population being studied (Gage and Dyke 1986; Gage 1989; Gavrilov and Gavrilova 1991). Parametric models have begun to be widely applied in demographic research only in the last two decades as advances in computer technology have facilitated the development, testing, and application of complex statistical models (Mode and Busby 1982; Mode and Jacobsen 1984; Gage 1988, 1989; Wood *et al.* 1992a; Gage and Mode 1993). These models are extremely promising for use with small paleodemographic samples because of their parsimony in describing mortality patterns with the smallest possible number of parameters.

Like relational models, fully parametric models of mortality can be used to smooth and correct inadequate mortality data. But they can be much more flexible than relational models. All mortality models impose a certain amount of *a priori* age structure onto the data being examined, but good parametric models make the fewest assumptions about what the detailed age pattern of mortality ought to be. In theory, this permits us to come closer to the "true" underlying age structure of mortality in the population being studied – assuming that we have selected the *right* parametric model.

A number of parametric models of the age patterns of mortality have been developed over the years, as attempts have been made to formulate a general "law of mortality" applicable to all human populations (for reviews, see Mode 1985:35–74; Gage 1989; Gavrilov and Gavrilova 1991; Wood *et al.* 1992a). In the following sections, we discuss models that we consider to be especially promising for paleodemography. Since paleodemographic cause-of-death analysis is (and will probably remain) poorly developed, all the models we consider deal with mortality from all causes simultaneously.

Weibull, Rayleigh, and bi-Weibull models

The two-parameter Weibull model (Weibull 1951) is widely used in industrial reliability testing, mainly to model the effects of accumulated damage on product breakage (Thompson 1988). By analogy, it may provide a reasonable model for human aging, which is a kind of "wear-out" process. The force of mortality in the standard Weibull model is

$$\mu(a) = \beta a^{\beta-1}/\eta^{\beta}. \tag{7.15}$$

The associated survival function is

$$S(a) = \exp[-(a/\eta)^{\beta}], \tag{7.16}$$

and the cohort PDF of ages at death is

$$f_0(a) = (\beta a^{\beta-1}/\eta^{\beta})\exp[-(a/\eta)^{\beta}]. \tag{7.17}$$

As Nordling (1953) first noted, the two-parameter Weibull specification can be used to model so-called multi-hit or multi-stage processes, in which a fixed number of insults or disease stages must be experienced before death ensues. Examples for which such models may be relevant include: cancer, in which two or more somatic mutations must occur before a cell line becomes malignant and metastatic; diabetic nephropathy, which is preceded by a fairly regular sequence of diabetic stages; and the formation of arterial plaques, for which multiple, sequential lesions in the arterial wall appear to provide a starting point (Whittemore and Keller 1978; Andersen 1988; Weiss and Chakraborty 1990).

Recently, a special case of the Weibull has been used for paleodemographic mortality analysis (Konigsberg and Herrmann 2000). This is the Rayleigh model, which is obtained from the Weibull by setting $\beta = 2$. By fixing one parameter, this model gains some efficiency in estimation, albeit at the cost of a corresponding loss in generality and flexibility.

A related model that has found some application in reliability testing is the bi-Weibull model (Evans *et al.* 2000:199–200). Reliability specialists have used this model to capture complex processes with both "burn-in" and "wear-out" stages, roughly paralleling the maturation and senescent phases of the human lifespan. The bi-Weibull is formed by adding together two Weibull mortality functions: the first a Weibull with two-parameters, λ and θ, that applies to all ages and the second a three-parameter Weibull that is added to the baseline hazard after $a = \gamma$, the earliest age at which wear-out affects the risk of death. To specify the force of mortality in the bi-Weibull, we need two separate equations:

$$\mu(a) = \lambda\theta(\lambda a)^{\theta-1}, \qquad 0 \le a < \gamma, \tag{7.18}$$

and

$$\mu(a) = \lambda\theta(\lambda a)^{\theta-1} + \left(\frac{\beta}{\eta}\right)\left(\frac{a-\gamma}{\eta}\right)^{\beta-1}, \qquad a \ge \gamma. \tag{7.19}$$

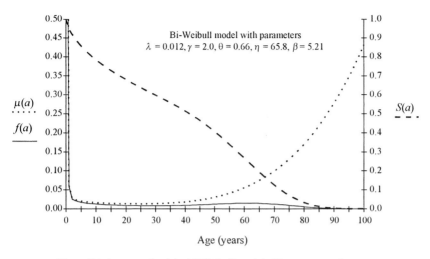

Figure 7.3. An example of the bi-Weibull model of human mortality.

The corresponding survival function is given by

$$S(a) = e^{-(\lambda a)^{\theta}}, \qquad 0 \le a < \gamma, \tag{7.20}$$

and

$$S(a) = \exp(-\{(\lambda a)^{\theta} + [(a - \gamma)/\eta]^{\beta}\}), \qquad a \ge \gamma. \tag{7.21}$$

The bi-Weibull model does a quite decent job of mimicking the bathtub curve of human mortality (Figure 7.3). So far as we know, however, it has never been used in paleodemography – or any other branch of demography of which we are aware. If we were willing to rely on evolutionary theory that suggests that senescent causes of death do not begin to be important until about the time of sexual maturation (Hamilton 1966), we could reduce the standard bi-Weibull specification to a four-parameter model by setting γ equal to, say, 15 years of age. One unfortunate feature of the bi-Weibull, incidentally, it that its force of mortality may be undefined at age zero if $\theta < 1$ (because it involves division by zero), making it impossible to estimate neonatal mortality.

The Gompertz model

The very first attempt to develop a parametric model of mortality was that of Gompertz (1825). Gompertz modeled the aging or senescent component of mortality with two parameters: a positive scale parameter α that sets the overall level of adult mortality, and a positive shape parameter β that determines how the risk of death accelerates with advancing age. The force of mortality in the Gompertz model is

$$\mu(a) = \alpha e^{\beta a}. \tag{7.22}$$

The corresponding cohort PDF is

$$f_0(a) = \alpha \exp\left[\beta a + \frac{\alpha}{\beta}(1 - e^{\beta a}) \right], \tag{7.23}$$

and the survival function is

$$S(a) = \exp\left[\frac{\alpha}{\beta}(1 - e^{\beta a}) \right]. \tag{7.24}$$

Gompertz, who was concerned exclusively with mortality associated with aging across the adult lifespan, assumed that the observed increase in adult mortality with age is a result of a negative exponential decline in physiological capacity (Gage 1989). A variety of other parametric models of aging have since been developed, some of them based on different assumptions about the aging process (e.g., linear rather than exponential decline in physiological capacity with age, or models of accumulated damage with age). Most of these ultimately reduce, or approximate, to the Gompertz equation (Wood *et al.* 1994; for reviews of these models, see Mode 1985; Gage 1989; Gavrilov and Gavrilova 1991).

The Gompertz–Makeham model

The earliest modification to the Gompertz model, proposed by Makeham (1860), involves adding a single parameter to capture age-independent adult mortality. This parameter represents mortality resulting from causes, such as accidents or sexually transmitted diseases, unrelated to either maturation or senescence. The Gompertz–Makeham model specifies the force of mortality as

$$\mu(a) = \alpha_1 + \alpha_2 e^{\beta a}. \tag{7.25}$$

The α_1 parameter in this expression represents the constant, age-independent component of mortality; the $\alpha_2\exp(\beta a)$ term is just a Gompertz function describing the senescent component.

The cohort PDF for the Gompertz–Makeham model is

$$f_0(a) = (\alpha_1 + \alpha_2 e^{\beta a}) \exp\left[-\alpha_1 a + \frac{\alpha_2}{\beta}(1 - e^{\beta a}) \right],\tag{7.26}$$

and the Gompertz–Makeham survival function is

$$S(a) = \exp\left[-\alpha_1 a + \frac{\alpha_2}{\beta}(1 - e^{\beta a}) \right].\tag{7.27}$$

The Gompertz–Makeham model fits well to empirical mortality distributions between the ages of 30 and 85 years (Finch 1990). Nearly all subsequent models of the age pattern of mortality have been extensions of the Gompertz–Makeham model, primarily intended to cover the rest of the lifespan – for example, by allowing for an early-adult accident hump (Thiele 1871; Heligman and Pollard 1980; Mode and Busby 1982; Mode and Jacobsen 1984; Gage 1989; Gavrilov and Gavrilova 1991). As we have already suggested, it is probably pointless for paleodemographers to concern themselves with a detail as small as the accident hump.

The Siler model

One of the most parsimonious parametric models of mortality across the *entire* lifespan, including pre-adult ages, is the Siler competing hazards model (Siler 1979, 1983). This model fits as well as or better than most other models to human mortality data (Gage and Dyke 1986; Gage and Mode 1993). Siler added a third component to the Gompertz–Makeham model to represent the earliest segment of life, when the risk of death often starts out high but then declines rapidly. The force of mortality in Siler's model is

$$\mu(a) = \alpha_1 e^{-\beta_1 a} + \alpha_2 + \alpha_3 e^{\beta_3 a}.\tag{7.28}$$

Note that the parameters of equation (7.25) have been renumbered here. Now α_1 is the level of neonatal mortality and β_1 is the rate of decline in early mortality with age. The second term is the constant (Makeham) component of the model, and the third term the senescent (Gompertz) component. The structure of the Siler model invites a simple interpretation of mortality as the sum of three components:

$$\mu(a) = \mu_1(a) + \mu_2 + \mu_3(a),\tag{7.29}$$

where each μ represents a distinct set of competing causes of death. Indeed, Siler (1979) called his model a competing hazards model precisely because

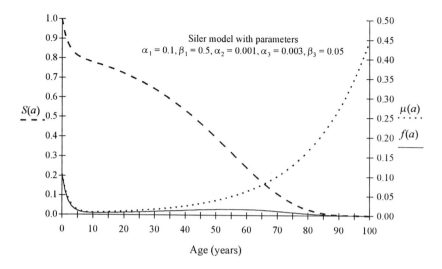

Figure 7.4. An example of the Siler model of human mortality.

he interpreted its three components as sets of risks that compete simultaneously throughout life. Because of the β parameters, however, the first component is unimportant after the earliest juvenile years, and the third component does not become dominant until adulthood.

The cohort PDF and survival function of the Siler model are

$$f_0(a) = (\alpha_1 e^{-\beta_1 a} + \alpha_2 + \alpha_3 e^{\beta_3 a}) \tag{7.30}$$

$$\times \exp\left[-\frac{\alpha_1}{\beta_1}(1 - e^{-\beta_1 a}) - \alpha_2 a + \frac{\alpha_3}{\beta_3}(1 - e^{\beta_3 a}) \right]$$

and

$$S(a) = \exp\left[-\frac{\alpha_1}{\beta_1}(1 - e^{-\beta_1 a}) - \alpha_2 a + \frac{\alpha_3}{\beta_3}(1 - e^{\beta_3 a}) \right]. \tag{7.31}$$

Figure 7.4 shows an example of the Siler model with parameters chosen to reflect a typical human mortality pattern. Despite the fact that the Siler model does not include an accident hump, it still fits reasonably well to human populations, including those that do have this feature (Gage and Mode 1993).

The three components of the Siler model – immature, age-independent, senescent – are assumed to be competing but noninteracting causes of death (or, somewhat more realistically, clusters of distinct causes of death). That is to say, individuals who survive one set of potential causes (e.g., age-independent ones) are just as susceptible as all other individuals to other causes (say, senescent ones).

Although the Siler model was not originally developed with much detailed etiology in mind (especially with regard to its immature component), Gage (1991) has shown empirically that the model has considerable etiological coherence. For example, mortality attributable to infectious diseases such as pneumonia and diarrhea is highly correlated with the immature and senescent components; degenerative causes of death are primarily associated with the senescent component; and accidents and maternal mortality fall largely into the age-independent component of the Siler model (Gage 1991). Maternal mortality is not, of course, truly age-independent; it simply is not associated with either immaturity or advanced age.

Gage, who pioneered the application of parametric mortality models in anthropological demography (Gage and Dyke 1986; Gage 1988, 1989), has used the Siler competing hazards model extensively for both empirical and theoretical investigations of the age patterns of mortality. He has examined international variation in human mortality (Gage 1990), the relationship of covariates to this variation (Gage 1994; Gage and O'Connor 1994), the age pattern of mortality in anthropological populations (Gage 1988, 1989), and even the age pattern of mortality in nonhuman primates (Gage and Dyke 1988; Dyke *et al.* 1993; Gage 1998). He has also examined hypotheses regarding the underlying etiology and epidemiology of disease processes and their relationships to the age pattern of mortality (Gage 1991, 1994). And one of his former students has used the Siler model extensively in paleodemographic analysis (O'Connor 1995; O'Connor *et al.* 1997).

Although the Siler model is unquestionably useful for investigating human mortality, it does have some limitations. Its immature component, for example, is often difficult to estimate and interpret. There are two distinct reasons for this difficulty. First, although the negative exponential specification of juvenile mortality fits most human data fairly well, it is not etiologically derived (Gage 1989). Second, juvenile mortality is difficult to estimate reliably from small samples because information on it comes primarily from a tiny subset of the data – those from the first five years or so of life. In most populations, mortality during this segment of the lifespan is high but declines rapidly with small increments in age; thus almost all the information about juvenile mortality must be extracted from an extremely narrow age range. With small samples, the scale of the juvenile component can sometimes be estimated reasonably well, but capturing the shape is more problematic (Gage 1989). This problem is worsened in paleodemography because of the common underrepresentation of infants and young children in skeletal samples owing to differential preservation (Gordon and Buikstra 1981; Waldron 1987; Walker *et al.* 1988). This whole issue is important because early juvenile deaths make up a large fraction of all deaths in most human populations, especially pre-industrial ones, and much of the variation in mortality among human populations falls in infancy and early childhood (see, e.g., Figure 7.1). For these reasons a better theoretical model of mortality at juvenile ages would be useful.

A second limitation of the Siler model is that it assumes individuals in a population to be homogeneous with respect to their genetic, physiological, environmental, and behavioral risks of death (Gage and Dyke 1986; Gage 1989). Variation in risk factors among individuals or subgroups in a population may influence the age pattern of mortality in ways that make comparative analyses difficult to interpret (Vaupel *et al.* 1979; Vaupel and Yashin 1985a,b; Gage 1989; Wood *et al.* 1992a,b; Himes 1994). We expand this point in the next section.

Interpreting competing hazards models when mortality is heterogeneous

In this section, we show that the competing hazard interpretation of the Siler model implies that the population being studied is homogeneous in mortality risk – that is, the population is made up of individuals who are all subject to exactly the same causes of death and are equally susceptible to them. In the presence of heterogeneity, the model's parameters cannot be interpreted in the conventional way proposed by Siler (1979). In other words, models like the Gompertz–Makeham and Siler are implicitly models of homogeneous risks. With heterogeneity among individuals in the risk of death, interpretation of the μ values on the right-hand side of equation (7.28) is not possible except under some not-very-plausible circumstances, as shown below.

Generally speaking, we do not believe that the members of any natural population, human or nonhuman, have exactly the same age-specific risks of death (for a discussion of this point, see Milner *et al.* 2000). For example, some individuals may be constitutionally frailer than others, a subset of individuals may engage in risky behavior, or some individuals may simply live in riskier environments, such as those associated with poverty. A number of recent advances in statistical methodology provide a framework for modeling heterogeneity among individuals in a population (see e.g.,

Heckman and Singer 1984; Manton *et al.* 1992). Another section of this chapter discusses several different methods for incorporating heterogeneity into parametric mortality models in ways that improve our ability to interpret the estimated parameters.

The simplest imaginable form of heterogeneity is one in which variation in risk comes packaged in the form of two distinct subgroups – but we observe only the mixture of the two. As we show in Appendix 7.2, the Siler model cannot be interpreted under this scenario as representing independent competing hazards. We will refer to models that are mixtures of two or more nonoverlapping subgroups as "mixed-hazards models" to distinguish them from competing-hazards models. Are there any possible two-component mixed-hazards models that can be interpreted in terms of independent competing causes? Appendix 7.2 shows that there are (see equations (A7.11)–(A7.12)), but also that they make little if any biological sense. If we believe that heterogeneity was likely to have existed in our target population – and it has almost certainly existed in every human population – then we should probably abandon models that purport to be competing-hazards models and replace them with specifications that can be interpreted explicitly in terms of mixtures of heterogeneous subgroups.

The mixed-Makeham model

In this section we develop a mixed-hazard model of human mortality that fits as well as the Siler model – and, just as importantly, has no more parameters. Consider a population made up of two subgroups, and assume that each subgroup has a different constant (Makeham) hazard but that both subgroups have the same senescent (Gompertz) hazard. The model is thus a mixture of two Gompertz–Makeham models, but constrained so that the two senescent components are identical. Accordingly, we call it the "mixed-Makeham model". The force of mortality in the mixture as a whole is

$$\mu(a) = p(a)(\alpha_1 + \alpha_3 e^{\beta_3 a}) + (1 - p(a))(\alpha_2 + \alpha_3 e^{\beta_3 a}) \qquad (7.32)$$
$$= p(a)\alpha_1 + (1 - p(a))\alpha_2 + \alpha_3 e^{\beta_3 a},$$

where α_1 now represents the constant hazard in the first, high-risk subgroup and α_2 represents the constant hazard in the second, low-risk subgroup. The term $p(a)$ is the fraction of high-risk individuals among all the individuals alive at age a, given by

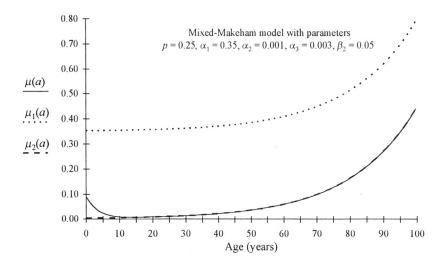

Figure 7.5. An example of the mixed-Makeham model of human mortality. The broken and dotted curves show the force of mortality in the low- and high-risk subgroups, respectively, whereas the solid curve shows the aggregate-level force of mortality in the mixture as a whole. Although neither subgroup curve has a distinct juvenile component, the aggregate curve displays a decline in juvenile mortality, reflecting selective mortality against the high-risk subgroup. As high-risk individuals are selected out of the population, the aggregate curve converges on the low-risk pattern.

$$p(a) = \frac{pS_1(a)}{pS_1(a) + (1-p)S_2(a)} \qquad (7.33)$$

$$= \frac{p\exp\left[-\alpha_1 a + \frac{\alpha_3}{\beta_3}(1 - e^{\beta_3 a})\right]}{p\exp\left[-\alpha_1 a + \frac{\alpha_3}{\beta_3}(1 - e^{\beta_3 a})\right] + (1-p)\exp\left[-\alpha_2 a + \frac{\alpha}{\beta_3}(1 - e^{\beta_3 a})\right]},$$

where p is the *initial* fraction of individuals in the high-risk subgroup (i.e. the fraction at birth). From the starting point p, $p(a)$ declines as high-risk individuals are selectively removed by death. As a result, the $p(a)\alpha_1$ term in equation (7.32) becomes smaller and smaller with age, and the overall force of mortality declines accordingly. Thus, even though there is no distinct juvenile component of mortality under the mixed-Makeham model, mortality declines during the early years of life as the aggregate mixture comes more and more to reflect the low-risk portion of the population (Figure 7.5). After a while, however, the shared senescent component begins to dominate the overall force of mortality, and the risk of death increases correspondingly at later ages in both subgroups.

The cohort PDF and survival function of the mixed-Makeham model are

$$
f_0(a) = p \exp\left[-\alpha_1 a + \frac{\alpha_3}{\beta_3}(1 - e^{\beta_3 a}) \right](\alpha_1 + \alpha_3 e^{\beta_3 a}) \tag{7.34}
$$

$$
+ (1 - p)\exp\left[-\alpha_2 a + \frac{\alpha_3}{\beta_3}(1 - e^{\beta_3 a}) \right](\alpha_2 + a_3 e^{\beta_3 a}),
$$

and

$$
S(a) = p \exp\left[-\alpha_1 a + \frac{\alpha_3}{\beta_3}(1 - e^{\beta_3 a}) \right] \tag{7.35}
$$

$$
+ (1 - p)\exp\left[-\alpha_2 t + \frac{\alpha_3}{\beta_3}(1 - e^{\beta_3 a}) \right].
$$

We have shown elsewhere that this model usually fits paleodemographic mortality profiles at least as well as the Siler model does (O'Connor 1995; Holman *et al.* 1997, 1998; O'Connor *et al.* 1997). The difference between this model and the Siler is that its parameters are easier to interpret and may provide clues about the existence of important forms of intrapopulation variation in material conditions that affect the risk of death. In addition, the α_1 and α_2 parameters of the mixed-Makeham model are estimated from observations drawn from the entire lifespan and are thus less sensitive to deficiencies in data on the very young than are the Siler parameters α_1 and β_1.

A more general approach to modeling heterogeneity

The above discussion has focused on discrete heterogeneity in which individuals can be assigned to one of two subgroups, each subgroup differing from the other but containing members who all share common mortality risks. This approach can be extended to any number of discrete subgroups. Subgroups may have risks of death that are all drawn from the same distribution but with different parameter values, or they may have different distributions altogether. Mixtures of different distributions have been used for a number of models in demography, for example to describe the postpartum resumption of menses (Ford and Kim 1987) and pregnancy loss (Wood 1989; Holman 1996). Recently, Louzada-Neto (1999) has proposed a "polyhazard" mortality model along these same lines.

A reasonable question to ask is whether we can justify adding risk groups without limit. Additional subgroups are perfectly easy to handle mathematically, but parameter estimation becomes increasingly difficult with each latent subgroup thrown into the pot. Most paleodemographic samples would not be able to cope with more than two or three subgroups. With many subgroups, moreover, we begin to lose the straightforward interpretation associated with the simple two-subgroup model. And once we forfeit the ability to interpret parameters, we descend from etiological modeling to empirical curve fitting.

Rather than blindly subdivide the population into hypothetical subgroups, we might consider a population that consists of such a large number of subgroups that the risk of death appears to vary continuously among individuals. We can then think in terms of a continuous probability density function of underlying risk rather than proportions falling into discrete categories of risk. If z is the individual-level component of the risk of death – that is, the part of the risk that varies among members of the population – then we can write $g(z)$ for the continuous distribution of risk. The age-at-death distribution that we observe is then the expectation over all values of z:

$$\bar{f}_0(a) = \int_{-\infty}^{\infty} g(z) f_0(a \mid z) \mathrm{d}z. \tag{7.36}$$

We can specify z in $f_0(a \mid z)$ in a number of ways, including as a covariate on a particular parameter or on the force of morality as a whole, as in the proportional hazards model (Cox 1972; Manton *et al.* 1986).

Several researchers have shown that parameter estimates can be disturbingly sensitive to the precise choice of equations for $g(z)$ or $f_0(a \mid z)$ (Heckman and Walker 1987; Manton *et al.* 1992; Moreno 1994; Rodríguez 1994). Consequently, specification of these terms should be based, whenever possible, on some theory about the underlying mechanisms that generate the heterogeneity in risk (see e.g., Weiss 1990; Wood 1998). The gamma, beta, and log-normal distributions are frequently used to model heterogeneity. For example, Gage (1989) has explored the behavior of the Siler model with gamma-distributed heterogeneity. But these specifications are often based on mathematical convenience rather than on any established biological principles.

Capturing the sex differential

There is one form of heterogeneity that can reasonably be captured by a simple dichotomous model: the difference between males and females. Since the one thing we know about human mortality is that it always differs between the sexes – and sometimes markedly so – it makes little sense to apply a single, homogeneous parametric model of mortality to a combined sample of male and female skeletons. Moreover, sex differences in mortality are interesting in their own right, and we would like to be able to say something about them. But to examine these differences using the Rostock Manifesto in its present form we must, in effect, cut our sample size in half by applying the method to the two sexes separately. Even worse, we have to throw out some important biological constraints on our parameter values: no matter what the difference in mortality between the sexes, the male and female segments of the population have to be growing or declining at the same rate r (Coale 1972:53–58), and meiosis re-establishes a sex ratio at birth that is always close to one-half. In addition, male and female age-specific mortality rates are not *completely* unrelated to each other, but differ in quite limited and specific ways (Keyfitz 1985:54–76). It would be a fine thing if we could make use of these universal constraints in estimating our model.

Imagine that our vector of skeletal traits c contains measures that provide information about sex as well as age in a sample made up both male and female skeletons. What is the probability, over the sample as a whole, of observing a particular c value – say, c_i? It is just the marginal density of c_i:

$$\Pr(c_i) = \sum_{k \in (0,1)} \int_0^{\infty} \Pr(c_i \mid a, k) f_r(a \mid k) \Pr(k) da \qquad (7.37)$$

$$= \sum_{k \in (0,1)} \int_0^{\infty} \Pr(c_i \mid a, k) f_r(a, k) da,$$

where k is an indicator variable for sex ($k = 0$ for females, 1 for males), and $f_r(a, k)$ is the joint distribution of deaths by age and sex in the target population. (The fact that this distribution is subscripted with an r indicates that it has been corrected for nonstationarity.) The likelihood function for the whole sample is $\Pi \Pr(c_i)$, where the product is taken over all n skeletons.

To use this likelihood we need two new quantities: an estimate of $\Pr(c_i \mid a, k)$ from a reference sample in which both age and sex are known, and a parametric expression for $f_r(a, k)$. The first is a purely statistical problem, and we ignore it here. We focus instead on finding an expression for $f_r(a, k)$.

We begin with the elementary relationship $\Pr(a, k) = \Pr(k|a)\Pr(a)$. It follows that

$$f_r(a, k) = \begin{cases} (1 - \rho(a))f_r(a), & \text{if } k = 0 \\ \rho(a)f_r(a), & \text{if } k = 1 \end{cases} \tag{7.38}$$

where $\rho(a)$ is the proportion of surviving people at age a for whom $k = 1$. That is, $\rho(a) = \Pr(k = 1|a)$. This quantity can be found as

$$\rho(a) = \frac{\rho(0)S_0(a)}{\rho(0)S_0(a) + (1 - \rho(0))S_1(a)}, \tag{7.39}$$

where $\rho(0)$ is the sex ratio at birth expressed as a proportion and the subscripts 0 and 1 refer to females and males, respectively. Now, everyone knows that $\rho(0)$ is not *exactly* equal to $\frac{1}{2}$, but it never strays very far from it (in some populations it soars to 0.51, in others it plunges to 0.49). So we assume from now on that $\rho(0) = \frac{1}{2}$. Thus, equation (7.39) reduces to

$$\rho(a) = \frac{S_0(a)}{S_0(a) + S_1(a)}. \tag{7.40}$$

Since the numbers of both sexes in a stable population must be changing at the same constant rate r, it must be the case that

$$f_r(a) = \frac{\bar{\mu}(a)\bar{S}(a)e^{-ra}}{\displaystyle\int_0^\infty \bar{\mu}(x)\bar{S}(x)e^{-rx}\,dx}. \tag{7.41}$$

In equation (7.41), the bars denote weighted averages over the two sexes. That is,

$$\bar{\mu}(a) = (1 - \rho(a))\mu_0(a) + \rho(a)\mu_1(a) \tag{7.42}$$

and

$$\bar{S}(a) = (1 - \rho(0))S_0(a) + \rho(0)S_1(a) \tag{7.43}$$
$$= \tfrac{1}{2}(S_0(a) + S_1(a))$$

if $\rho(0) = \frac{1}{2}$.

How should we model $\mu_k(a)$ and $S_k(a)$ themselves? As a general strategy, we propose treating the mortality of one sex as a baseline and letting the other sex differ from it in what might be called "quasi-proportional" fashion:

$$\mu_0(a) = \text{baseline hazard}, \tag{7.44}$$

and

$$\mu_1(a) = \mu_0(a)e^{\delta(a)}, \tag{7.45}$$

where $\delta(a)$ is some function of age that models the sex differential $\ln(\mu_1(a)/\mu_0(a))$. We have tested several specifications of $\delta(a)$ against data from the empirical life tables compiled by Keyfitz and Flieger (1968, 1990). Although we find that $\delta(a)$ is positive at all ages in almost all human populations (male mortality is almost always greater than female mortality), neither a constant difference $\delta(a) = \kappa$ nor the linear function $\delta(a) = \alpha + \beta a$ captures the real age pattern of the sex differential. Instead, the empirical differential is typically bimodal by age, peaking at ages 20–25 years and again at 55–65 years (sometimes one mode is higher than the other; sometimes a mode is missing). If our quasi-proportional model is to be implemented, we will eventually need to identify a simple function that duplicates this pattern.

What happens from this point on depends in its details on the precise way we decide to specify $\delta(a)$. For the present, we will assume that $\delta(a)$ acts as a true proportional hazard so that we can sketch out the rest of the method as simply as possible. If we can also assume that $\rho(0) = \frac{1}{2}$, then

$$\bar{\mu}(a) = \frac{\mu_0(a)}{2S(a)}(S_0(a) + S_1(a)e^{\delta(a)}). \tag{7.46}$$

Consequently,

$$\bar{\mu}(a)\bar{S}(a) = \tfrac{1}{2}\mu_0(a)(S_0(a) + S_1(a)e^{\delta(a)}), \tag{7.47}$$

which is what we need to substitute in equation (7.41).

Combining all these results and rearranging, the likelihood of a set of observed age- and sex-related traits in a sample of n skeletons is

$$L = \prod_{i=1}^{n} \sum_{k \in (0,1)} \int_0^\infty \Pr^*(c_i | a, k) f_r(a, k) da \tag{7.48}$$

$$= \prod_{i=1}^{n} \sum_{k \in (0,1)} \int_0^\infty \Pr^*(c_i | a, k) \left(\frac{S_k(a)}{S_0(a) + S_1(a)} \right) f_r(a) da,$$

where, as before, the asterisk (*) denotes an estimate made from data on a reference sample, and

$$f_r(a) = \frac{\mu_0(a)(S_0(a) + S_1(a)e^{\delta(a)})e^{-ra}}{\displaystyle\int_0^\infty \mu_0(x)(S_0(x) + S_1(x)e^{\delta(x)})e^{-rx}dx}. \tag{7.49}$$

Once we specify parametric models for $\mu_0(a)$ and $\delta(a)$, we can use equations (7.48) and (7.49) to estimate $f_r(a, k)$ from the target sample by maximum likelihood. And once we have that in hand, we have both the mortality profile (by sex) and the population growth rate of the target population. We can also say something about how old an individual skeleton in the target population is likely to be and what its probable sex is – things we would like to know for paleopathological purposes – by plugging our estimates of $f_r(a, k)$ into the multivariate generalization of Bayes's theorem:

$$\widehat{\Pr}(a, k | c_i) = \frac{\Pr^*(c_i | a, k)\hat{f}_r(a, k)}{\displaystyle\sum_{y \in (0,1)} \int_0^\infty \Pr^*(c_i | x, y)\hat{f}_r(x, y)\mathrm{d}x} \tag{7.50}$$

$$= \frac{\Pr^*(c_i | a, k)\hat{f}_r(a, k)}{\widehat{\Pr}(c_i)},$$

where the hats (ˆ) denote maximum likelihood estimates from the target sample. This expression, which is a straightforward extension of the original Rostock Manifesto, ought to provide us with the proper error structure for both our age estimates and our classifications by sex.

Discussion

In this chapter, we have reviewed several parametric models of mortality processes that can be used in conjunction with the Rostock approach to paleodemographic mortality analysis. Since paleodemographers will never be able to fit complicated models to their skeletal data, we have emphasized simple models that still do a reasonable job of capturing the main features of the human mortality curve. (The fact that the equations describing these models often look dauntingly complicated should not obscure their underlying simplicity.) At the same time, we have tried to focus most of our attention on models that support at least a certain amount of etiological interpretation, so that we may actually stand to learn something interesting from our skeletal samples instead of just fitting meaningless curves to them.

On biological grounds, we believe that within-population heterogeneity in health and the risk of death ought to be a central theoretical concern of paleodemography (see Wood *et al.* 1992b; Wood 1998; Milner *et al.* 2000). Accordingly, we have spent a fair amount of effort in exploring the implications of heterogeneity for etiological models of mortality. One form of heterogeneity that is always with us – *viva la hétérogènéité!* – is the difference between males and females. As it happens, sex is also one of the fundamental dimensions along which we would like to be able to classify our skeletons. Therefore, we have proposed an extension of the Rostock approach that estimates the sex differential at the same time as it probabilistically assigns age and sex to our skeletons. One of the challenges in applying this extension will be to find a simple parameterization of the sex differential in risk of death. In other words, we need even more parametric models, not fewer.

Acknowledgments

This chapter has benefited enormously from the general discussion that took place at the meeting on paleodemographic age estimation held at the Max Planck Institute for Demographic Research, Rostock, Germany, in the summer of 2000. We thank all the meeting participants for their lively contributions to that discussion. We are especially grateful to Jesper Boldsen, Rob Hoppa, Lyle Konigsberg, Brad Love, George Milner, Bethany Usher, and Jim Vaupel for helpful suggestions, which we have not always been wise enough to follow.

Appendix 7.1

The age-at-death distribution for skeletons deposited over time

In a series of famous papers, Lotka (1907, 1922, 1931) worked out the characteristics of the stationary and stable population at any instant in time. In examining skeletons from archaeological sites, however, we are never dealing with a single instant of time, but rather with some more or less prolonged (and usually unknown) period during which skeletons are laid down. How do we go from the stable or stationary age-at-death distribution at one time to the corresponding distribution over the entire period of deposition?

If skeletons are accumulated over a span of time equal to ω, then

$$\Pr(a) = \kappa \int_0^\omega \frac{f_r(a,t)}{\int_0^\infty f_r(x,t)\,\mathrm{d}x}\,\mathrm{d}t, \qquad (A7.1)$$

where $f_r(a,t)$ is the age-at-death distribution (corrected for nonstationarity) at time t, and κ is a normalizing constant ensuring that $\Pr(a)$ integrates to 1. If the population is stationary, $r = 0$ and

$$f_0(a,t) = \frac{\mu(a)S(a)}{\displaystyle\int_0^\infty \mu(x)S(x)dx} \tag{A7.2}$$

(Lotka 1907). Since nothing on the right-hand side of equation (A7.2) varies with t, its integral is simply a constant equal to $f_0(a,t)$ itself:

$$\Pr(a) = \kappa \int_0^\omega \frac{f_0(a,t)}{\displaystyle\int_0^\infty f_0(x,t)dx}\, dt = \frac{\mu(a)S(a)}{\displaystyle\int_0^\infty \mu(x)S(x)dx}. \tag{A7.3}$$

Note that the right-hand portion of this expression does not contain ω. Thus, the fact that we usually do not know the exact period over which skeletons were deposited is of no concern.

If the population is stable but not stationary ($r \neq 0$), we must take into account the fact that the number of skeletons being deposited each year changes in proportion to population growth or decline. In general, the number of deaths of age a at time t is $n(a,t)\mu(a)$, where $n(a,t)$ is the number of *living* individuals age a at risk of death at time t. But since a stable population is closed to migration, $n(a,t) = n(0, t-a)S(a)$. And since $f_0(a) = \mu(a)S(a)$, the number of deaths at a in t, $n(a,t)\mu(a)$, becomes $n(0, t-a)f_0(a)$. Lotka (1907) showed that the number of births changes exponentially in a stable population. Thus, the number of deaths age a at t can be rewritten as

$$n(0,0)e^{r(t-a)}f_0(a) = n(0,0)e^{rt}f_0(a)e^{-ra}. \tag{A7.4}$$

Substituting in equation (A7.1), we have

$$\Pr(a) = \kappa \int_0^\omega \frac{f_r(a,t)}{\displaystyle\int_0^\infty f_r(x,t)}\, dt \tag{A7.5}$$

$$= \kappa \int_0^\omega \frac{n(0,0)e^{rt}f_0(a,t)e^{-ra}}{\displaystyle\int_0^\infty n(0,0)e^{rt}f_0(x,t)e^{-rx}dx}.$$

Since the term $n(0,0)e^{rt}$ in the denominator of the right-hand side of equation (A7.5) does not vary with x, we can pull it out of the inner integral and cancel it from the numerator and denominator. We are left with the relation

$$\Pr(a) = \frac{\mu(a)S(a)e^{-ra}}{\displaystyle\int_0^\infty \mu(x)S(x)e^{-rx}dx} \tag{A7.6}$$

in a stable population with growth rate r. Again, this expression does not contain ω, so we do not need to know its value. If $r = 0$, this equation reduces to equation

(A7.3), which highlights the fact that the stationary population is just a special case of the stable population. It also shows that we can use equation (A7.6) in our likelihood function to estimate r whether it is zero or nonzero, positive or negative.

Appendix 7.2

The implications of heterogeneity for competing hazards models

Can models such as the Siler model, which are normally interpreted as models of competing hazards, support such an interpretation when the population involved is heterogeneous in the risk of death? Consider a population for which there are only two types of individuals. Individuals of type 1 are all at hazard $\mu_1(a)$ and individuals of type 2 are all at hazard $\mu_2(a)$. Assume that, within the two subgroups, individuals are homogeneous for mortality risk, and let the proportion of newborns in group 1 be p and in group 2 be $(1 - p)$. Since $f_0(a)$ and $S(a)$ are probabilities, they can be found for the mixture of the two groups by using the law of total probability:

$$S(a) = pS_1(a) + (1 - p)S_2(a) \tag{A7.7}$$

and

$$f_0(a) = pf_{0,1}(a) + (1 - p)f_{0,2}(a). \tag{A7.8}$$

Using equation (7.6), we can now write the mortality function for the entire population as

$$\mu(a) = \frac{f_0(a)}{S(a)} = \frac{pf_{0,1}(a) + (1 - p)f_{0,2}(a)}{pS_1(a) + (1 - p)S_2(a)}. \tag{A7.9}$$

Clearly, equation (A7.9) does not take the form $\mu_1(a) + \mu_2(a)$. It does not even take the form of a simple weighted average of the two subgroups: $p\mu_1(a) + (1 - p)\mu_2(a)$. The proper total hazard in terms of both the subcomponent hazards is $\mu(a) = p(a)\mu_1(a) + (1 - p(a))\mu_2(a)$. In this expression, $p(a)$ is the fraction of those individuals surviving to age a who belong to group 1, equal to

$$p(a) = \frac{pS_1(a)}{S(a)} = \frac{pS_1(a)}{pS_1(a) + (1 - p)S_2(a)}. \tag{A7.10}$$

The numerator is the fraction of survivors in group 1 at age a and the denominator is the fraction of all survivors at age a.

The above exercise shows that interpreting the individual components of a "competing-hazards" model as if they really were independent competing causes of death may be inappropriate when the population consists of two subgroups. Can the parameters of a two-subgroup mixed-hazards model *ever* be interpreted as a competing hazards model? Some algebra reveals that this is permissible if

$$\mu_1(a) + \mu_2(a) = \frac{pf_{0,1}(a) + (1-p)f_{0,2}(a)}{pS_1(a) + (1-p)S_2(a)}, \qquad (A7.11)$$

$$\frac{f_{0,1}(a)}{S_1(a)} + \frac{f_{0,2}(a)}{S_2(a)} = \frac{pf_{0,1}(a) + (1-p)f_{0,2}(a)}{pS_1(a) + (1-p)S_2(a)},$$

$$\frac{f_{0,1}(a)S_2 + f_{0,2}(a)S_1}{S_1(a)S_2(a)} = \frac{pf_{0,1}(a) + (1-p)f_{0,2}(a)}{pS_1(a) + (1-p)S_2(a)}.$$

Since $f_0(a) = -dS(a)/da$, *the equivalencies in equation* ($A7.11$) *hold when*

$$p = \frac{f_{0,1}(a)S_2(a)^2}{f_{0,1}(a)S_2(a)^2 + f_{0,2}(a)S_1(a)^2}, \qquad (A7.12)$$

or in the trivial case in which each subgroup experiences exactly the same risk, $\mu_1(a) = \mu_2(a)$. If one of these conditions – the first of which is completely arbitrary and the second not a model of heterogeneity at all – is not met, competing-hazards models such as the Siler model are inappropriate and cannot be interpreted properly. It can be shown that similar conditions hold when more than two heterogeneous subgroups exist in the population.

References

Aalen OOA (1989) A linear regression model for the analysis of life times. *Statistics in Medicine* **8**, 907–925.

Acsádi G and Nemeskéri J (1970) *History of human life span and mortality.* Budapest: Akadémiai Kiadó.

Alesan A, Malgosa A, and Simó C (1999) Looking into the demography of an Iron Age population in the western Mediterranean. I. Mortality. *American Journal of Physical Anthropology* **110**, 285–301.

Andersen PK (1988) Multistate models in survival analysis: a study of nephropathy and mortality in diabetes. *Statistics in Medicine* **7**, 661–670.

Angel JL (1969) The bases of paleodemography. *American Journal of Physical Anthropology* **30**, 427–438.

Benedictow OJ (1996) *The medieval demographic system of the Nordic countries,* revised edition. Oslo: Middelalderforlaget.

Bourgeois-Pichat J (1971) Stable, semi-stable populations and growth potential. *Population Studies* **25**, 235–254.

Brass W (1971) On the scale of mortality. In W Brass (ed.): *Biological aspects of demography.* London: Taylor and Francis, pp. 69–110.

Brass W (1975) *Methods for estimating fertility and mortality from limited and defective data.* Chapel Hill, NC: Carolina Population Center, University of North Carolina.

Brass W and Coale AJ (1968) Methods of analysis and estimation. In Brass W (ed.): *The demography of tropical Africa.* Princeton, NJ: Office of Population Research, Princeton University, pp. 88–150.

Brooks A, Lithgow GJ, and Johnson TE (1994) Mortality rates in a genetically heterogeneous population of *Caenorhabditis elegans*. *Science* **263**, 668–671.

Carey JR, Liedo P, Orozco D, and Vaupel JW (1992) Slowing of mortality rates at older ages in large medfly cohorts. *Science* **258**, 457–461.

Carrier NH and Hobcraft J (1971) *Demographic estimation for developing societies*. London: Population Investigation Committee, London School of Economics.

Chowdhury MK, Becker S, Razzaque A, Sarder AM, Shaikh K, and Chen LC (1981) *Demographic surveillance system – Matlab: vital events and migration 1978*. Scientific Report no. 47. Dhaka, Bangladesh: International Centre for Diarrheal Disease Research.

Coale AJ (1972) *The growth and structure of human populations: a mathematical investigation*. Princeton, NJ: Princeton University Press.

Coale AJ and Demeny P (1966) *Regional model life tables and stable populations*. New York: Academic Press.

Cox DR (1962) *Renewal theory*. London: Chapman & Hall.

Cox DR (1972) Regression models and life-tables (with discussion). *Journal of the Royal Statistical Society (Series B)* **34**, 187–220.

Dyke B, Gage TB, Ballou JD, Petto AJ, Tardif AD, and Williams LE (1993) Model life tables for the smaller New World monkeys. *American Journal of Primatology* **29**, 269–285.

Evans M, Hastings N, and Peacock B (2000) *Statistical distributions*, third edition. New York: John Wiley and Sons.

Ewbank DC, Gomez de Leon JC, and Stoto MA (1983) A reducible four-parameter system of model life tables. *Population Studies* **37**, 105–127.

Finch CE (1990) *Longevity, senescence, and the genome*. Chicago: University of Chicago Press.

Ford K and Kim Y (1987) Distributions of postpartum amenorrhea: some new evidence. *Demography* **24**, 413–430.

Fukui HH, Xiu L, and Curtsinger JW (1993) Slowing of age-specific mortality rates in *Drosophila melanogaster*. *Experimental Gerontology* **28**, 585–599.

Gage TB (1988) Mathematical hazard models of mortality: an alternative to model life tables. *American Journal of Physical Anthropology* **76**, 429–441.

Gage TB (1989) Bio-mathematical approaches to the study of human variation in mortality. *Yearbook of Physical Anthropology* **32**, 185–214.

Gage TB (1990) Variation and classification of human age patterns of mortality: analysis using competing hazards models. *Human Biology* **62**, 589–614.

Gage TB (1991) Causes of death and the components of mortality: testing the biological interpretations of a competing hazards model. *American Journal of Human Biology* **3**, 289–300.

Gage TB (1994) Population variation in cause of death: level, gender, and period effects. *Demography* **31**, 271–296.

Gage TB (1998) The comparative demography of primates, with some comments on the evolution of life histories. *Annual Review of Anthropology* **27**, 197–221.

Gage TB and Dyke B (1986) Parameterizing abridged mortality tables: the Siler three-component hazard model. *Human Biology* **58**, 275–291.

Gage TB and Dyke B (1988) Model life tables for the larger Old World monkeys. *American Journal of Primatology* **16**, 305–320.

Gage TB and Mode CJ (1993) Some laws of mortality: how well do they fit? *Human Biology* **65**, 445–461.

Gage TB and O'Connor KA (1994) Nutrition and the variation in level and age patterns of mortality. *Human Biology* **66**, 77–103.

Gavrilov LA and Gavrilova NS (1991) *The biology of life span: a quantitative approach.* London: Harwood Academic Publishers.

Gompertz B (1825) On the nature of the function expressive of the law of human mortality, and on a new mode of determining the value of life contingencies. *Philosophical Transactions of the Royal Society of London (Series A)* **115**, 513–585.

Gordon CC and Buikstra JE (1981) Soil pH, bone preservation, and sampling bias at mortuary sites. *American Antiquity* **46**, 566–571.

Green S, Green S, and Armelagos GJ (1974) Settlement and mortality of the Christian site (1050 A.D.–1300 A.D.) of Meinarti (Sudan). *Journal of Human Evolution* **3**, 297–316.

Greene DL, Van Gerven DP, and Armelagos GJ (1986) Life and death in ancient populations: bones of contention in paleodemography. *Human Evolution* **1**, 193–207.

Hamilton WD (1966) The moulding of senescence by natural selection. *Journal of Theoretical Biology* **12**, 12–45.

Heckman JJ and Singer B (1984) Econometric duration analysis. *Journal of Econometrics* **24**, 63–132.

Heckman JJ and Walker JR (1987) Using goodness of fit and other criteria to choose among competing duration models: a case study of Hutterite data. In C Clogg (ed.): *Sociological methodology 1987.* New York: American Sociological Association, pp. 247–307.

Heligman L and Pollard JH (1980) The age pattern of mortality. *Journal of the Institute of Actuaries* **107**, 49–80.

Himes CL (1994) Age patterns of mortality and cause-of-death structures in Sweden, Japan, and the United States. *Demography* **31**, 633–650.

Holman DJ (1996) Fecundability and total fetal loss in Bangladesh. Doctoral dissertation, Pennsylvania State University, University Park, PA.

Holman DJ, O'Connor KA, Wood JW, and Boldsen JL (1997) Correcting for nonstationarity in paleodemographic mortality models [abstract]. *American Journal of Physical Anthropology, Supplement* **24**, 132.

Holman DJ, O'Connor KA, Wood JW, and Boldsen J (1998) Estimating population growth rates from skeletal samples. Paper presented at the annual meeting of the American Anthropological Association, Philadelphia, PA.

Horiuchi S and Coale AJ (1990) Age patterns of mortality for older women: an analysis using age-specific rate of mortality change with age. *Mathematical Population Studies* **2**, 245–267.

Johannson SR and Horowitz S (1986) Estimating mortality in skeletal populations: influence of the growth rate on the interpretation of levels and trends during the transition to agriculture. *American Journal of Physical Anthropology* **71**, 233–250.

Kannisto V (1994) *Development of oldest-old mortality, 1950–1990: evidence from 28 developed countries.* Odense, Denmark: Odense University Press.

Keyfitz N (1968) *Introduction to the mathematics of population.* Reading, MA: Addison-Wesley.

Keyfitz N (1985) *Applied mathematical demography,* second edition. Berlin: Springer-Verlag.

Keyfitz N and Flieger W (1968) *World population: an analysis of vital data.* Chicago: University of Chicago Press.

Keyfitz N and Flieger W (1990) *World population growth and aging: demographic trends in the late twentieth century.* Chicago: University of Chicago Press.

Konigsberg LW and Frankenberg SR (1992) Estimation of age structure in anthropological demography. *American Journal of Physical Anthropology* **89**, 235–256.

Konigsberg LW and Frankenberg SR (1994) Paleodemography: "Not quite dead". *Evolutionary Anthropology* **3**, 92–105.

Konigsberg LW and Herrmann NP (2000) Estimation of age-at-death distributions: further examples from Indian Knoll. Presented at the Workshop on Paleodemographic Age Estimation, Max Planck Institute for Demographic Research, Rostock, Germany.

Konigsberg LW, Frankenberg SR, and Walker RB (1997) Regress what on what? Paleodemographic age estimation as a calibration problem. In RR Paine (ed.): *Integrating archaeological demography: multidisciplinary approaches to prehistoric population.* Carbondale, IL: Center for Archaeological Investigations, Southern Illinois University, pp. 64–88.

Lanphear KM (1989) Testing the value of skeletal samples in demographic research: a comparison with vital registration samples. *International Journal of Anthropology* **4**, 185–193.

Ledermann S and Breas J (1959) Les dimensions de la mortalité. *Population* **14**, 637–682.

Lopez A (1961) *Problems in stable population theory.* Princeton, NJ: Office of Population Research, Princeton University.

Lotka AJ (1907) Relation between birth rates and death rates. *Science* **26**, 21–22.

Lotka AJ (1922) The stability of the normal age distribution. *Proceedings of the National Academy of Sciences* **8**, 339–345.

Lotka AJ (1931) The structure of a growing population. *Human Biology* **3**, 459–493.

Louzada-Neto F (1999) Polyhazard models for lifetime data. *Biometrics* **55**, 1281–1285.

Lovejoy CO, Meindl RS, Pryzbeck TR, Barton TS, Heiple KG, and Kotting D (1977) Paleodemography of the Libben site, Ottawa County, Ohio. *Science* **198**, 291–293.

Luder HU (1993) Hazard rates and causes of death in a captive group of crab-eating monkeys (*Macaca fascicularis*). *American Journal of Primatology* **39**, 40–50.

Makeham WM (1860) On the law of mortality. *Journal of the Institute of Actuaries* **13**, 325–358.

Manton KG and Stallard E (1988) *Chronic disease modelling: measurement and evaluation of the risks of chronic disease processes.* London: Charles Griffin.

Manton KG, Stallard E, and Vaupel JW (1986) Alternative models for the heterogeneity of mortality risks among the aged. *Journal of the American Statistical Association* **81**, 635–644.

Manton KG, Singer B, and Woodbury MA (1992) Some issues in the quantitative characterization of heterogeneous populations. In J Trussell, R Hankinson, and J Tilton (eds.): *Demographic applications of event history analysis*. Oxford: Oxford University Press, pp. 9–37.

Mays S (1992) Taphonomic factors in a human skeletal assemblage. *Circaea* **9**, 54–58.

Mensforth RP (1990) Paleodemography of the Carlston Annis (Bt–5) Late Archaic skeletal population. *American Journal of Physical Anthropology* **82**, 81–99.

Milner GR, Wood JW, and Boldsen JL (2000) Paleodemography. In SR Saunders and MA Katzenberg (eds.): *Biological anthropology of the human skeleton*. New York: Wiley-Liss, pp. 467–497.

Mode CJ (1985) *Stochastic processes in demography and their computer implementation*. Berlin: Springer-Verlag.

Mode CJ and Busby RC (1982) An eight-parameter model of human mortality: the single decrement case. *Bulletin of Mathematical Biology* **44**, 647–659.

Mode CJ and Jacobsen ME (1984) A parametric algorithm for computing model period and cohort human survival functions. *International Journal of Bio-Medical Computing* **15**, 341–356.

Moore JA, Swedlund AC, and Armelagos GJ (1975) The use of life tables in paleodemography. *American Antiquity* **40**, 57–70.

Moreno L (1994) Frailty selection in bivariate survival models: a cautionary note. *Mathematical Population Studies* **4**, 225–233.

Nam CB (1990) Mortality differentials from a multiple-cause-of-death perspective. In J Vallin, S D'Souza, and A Palloni (eds.): *Measurement and analysis of mortality: new approaches*. Oxford: Oxford University Press, pp. 328–342.

Nordling CO (1953) A new theory on the cancer inducing mechanism. *British Journal of Cancer* **7**, 68–72.

O'Connor KA (1995) The age pattern of mortality: a micro-analysis of Tipu and a meta-analysis of twenty-nine paleodemographic samples. Doctoral dissertation, State University of New York, Albany, NY.

O'Connor KA, Holman DJ, Boldsen J, Wood JW, and Gage TB (1997) Competing and mixed hazards models of mortality: osteological applications [abstract]. *American Journal of Physical Anthropology, Supplement* **24**, 180.

Paine RR (1989) Model life table fitting by maximum likelihood estimation: a procedure to reconstruct paleodemographic characteristics from skeletal age distributions. *American Journal of Physical Anthropology* **79**, 51–61.

Parlett B (1970) Ergodic properties of populations. I. The one sex model. *Theoretical Population Biology* **1**, 191–207.

Preston SH (1976) *Mortality patterns in national populations, with special reference to recorded causes of death*. New York: Academic Press.

Rodríguez G (1994) Statistical issues in the analysis of reproductive histories using hazard models. *Annals of the New York Academy of Sciences* **709**, 266–279.

Sattenspiel L and Harpending H (1983) Stable populations and skeletal age. *American Antiquity* **48**, 489–498.

Schoen R (1975) Constructing increment-decrement life tables. *Demography* **12**, 313–324.

Siler W (1979) A competing-risk model for animal mortality. *Ecology* **60**, 750–757.

Siler W (1983) Parameters of mortality in human populations with widely varying life spans. *Statistics in Medicine* **2**, 373–380.

Thatcher AR, Kannisto V, and Vaupel JW (1997) *The force of mortality from age 80 to 120.* Odense, Denmark: Odense University Press.

Thiele PN (1871) On a mathematical formula to express the rate of mortality throughout the whole of life. *Journal of the Institute of Actuaries* **16**, 313–329.

Thompson WA (1988) *Point process models with applications to safety and reliability.* London: Chapman & Hall.

United Nations (1955) *Age and sex patterns of mortality: model life tables for underdeveloped countries.* Population Studies, no. 22. New York: United Nations.

United Nations (1956) *Methods for population projections by age and sex.* Population Studies, no. 25. New York: United Nations.

Vaupel JW (1997) Trajectories of mortality at advanced ages. In KW Wachter and CE Finch (eds.): *Between Zeus and the salmon: the biodemography of longevity.* Washington, DC: National Academy Press, pp. 17–37.

Vaupel JW and Yashin AI (1985a) Heterogeneity's ruses: some surprising effects of selection on population dynamics. *American Statistician* **39**, 176–185.

Vaupel JW and Yashin AI (1985b) The deviant dynamics of death in heterogeneous populations. In NB Tuma (ed.): *Sociological methodology 1985.* San Francisco: Jossey-Bass, pp. 179–211.

Vaupel JW, Manton KG, and Stallard E (1979) The impact of heterogeneity in individual frailty on the dynamics of mortality. *Demography* **16**, 439–454.

Vaupel JW, Johnson TE, and Lithgow GJ (1994) Rates of mortality in populations of *Caenorhabditis elegans. Science* **266**, 826.

Vaupel JW, Carey JR, Christensen K, Johnson TE, Yashin AI, Holm NV, Iachine IA, Kannisto V, Khazaeli AA, Liedo P, Longo VD, Zeng Y, Manton KG, and Curtsinger JW (1998) Biodemographic trajectories of longevity. *Science* **280**, 855–860.

Waldron T (1987) The relative survival of the human skeleton: implications for paleopathology. In A Boddington, AN Garland, and RC Janaway (eds.): *Death, decay, and reconstruction.* Manchester: Manchester University Press, pp. 55–64.

Walker PL, Johnson JR, and Lambert PM (1988) Age and sex biases in the preservation of human skeletal remains. *American Journal of Physical Anthropology* **76**, 183–188.

Weibull W (1951) A statistical distribution function of wide applicability. *Journal of Applied Mechanics* **18**, 293–297.

Weiss KM (1973) *Demographic models for anthropology.* Washington, DC: Society for American Archaeology.

Weiss KM (1990) The biodemography of variation in human frailty. *Demography* **27**, 185–206.

Weiss KM and Chakraborty R (1990) Multistage models and the age patterns of cancer: does the statistical analogy imply genetic homology? In L Herrera (ed.): *Familial adenomatous polyposis*. New York: Wiley-Liss, pp. 77–89.

Whittemore AS and Keller J (1978) Quantitative theories of carcinogenesis. *SIAM Review* **20**, 1–30.

Wood JW (1987a) Problems of applying model fertility and mortality schedules to demographic data from Papua New Guinea. In TM McDevitt (ed.): *The survey under difficult conditions: population data collection and analysis in Papua New Guinea*. New Haven, Conn.: Human Relations Area File Press, pp. 27–53.

Wood JW (1987b) The genetic demography of the Gainj of Papua New Guinea. 2. Determinants of effective population size. *American Naturalist* **129**, 165–187.

Wood JW (1989) Fecundity and natural fertility in humans. *Oxford Review of Reproductive Biology* **11**, 61–109.

Wood JW (1998) A theory of preindustrial population dynamics: demography, economy, and well-being in Malthusian systems. *Current Anthropology* **39**, 99–135.

Wood JW, Holman DJ, Weiss KM, Buchanan AV, and LeFor B (1992a) Hazards models for human population biology. *Yearbook of Physical Anthropology* **35**, 43–87.

Wood JW, Milner GR, Harpending H, and Weiss KM (1992b) The osteological paradox: problems of inferring prehistoric health from skeletal samples. *Current Anthropology* **33**, 343–370.

Wood JW, Weeks SC, Bentley GR and Weiss KM (1994) Human population biology and the evolution of aging. In DE Crews and RM Garruto (eds.): *Biological anthropology and aging: perspectives on human variation over the life span*. Oxford: Oxford University Press, pp. 19–75.

Zaba B (1979) The four-parameter logit life table system. *Population Studies* **33**, 79–100.

Zaba B (1981) Use of the relational Gompertz model in analysing data collected in retrospective surveys. *Centre for Population Studies Working Paper* no. 81-2. London: London School of Hygiene and Tropical Medicine.

8 Linking age-at-death distributions and ancient population dynamics: a case study

RICHARD R. PAINE AND JESPER L. BOLDSEN

Introduction

Skeletal series recovered by archaeologists frequently display patterns of death that differ from those of typical living, or historically documented, populations. Some of these prehistoric patterns are extremely widespread. Widespread patterns include notably small proportions of infants (see e.g., Acsádi and Nemeskéri 1970; Lovejoy et al. 1977; Buikstra et al. 1986), high proportions of older children and young adults (see e.g., Acsádi and Nemeskéri 1970; Weiss 1973; Lovejoy et al. 1977; Keckler 1997; Paine 1997), and an apparent excess of female death during the young adult years (Acsádi and Neméskeri 1970; Boldsen and Paine 1995, 1999). Most paleodemographers would agree that the small proportion of infants is primarily an issue of preservation and recovery (e.g., Buikstra et al. 1986). The other patterns have produced a wide range of explanations ranging from concerns about the archaeological process and paleodemographic methods (Bocquet-Appel and Masset 1982, 1996; Walker et al. 1988; Konigsberg and Frankenberg 1994; Konigsberg et al. 1997), to epidemiological ones (e.g., Lovejoy et al. 1977).

Relationships between demographic characteristics of a living population and a skeletal series recovered from it are not straightforward (Sattenspiel and Harpending 1983; Wood et al. 1992; Paine 1997). If we wish to understand the demography of the living population, we must develop explicit, testable models (see e.g., Keckler 1997; Paine 1997, 2000) that clearly define relationships between the two (Howell 1982; Wood et al. 1992). This chapter outlines preliminary attempts to develop a model to test one possible explanation of two persistent trends in the shape of childhood death.

The problem

The Historical Perspectives on Human Demography Database

The Historical Perspectives on Human Demography Database (HPHD) was compiled from existing site reports and more widely published data. It includes 14 089 anatomically aged individuals, 2 years of age and older at death, from more than 75 sites in central Europe, primarily Germany, Austria, Hungary and the Czech Republic. The database is large, but, because of difficulties of data control and compatibility, it is better used as a source of hypotheses than definitive data. Skeletal age-at-death estimates in the database were produced by a large number of osteologists using a variety of techniques. Despite recent and ongoing attempts to better quantify estimation techniques (Boldsen 1988, 1997; Konigsberg and Frankenberg 1992; Skytthe and Boldsen 1993; Konigsberg *et al.* 1997; Milner *et al.* 1997) traditional methods rely on unquantifiable, often investigator-specific, weightings of categorical observations (Maples 1989). Interobserver differences are an obvious problem in aggregated samples such as this. The sample also includes skeletons from a wide range of preservation conditions. Age estimates for subadults, which are based on developmental stages (e.g., dentition, epiphyseal union) are generally considered to be the most accurate. We believe the age categories used in the analysis that produced Figure 8.1 (2–5 years, 5–18 years, 18+ years) are sufficiently conservative as to minimize the problem of interobserver differences in age estimation.

Preliminary examinations of the HPHD database (Boldsen and Paine 1995, 1999, unpublished data; Paine and Boldsen 1997) have yielded a series of age-at-death patterns that diverge from modern or historical patterns, but resemble paleodemographic patterns found elsewhere. These include a general lack of infants, which probably results from factors of preservation and recovery, the often cited mid-age bulge, apparent sex differences in adult mortality (Boldsen and Paine 1995), and two very persistent trends in childhood death, which were to be the focus of the modeling exercise presented in this chapter.

Between the Mesolithic period and the Iron Age, the weight of child mortality, as measured by the death rate ratio[1] or DRR (JL Boldsen and RR Paine, unpublished data), shifts toward older childhood (Figure 8.1).

---

[1] The death rate ratio (DRR) is computed as $d_{5\text{-}18}/d_{2\text{-}5}$ where $d_{2\text{-}5}$ is the mean death rate from age 2 to 5 years: $d_{2\text{-}5} = 1 - [S(5)/S(2)]^{1/3}$ and $d_{5\text{-}18}$ is the mean death rate from age 5 to 18 years: $d_{5\text{-}18} = 1 - [S(18)/S(5)]^{1/13}$. Children under 2 years were omitted from the analysis to avoid the influence of differential preservation and recovery of infant skeletons.

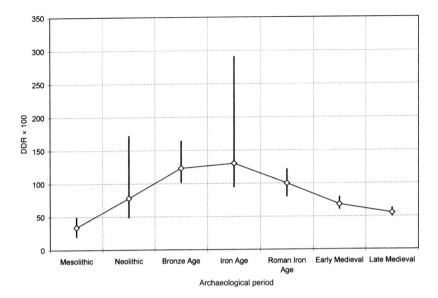

Figure 8.1. The death rate ratio (DRR) tracks the ratio of late childhood (5–18 years) to early childhood (2–5 years) death, by archaeological period. Higher DRR indicates relatively higher death rates among older children. Error bars are bootstrapped 95% confidence intervals.

After the Iron Age, the trend reverses and child death becomes concentrated in earlier ages. The DRR is a good statistic for paleodemographic cross-period comparisons; it is limited to broad age categories, and is relatively insensitive to changes in population growth (JL Boldsen and RR Paine, unpublished data).

The consistency of the pattern, both before and after the reversal point in the Iron Age, led us to believe that the pattern implied more than changing archaeological recovery conditions or biases in skeletal aging techniques. We sought an explanation that would be biologically meaningful, fit with archaeologically and historically derived records of population change, and be testable. Relationships between the growth of large settled populations and increases in disease have long been a focus of paleodemographic interest (e.g., Cohen 1977; Cohen and Armelagos 1984; Wood *et al.* 1992). We decided to test the hypothesis that the frequency of epidemic events increased as the European population grew and became increasingly connected to the larger Old World population system.

The hypothesis makes biological sense. The microorganisms that cause epidemic diseases require a constant supply of new hosts to survive. Both population size and density increased in Europe during the period covered by the HPHD. Though this growth was not necessarily even over either time or space, the overall pattern is clear. Connections between the northern and central European populations represented by the HPHD and the larger Old World population system, particularly Asia and the Mediterranean, also increased. Specific historical instances, including the intrusions of such groups as the Romans and the Avars, are dramatic illustrations of this process, which culminated in the highly integrated trade economy of the later Middle Ages. These factors would have combined to expand the pool of new hosts available to maintain epidemic diseases.

One of the best tools paleodemographers have for testing hypotheses is computer modeling. Computer models enable us to link demographic processes in living populations to the skeletal record (see e.g., Keckler 1997; Paine 1997, 2000). The purpose of the analysis presented here was to test whether increasing the frequency of epidemic events, and obeying some very basic assumptions, can create the general pattern of child death we observed in the HPHD. Future research will refine the model, making it more biologically realistic, but staying within the bounds of paleodemographic data (J.L. Boldsen and R.R. Paine, unpublished data).

Modeling procedure

We decided to simulate the effects of epidemic events, occurring at decreased intervals, through a series of Leslie matrix projections. Contemporary demographers use Leslie matrices (Leslie 1945) to project population size and age structure forward in time. Data from a Leslie matrix projection can be used to compute vital rates, as well as full life tables, for projected populations at any stage of the projection. This is particularly interesting when, as part of the projection, a model population is perturbed and becomes unstable. The short- and long-term effects of the perturbation can then be tracked through the projection (for a paleodemographic example, see Paine 2000).

A Leslie matrix projection requires three pieces of data: (a) a set of age-specific fertility rates (ASFRs) for the projected population; (b) age-specific probabilities of survival (P_x); and (c) a population to project. The ASFRs comprise the top row of the matrix. The P_x values are found on the subdiagonal. All remaining cells of the matrix are zeros. The population to be projected is entered into a column vector, which is postmultiplied by the matrix to produce a new population structure. For particularly clear discussions of Leslie matrices see Bradley and Meek (1986) and Caswell (1989).

Table 8.1. *Demographic characteristics of the model stable population used in the projection. The first two columns are parameter values for the Brass (1971) relational model life tables. The other demographic values were derived from the model life table*

α	β	e_0	TFR	CBR	CDR	r
0.65	0.95	22.05	6.1	45.23	44.49	0.00074

e_0, life expectancy at birth; TFR, total fertility rate; CBR, crude birth rate; CDR, crude death rate.

The base population was designed for general utility (Paine 2000). It is not intended as a precise estimate of past conditions, rather it is intended to present a possible picture that is broadly acceptable enough to allow the focus of attention to remain the analysis of epidemic intervals. We used the Brass (1971) logit life table models to define the parameters of the basic population matrix. The Brass standard model fertility schedule was set to yield a total fertility rate (TFR) of 6.1. This corresponds to the average TFR for natural fertility populations surveyed by Campbell and Wood (1988). The survivorship probabilities were produced from a Brass standard model with $\alpha = 0.65$, and $\beta = 0.95$. This yields mortality characteristics close to anthropologists' stereotypes of pre-industrial agrarian populations (Table 8.1; Paine 2000).

The Leslie matrix generated from these population characteristics (labeled **S** for stable) serves several purposes. It is the source of the stable population distribution used to initialize each projection (see below). It provides a baseline for constructing the matrices to represent epidemic years. Finally, it represents the model population's demographic behavior for all the nonepidemic years in each projection.

Given very loose conditions,[2] which are met in the Brass models, any Leslie matrix that is projected long enough will produce a stable age distribution with stable demographic rates, regardless of the initial population. The number of intervals required to approach stability varies with the size of the matrix (the number of intervals of lifespan). The initial population vector was generated by projecting the Leslie matrix (**S**) described above for 100 cycles (representing 100 years). At that point the population vector was stable. The crude rates in Table 8.1 are those of the stable

---

[2] These conditions are set out in the theorem of Perron and Frobenius (summarized by Pollard (1973)). The primary condition is that two consecutive F_j values (the age-specific fertility rates, represented in the top row of the Leslie matrix) be positive. This is true of virtually all models of human fertility.

population. Note that, though the model population is stable, it is growing slowly.

Epidemic cycles

Exposure to an acute, epidemic disease typically results in one of two outcomes: (a) the host dies, or (b) the host successfully defends itself against the disease and develops long-term resistance. It is also reasonable to assume that individuals who survive repeated insults are less frail than those who succumb to them. Resistance is a central assumption of our hypothesis.

During the projection, plague years, represented by their own matrices, are interspersed at regular intervals from 3 years to 96 years. Nonepidemic years are represented by the same base matrix (**S**), regardless of projection. Each projection represents 75 years (75 cycles). Arbitrarily, the first epidemic year is always year 2 of the projection. Epidemic cycles then repeat according to the interval being simulated. For example, in the six-year interval projection, the stable population vector is postmultiplied by the stable matrix **S** in the first year. The new population vector is postmultiplied by the six-year interval epidemic matrix (E_6), which perturbs the population structure. The new population vector is then postmultiplied by **S** for six intervals, followed by E_6 again, etc. Each new population vector is recorded on a spreadsheet where crude birth rates, death rates and population growth, as well as the age structure of death can be tracked.

The rules for the projections were purposely kept simple. In each projection, the first time a cohort was subjected to an epidemic year each member's probability P of surviving that year was reduced by 30%, for example in the 12-year interval projection (represented by matrix E_{12}) the P of 9-year-olds decreases from 0.993 to 0.693. During subsequent epidemic years, survivors of those cohorts that have been subjected to a single epidemic year have their probability of survival reduced by 10%, so in the six-year interval projection the P of 9-year-olds decreases from 0.993 to 0.893. If a cohort is subjected to more than two epidemic years, the probability of survival is not affected. So, our same 9-year-olds are unaffected in the three-year interval, because 9-year-old survivors in the living population vector have been subjected to two previous epidemic years.

We do not envision the epidemic matrices as the result of singular epidemic events. It would be naive to suggest that there was only one disease active in a population during a given period. The epidemic matrices are intended as proxies for the cumulative effect of all acute, epidemic

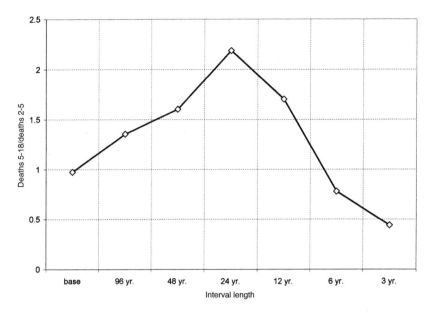

Figure 8.2. The ratio of older child deaths (5–18 years) to younger child deaths (2–5 years) for seven population projections. Deaths are cumulative over the course of 75-year projections. The *x*-axis indicates the interval length between epidemic years in each projection.

diseases active in the given time. The cycle length represents the average cycling length for the suite of diseases. One alternative would be to include multiple, less virulent diseases in the same projection. If the diseases had the same interval, the overall pattern of death would not vary appreciably from patterns produced under the present assumption, but the consequences for the living population might be different.

Results

Decreasing the interval between epidemic years does mimic the changes in child age-at-death seen in the HPHD (Figure 8.2). The projections capture both the shift toward later childhood death and the later recompression of death into early childhood. As long as the interval between epidemic years is longer than 18 years, shortening it increases the proportion of older child death by increasing the number of intervals where subadult (for present purposes 2–18 years) mortality is dominated by age-independent death (Figure 8.3). When the interval is shortened below 18 years, childhood

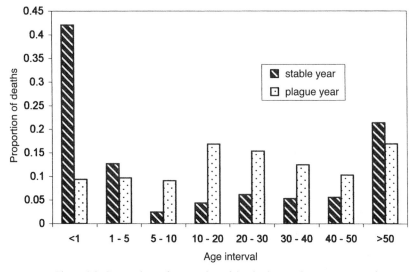

Figure 8.3. Comparison of proportion of deaths, by age, between a normal mortality year and an epidemic year (96-year interval model). The distribution of deaths for childhood ages (under 18 years) is the same as shown in all models where epidemic interval is > 18 years.

mortality is slowly compressed into younger ages as epidemic mortality in childhood is no longer age independent (Figure 8.4).

Discussion

The goal of this study was, before investing more resources in it, to provide a quick-and-dirty test of the hypothesis that the childhood mortality trends observed in the HPHD resulted from changes in the frequency of epidemic events. The projection could have effectively refuted the hypothesis by producing a conflicting pattern of childhood death (as in Paine 1997). We cannot refute other hypotheses with this projection study. Eliminating alternatives and testing more refined versions of hypotheses about the impact of epidemic events will be the subject of future studies.

Future versions of the model will add biological realism, but within the limitations of the data. Several areas need to be addressed. How should very young (< 2 years) children be affected by epidemic events? Wrigley and colleagues (1997) reported that very young children had a low risk in epidemic events of the 16th–18th centuries. This may result from immunities associated with lactation or it may reflect the importance of competing

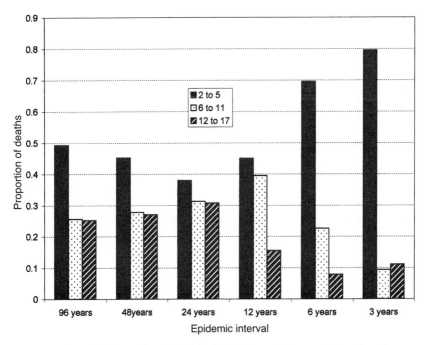

Figure 8.4. Proportion of child deaths for six population projections, based on cumulative deaths at the end of the projection.

causes of death among the very young. What is a reasonable level of mortality from epidemic causes? Levels of epidemic mortality presented in this analysis represent a worst-case model, based primarily on levels of death attributed to the Black Death (e.g., McNeil 1977). They are useful because they produce clear patterns. They are also unrealistic. If extended for longer periods, all the epidemic interval models presented here produce demographic collapse. It is both a historical fact, and an underlying assumption of our hypothesis, that populations (in the long run) were growing throughout the period represented by the HPHD.

One problem with the short projection presented here is that when the projection is started with a stable age structure the short-interval scenarios take longer to fully affect the population and their demographic implications are underestimated. This is because it takes more (between 2 and 12) projected years for the first cohorts that were reduced by epidemic mortality to reach reproductive age. In scenarios where the interval between episodes is longer than the prereproductive period crude birth rates are affected immediately. Therefore, the projections will have to be longer, and the analysis more sophisticated, when the goal of the projection study is to compare the demographic consequences of epidemic mortality rather than to search for general patterns.

We do not believe the data justify trying to tie specific epidemic interval lengths to specific time periods based on child age-at-death ratios. The ratios presented in Figure 8.1, where older children appear to have *higher* death rates than younger ones during some periods, are highly improbable from a demographic standpoint. Other factors, especially issues of preservation and recovery, probably influence these ratios to a large but unmeasurable extent. Even if the interval between epidemic events does explain the overall trends, the actual ratio values are most likely the result of epidemic cycles in combination with other factors, including preservation and recovery.

Paleodemography aspires to be taken seriously by both anthropologists and contemporary demographers. To do so we must possess a credible body of theory (Wood 1999), reliable data (Bocquet-Appel and Masset 1982, 1996; Walker *et al.* 1988; Konigsberg and Frankenberg 1994; Konigsberg *et al.* 1997), and the means to evaluate our hypotheses effectively, which includes testable models of population processes (Wood *et al.* 1992; Keckler 1997; Paine 1997, 2000). Other chapters in this volume address one of the most vexing problems associated with paleodemographic data, the bias introduced by the age distribution of our reference samples (Bocquet-Appel and Masset 1982). However, even if we can eliminate bias in age estimates and improve their accuracy (even to the point of perfect accuracy), we will still be faced with the problem of linking living population processes to skeletal age distributions (Wood *et al.* 1992 among others). Practical models of living population processes, which include their effects on patterns of death, are a means of establishing those links.

References

Acsádi G and Nemeskéri J (1970) History of human lifespan and mortality. Budapest: Akadémai Kiadó.

Bocquet-Appel JP and Masset C (1982) Farewell to paleodemography. *Journal of Human Evolution* **11**, 321–333.

Bocquet-Appel JP and Masset C (1996) Paleodemography: expectancy and false hope. *American Journal of Physical Anthropology* **99**, 571–583.

Boldsen JL (1988) Two methods for the reconstruction of the empirical mortality profile. *Human Evolution* **3**, 335–342.

Boldsen JL (1997) Transitional analysis: a method for unbiased age estimation from skeletal traits. (Abstract) *American Journal of Physical Anthropology Supplement* **24**, 79.

Boldsen JL and Paine RR (1995) Defining extreme longevity from the Mesolithic to the Middle Ages: estimates based on skeletal data. In B Jeune and J W Vaupel (eds.): *Exceptional longevity: from prehistory to present.* Odense: Odense University Press, pp. 25–36.

Boldsen JL and Paine RR (1999) Human longevity since the ice age. Third European-American Research Colloquium on Social and Biological Determinants of Longevity, Max Planck Institute for Demographic Research, Rostock, Germany.

Bradley I and Meek RL (1986) *Matrices and society: matrix algebra and its applications in the social sciences.* Princeton, NJ: Princeton University Press.

Brass W (1971) On the scale of mortality. In W Brass (ed.): *Biological aspects of demography.* London: Taylor and Francis, pp. 69–110.

Buikstra JE, Konigsberg LW, and Bullington J (1986) Fertility and the development of agriculture in the prehistoric Midwest. *American Antiquity* **51**, 528–546.

Campbell KL and Wood JW (1988) Fertility in traditional societies. In P Diggory, M Potts, and S Teper (eds.): *Natural human fertility: social and biological determinants.* London: Macmillan, pp. 39–69.

Caswell H (1989) *Matrix population models.* Sunderland, MA: Sinauer Associates.

Cohen MN (1977) *The food crisis in prehistory.* New Haven, CT: Yale University Press.

Cohen MN and Armelagos GR (eds.) (1984) *Paleopathology at the origins of agriculture.* Orlando, FL: Academic Press.

Howell N (1982) Village composition implied by a paleodemographic life table. *American Journal of Physical Anthropology* **59**, 263–269.

Keckler CNW (1997) Catastrophic mortality in simulations of forager age-at-death: where did all the humans go? In RR Paine (ed.): *Integrating archaeological demography: multidisciplinary approaches to prehistoric population.* Carbondale, IL: Center for Archaeological Investigations, Occasional Papers 24, pp. 205–228.

Konigsberg LW and Frankenberg SR (1992) Estimation of age structure in anthropological demography. *American Journal of Physical Anthropology* **89**, 235–256.

Konigsberg LW and Frankenberg SR (1994) Paleodemography: "Not quite dead". *Evolutionary Anthropology* **3**, 92–105.

Konigsberg LW, Frankenberg SR, and Walker RB (1997) Regress what on what? Paleodemographic age estimation as a calibration problem. In RR Paine (ed.): *Integrating archaeological demography: multidisciplinary approaches to prehistoric population.* Carbondale, IL: Center for Archaeological Investigations, Occasional Papers 24, pp. 64–88.

Leslie PH (1945) On the uses of matrices in certain population mathematics. *Biometrika* **33**, 183–212.

Lovejoy CO, Meindl RS, Pryzbeck TR, Barton TS, Heople KG, and Kotting D (1977) Paleodemography of the Libben Site, Ottawa County, Ohio. *Science* **198**, 291–293.

Maples WR (1989) An improved technique using dental histology for estimation of adult age. *Journal of Forensic Science* **24**, 168–172.

McNeil WH (1977) *Plagues and peoples.* New York: Doubleday.

Milner GR, Boldsen JL, and Usher BM (1997) Age at death determination using revised scoring procedures for age-progressive skeletal traits. *American Journal of Physical Anthropology, Supplement,* **24**, 170.

Paine RR (1997) The role of uniformitarian models in osteological paleodemography. In RR Paine (ed.): *Integrating archaeological demography: multidisciplinary approaches to prehistoric population.* Carbondale, IL: Center for Archaeological Investigations, Occasional Papers 24, pp. 191–204.

Paine RR (2000) If a population crashes in prehistory, and there is no paleodemographer there to hear it, does it make a sound? *American Journal of Physical Anthropology* **112**, 181–190.

Paine RR and Boldsen JL (1997) Long-term trends in mortality patterns in preindustrial Europe. (Abstract) *American Journal of Physical Anthropology,* Supplement **24**, 183.

Pollard JH (1973) *Mathematical models for the growth of human populations.* Cambridge: Cambridge University Press.

Sattenspiel LR and Harpending HC (1983) Stable populations and skeletal age. *American Antiquity* **48**, 489–498.

Skytthe A and Boldsen JL (1993) A method for computer aided estimation of age at death from skeletons. (Abstract) *American Journal of Physical Anthropology,* Supplement **16**, 182.

Walker PL, Johnson J, and Lambert P (1988) Age and sex biases in the preservation of human skeletal remains. *American Journal of Physical Anthropology* **76**, 183–188.

Weiss KM (1973) *Demographic models for anthropology.* Society for American Archaeology, Memoir 27. Published as *American Antiquity* **38**, Part 2.

Wood JW, Milner GR, Harpending HC, and Weiss KM (1992) The osteological paradox: problems of inferring prehistoric health from skeletal samples. *Current Anthropology* **33**, 343–358.

Wrigley EA, Davies RS, Oeppen JE, and Schofield RS (1997) *English population history from family reconstitution 1580–1837.* Cambridge: Cambridge University Press.

9 A solution to the problem of obtaining a mortality schedule for paleodemographic data

BRADLEY LOVE AND HANS-GEORG MÜLLER

Introduction

In this chapter, we present some thoughts on how to think about age estimation problems in paleodemography. After this has been addressed, we offer statistical solutions to the problems that arise, expanding on the results of Müller *et al.* (2001). Finally, we point out several problems that may be of future interest to researchers, both in practice and in theory.

The problem

One problem that arises from paleodemographic data is that they do not lend themself to the typical methods of demography. Since the age-at-death is not known, classical demographic and statistical methods encounter problems when the aim is the construction of a mortality schedule.

The available data typically consist of a classification of age indicator stages from skeletal remains. Such characteristics are scored by the physical anthropologist, and are often assigned to categorical stages or classes. Ideally the mapping from skeleton to stage is such that each age class is assigned to a unique stage. In practice, however, stages overlap substantially and are fraught with error, and information is sparse. The only information available to the paleodemographer is the observed frequency counts resulting from the classification by the physical anthropologist.

For the proposed approach we require two distinct datasets. The first dataset, the reference or training set, contains both actual age-at-death and the age indicator stage to which the skeletal remain is assigned. Ideally there would exist a standard reference/training set, i.e., a scoring technique would be evaluated based on a single reference set. Of course the standard training set is hard to obtain in reality, since the classification or stage assignment will depend not only on the scoring or staging method but also

181

on the person who is doing the scoring. It is not easy to deal with evaluator effects, and problems with inter- and intra-observer error will render many reference datasets less than ideal. One idea is that each physical anthropologist develops his or her own reference sample for each scoring method. In a perfect world, every anthropologist using the same staging method would make the same assignment into a stage for given skeletal remains. In practice we can only hope for the probabilities of assigning into the same stage being the same. A worse scenario comes into place if anthropologists differ systematically in their assignments. Reference samples can be obtained from anatomical collections such as the Terry and the Hamman–Todd collections or from historical collections that include documented age-at-death records, e.g., Spitalfields, St Bride's Crypt, etc. (see Usher, Chapter 3, this volume).

The second dataset is the actual target sample. This is the dataset that is of interest to the paleodemographer or physical anthropologist and for which the mortality schedule, i.e., the distribution of the lifetimes, is desired. This dataset contains only the observed frequency counts of the stages, obtained according to the chosen scoring technique. The reference and the target datasets are independent of each other, and we will take advantage of this fact in the statistical analysis.

To formalize the notation, suppose that an age indicator state has I distinct categories. These I categories will be labeled by $1, 2, \ldots, I$, and the indicator state by C. For example, $C = i$ means that the i-th category is assigned. The actual age-at-death will be denoted A and is assumed to be a continuous random variable. The number of observed subjects, i.e., skeletal remains, will be denoted n, where $n_1, n_2, \ldots, n_I$ denotes the number of observations in categories labeled by $1, \ldots, I$, respectively. Note that $n_1 + n_2 + \ldots + n_I = n$. To minimize confusion over the two datasets we will superscript ages, categories and frequencies with either R, for the reference population, or T, for the target population.

Of main interest is the unknown mortality schedule of the population to which the available skeletal remains belong. The mortality schedule can be quantified in one of the following formats: force of mortality (hazard function), density function, or survival function, all pertaining to the lifetime distribution. We chose to characterize the mortality schedule via estimation of the probability density function of the time of deaths for the target sample. We will denote this function $f^T(a)$. It is useful to note that the probability density function can be expressed in many ways,

$$f^T(a) = \frac{dF^T(a)}{da},$$

$$(9.1)$$

$$= -\frac{dS^{\mathrm{T}}(a)}{da},$$

$$= h^{\mathrm{T}}(a)S^{\mathrm{T}}(a),$$

where $F^{\mathrm{T}}(a)$ is the cumulative distribution function, $S^{\mathrm{T}}(a)$ is the survival function, and $h^{\mathrm{T}}(a)$ is the force of mortality (hazard function). It can be shown that with one of these functions identified, all other forms are determined as well. For example, estimating the probability density function will also provide an estimate for the hazard function.

The reference dataset can be viewed as a bivariate dataset $(A_j^{\mathrm{R}}, C_j^{\mathrm{R}})$ for $j = 1, 2, \ldots, n^{\mathrm{R}}$, where C_j^{R} denotes the indicator stages of subject j in the reference sample and A_j^{R} denotes the age-at-death of subject j in the reference sample. The target dataset is a univariate dataset consisting of C_j^{T}, the assigned categories, for $j = 1, 2, \ldots, n^{\mathrm{T}}$, or can be equivalently represented as the observed frequency counts $n_1^{\mathrm{T}}, n_2^{\mathrm{T}}, \ldots, n_I^{\mathrm{T}}$, of those observations falling into category j, where $1 \leq j \leq I$. Note that the age-at-death is unobserved.

The scoring techniques and their complications deserve some discussion. Assigning ages into categories constitutes a large loss of information regarding the age-at-death of the individual. Since many different ages are assigned into the same category, it is impossible to differentiate between various ages given the assigned category. Furthermore, the category assignments typically overlap with respect to the ages that are assigned into the categories. This means that skeletal remains of a given age-at-death A have a good chance to be assigned to each of several categories.

Ideally, available data would include the actual age-at-death for the target sample, i.e., $A_1^{\mathrm{T}}, A_2^{\mathrm{T}}, \ldots, A_{n^{\mathrm{T}}}^{\mathrm{T}}$, so that commonly available methods for estimating $f^{\mathrm{T}}(a)$, such as maximum likelihood for parametric models or smoothing methods under nonparametric assumptions, could be used. It is worth mentioning that new and more accurate age determination methods are emerging that will allow physical anthropologists to construct improved estimates for age-at-death from skeletal remains (see other chapters in this volume).

The primary aim of reconstructing age-at-death has led many researchers down the incorrect path of constructing a demographic mortality schedule from individual age-at-death estimates. If indeed the actual age-at-death were known, then one could proceed to estimate the probability density function parametrically with maximum likelihood or nonparametrically with smoothing techniques (see Lehmann and Casella 1988; Fan and Gijbels 1996). But, in the available data for the target sample, the actual age-at-death is unknown. A flawed but often used procedure is the following. In a first step one uses the reference sample to obtain an individual age-at-death estimate for each individual from the incomplete data of the target sample for each individual. One then proceeds as if complete age-at-death data were available. The problem with this method of analysis is that it assumes that the prediction of age-at-death can be based on the mortality schedule as observed in the reference sample, which requires that the mortality schedule of the target sample be the same as that for the reference sample. Then, when the probability distribution function is estimated from the predicted age-at-death data, the phenomenon of "age mimicry" arises, namely that the observed age-at-death distribution in the reference sample inappropriately influences the estimated age-at-death distribution in the target sample.

A better solution is as follows. First, we define invariant weight functions that can be estimated from the reference sample, quantifying the chance that a skeleton with given age-at-death is assigned to a specific category. Second, we use these weight functions and the observed data to estimate a probability density function for the mortality schedule of the target sample. Only in a third and final step do we use the estimated probability density function and the observed data to estimate individual age-at-death. Note that individual age estimation is a last step rather than a first step as in the incorrect solution to this problem. In addition we include methods of statistical model checking, a critical step that is all too often ignored.

Solution: Part I   The weight functions

An alternative name for this section would be "extracting relevant information from the reference dataset". Weight functions provide us with insight into the nature of the scoring method, i.e., the assignment of skeletons of age A^R to the stage C^R, as well as with the first step of our proposed solution.

Some theory behind the weight functions

Weight functions emerge as a relevant measure of the association between the age-at-death and the categories that are assigned on the basis of skeletal characteristics. The weight functions are the conditional probabilities that a skeletal remain with age-at-death A is assigned into category C. Formally, the i-th weight function is defined as

$$w_i(a) = \Pr(C = i \mid A = a) \tag{9.2}$$

for $i = 1, 2, \ldots, I$. This implies

$$\sum_{i=1}^{I} w_i(a) = 1 \tag{9.3}$$

for all ages a, so that there are $I - 1$ weight functions that characterize the chances of assignment of categories to remains of specific age-at-death.

Furthermore, we assume that the weight functions are invariant, i.e., that the weight functions solely represent a characteristic feature of the osteological staging procedure. In particular, the weight functions do not depend on the population that is being studied. This is an assumption similar to that made by Howell (1976). In essence it means that a skeletal remain with age-at-death A has the same probability of being assigned into category C for all populations, and the population from which the skeletal remain is derived does not influence the assignment. This is a minimal assumption that must be made to analyze the target data. Any assumption that is weaker would make the analysis virtually impossible.

To gain a better understanding of the information contained in the weight functions, we apply Bayes' theorem to obtain

$$w_i(a) = \Pr(C = i \mid A = a) \tag{9.4}$$

$$= \frac{f(a \mid C = i) P(C = i)}{f(a)},$$

where $f(a \mid C = i)$ is the conditional density of lifetime a given an assigned category C, and $f(a)$ is the density of the distribution of ages-at-death, the mortality schedule. Then

$$E(w_i(A)) = \int w_i(a) f(a) da \tag{9.5}$$

$$= \int \frac{f(a \mid C = i) \Pr(C = i)}{f(a)} f(a) da$$

$$= \Pr(C = i) \int f(a \mid C = i) da$$

$$= \Pr(C = i)$$

$$= \pi_i.$$

The last line of equation (9.5) represents the prevalence of the i-th category in the population. In terms of our problem this gives,

$$\int w_i(a) f^{\mathrm{T}}(a) da = \pi_i^{\mathrm{T}}, \tag{9.6}$$

for $i = 1, 2, \ldots, I$. We refer to these equations as the estimating equations for the mortality schedule or target density $f^{\mathrm{T}}(a)$. The estimating equations provide an inverse problem. This is because we can estimate the weight functions from the reference data, and π_i^{T} can be estimated from the observed frequency counts of the target data. This provides constraints for the unknown density $f^{\mathrm{T}}(a)$ of the target distribution and the resulting estimating equations provide the basis for inference for $f^{\mathrm{T}}(a)$.

Estimating the weight functions

Actually estimating the weight functions from the reference data is not a trivial task. Different people will use different methods to do this, the main choice being between parametric and nonparametric approaches (there are various methods included in this book). Here we will attempt to describe a very general approach requiring as few assumptions as possible to estimate the weight functions. Furthermore, from our experience of analyzing of actual data, it appears that simple parametric models for the weight functions generally do not work, as they do not fit observed datasets. In Konigsberg and Frankenberg (1992), Gaussian densities were proposed for what corresponds to the weight functions in our approach. But our data cannot be fitted with such relatively simple weight function models.

Considering estimation of the weight functions, note that

$$
\begin{aligned}
w_i(a) &= \Pr(C = i \mid A = a) \\
&= E(1_{\{C = i\}} \mid A = a),
\end{aligned}
\tag{9.7}
$$

where E is the expected value. The indicator variable has the property that $1_{\{C = i\}} = 1$ if $C = i$ and $1_{\{C = i\}} = 0$ if $C \neq i$. Expressing the weight function as a conditional expectation allows us to view the problem of estimating a weight function as a regression problem.

Making as few assumptions as possible, we will use a nonparametric regression procedure to estimate the weight function. We suggest that using nonparametric regression should always be the first step when exploring new weight functions for various scoring techniques. The main reason for this is that the functional form of the weight functions is unknown, and in fact varies widely. The estimation procedure should not be biased by the method chosen, as is the case for parametric fitting whenever the model is not adequate for the data at hand. Due to the peculiar nature of the weight functions this will be the case more often than not.

The strength of the nonparametric regression approach is that it is always unbiased for large samples, but the downside is that it is computationally more complex and difficult and that one does not gain a simple functional form that can be written down in the end. The nice part with this type of analysis is that it works extremely well as an exploratory tool. If the nonparametric forms look similar to some known parametric model, one can then go forward with a parametric analysis, suggested by this preliminary step. In practice, quite often one will, however, be stuck with the nonparametric approach, as it is often impossible to find a satisfactory parametric model.

There are many different forms of nonparametric regression available such as smoothing or regression splines, wavelets or various kernel estimators (see Müller 1988; Fan and Gijbels 1996; Simonoff 1997). Here we will focus on using the Nadaraya–Watson kernel estimator (Nadaraya 1964; Watson 1964; Bhattacharya and Müller 1993) to estimate weight functions. The formula reduces to

$$
\hat{w}_i(a) = \frac{\sum_{j=1}^{n^R} K\left(\frac{a - A_j^R}{h}\right) 1_{\{C_j^R = i\}}}{\sum_{j=1}^{n^R} K\left(\frac{a - A_j^R}{h}\right)},
\tag{9.8}
$$

where

$$
K\left(\frac{a - A_j^R}{h}\right) =
\begin{cases}
1 - \left(\frac{a - A_j^R}{h}\right)^2 & \text{if } \left(\frac{a - A_j^R}{h}\right)^2 < 1 \\
0 & \text{otherwise}
\end{cases}
\tag{9.9}
$$

and h is the bandwidth or smoothing parameter. There exists a whole body of literature on how to choose the correct h, including cross-validation schemes. A very rough rule is simply to set h as 10% of the range of the data. Additional details on smoothing can be found in Bhattacharya and Müller (1993), Fan and Gijbels (1996) or Simonoff (1997).

Solution: Part II Estimating the mortality schedule

The probability density of age-at-death for the population from which the target sample is derived is the goal of our inference. The information provided in the target sample, which consists of assigned categories, will be combined with the estimated weight functions, i.e., the knowledge that we have about the scoring method, in order to estimate the mortality schedule.

The target dataset consists of frequency counts, resulting from applying the scoring scheme. In our notation these counts are $n_1^T, n_2^T, \ldots, n_I^T$. Accordingly, the frequency counts follow a multinomial distribution with parameters $n^T, \pi_1^T, \pi_2^T, \ldots, \pi_{I-1}^T$, where n^T is the total number of observations in the target sample and π_i^T is the true unknown proportion of the skeletal remains in the target population that would be assigned to the i-th category, according to the true weight functions. Note that here we do not include π_I^T as a parameter, since $\sum_{i=1}^{I} \pi_i^T = 1$. For the multinomial distribution, denoting $(N_1^T, \ldots, N_I^T)$ as the random variable of the counts and $(n_1^T, \ldots, n_I^T)$ as the observed counts,

$$\Pr(N_1^T = n_1^T, N_2^T = n_2^T, \ldots, N_I^T = n_i^T) \tag{9.10}$$

$$= \frac{n^T}{n_1^T! n_2^T! \ldots n_I^T!} \pi_1^{T n_1^T} \pi_2^{T n_2^T} \ldots \pi_I^{T n^T}.$$

Using maximum likelihood methods we can estimate the unknown multinomial parameters

$$\pi_1^T, \pi_2^T, \ldots, \pi_I^T \text{ by } \hat{\pi}_1^T = \frac{n_1^T}{n^T}, \hat{\pi}_2^T = \frac{n_2^T}{n^T}, \ldots, \hat{\pi}_I^T = \frac{n_I^T}{n^T}.$$

Notice that

$$\hat{\pi}_I^T = 1 - \hat{\pi}_1^T - \ldots - \hat{\pi}_{I-1}^T.$$

We will now assume that the mortality schedule follows a parametric distribution. This means that $f^T(a) = f^T(a|\theta)$, where θ are the parameters of the mortality schedule. The functional form of the lifetime distribution is determined once the parameter θ is known. Note that θ can be a univariate or multivariate. The number of parameters can be at most the number of categories minus 2.

Using the fact that the frequency counts are multinomially distributed and combining this with the estimating equations,

$$\pi_i^T = \int w_i(a) f^T(a|\theta) da \tag{9.11}$$

for $i = 1, 2, \ldots, I$, will lead to the proposed solution, see Müller et al. (2001). We plug the estimating equations into equation (9.10) and use maximum likelihood techniques (9.11), to solve for the unknown parameter θ. Of course, instead of using $w_i(a)$ we will have to use the estimates $\hat{w}_i(a)$, constructed in part I of the solution.

Once the likelihood for θ has been maximized at $\hat{\theta}$, the estimate for the morality schedule is simply $f(a|\hat{\theta})$.

Computationally, this poses the task of maximizing an estimated likelihood. This is nontrivial because of the nonparametric nature of the estimates of the weight functions. Since we have estimated the weight functions nonparametrically, we must solve for the likelihood function (if θ is only one parameter) or surface (if θ is more than one parameter) numerically. We implement this step by means of Broyden's method for maximizing a computed surface. (For more information about this technique see Press *et al.* 1996.)

Solution: Part III   Estimating age-at-death for an individual

Since it is often of interest to estimate an individual's age-at-death from a skeletal remain, we will provide a method for doing this, utilizing the framework developed here. The conditional expectation for age-at-death, given an individual has been assigned to the i-th category, is

$$E(A^{\mathrm{T}}|C^{\mathrm{T}} = i) = \int af^{\mathrm{T}}(a|C^{\mathrm{T}} = i)da. \tag{9.12}$$

This corresponds to the average age-at-death of a skeletal remain that has been assigned to category i. Thus we have reduced the age-at-death estimation problem to estimating $f^{\mathrm{T}}(a|C^{\mathrm{T}} = i)$. Recall that the weight functions can be expressed as

$$w_i(a) = \frac{f^{\mathrm{T}}(a|C^{\mathrm{T}} = i)P(C^{\mathrm{T}} = i)}{f^{\mathrm{T}}(a)}, \tag{9.13}$$

from equation (9.4). We can then solve the above equation for $f^{\mathrm{T}}(a|C^{\mathrm{T}} = i)$ and, using $P(C^{\mathrm{T}} = i) = \int w_i(a)f^{\mathrm{T}}(a)da$ via the estimating equations, obtain

$$f^{\mathrm{T}}(a|C^{\mathrm{T}} = i) = \frac{w_i(a)f^{\mathrm{T}}(a)}{\int w_i(a)f^{\mathrm{T}}(a)da}. \tag{9.14}$$

Plugging this result into equation (9.12) we arrive at

$$E(A^T|C^T = i) = \frac{\int aw_i(a)f^T(a)da}{\int w_i(a)f^T(a)da}. \tag{9.15}$$

The quantities on the right-hand side can be estimated, using the estimates $\hat{w}_i(a)$ for the weight functions $w_i(a)$ from part I of the solution, and $f^T(a|\hat{\theta})$ for $f^T(a)$ from part II. We then arrive at the age-at-death estimates,

$$\hat{E}(A^T|C^T = i) = \frac{\int a\hat{w}_i(a)f^T(a|\hat{\theta})da}{\int \hat{w}_i(a)f^T(a|\hat{\theta})da}. \tag{9.16}$$

Again the problem is a little more difficult than stated, since we have estimated the weight functions nonparametrically, and hence have to numerically estimate the integrals. But this is a fairly straightforward numerical calculation (see Press et al. 1996). For example, using the extended Simpson's method is a good option here.

Also note that we have in essence flipped the customary approach around. Previously, individual age estimates were estimated first, and then from these age estimates the distribution of lifetimes was obtained. The problem with this technique is that, when individual age-at-death is estimated first, this implicitly assumes that the target data come from a population with the same mortality schedule as the reference population. In contrast, in our solution we use the information contained in the frequency counts for the target dataset to estimate the mortality schedule first. The estimated mortality schedule then is a prerequisite for estimating individual age-at-death.

Solution: Part IV   Goodness-of-fit

Of course it is never correct to apply a model and not to check whether the assumed model actually fits the observed data. All too often models are fitted and never checked for accuracy. In order to construct a goodness-of-fit test, we first observe that the model predicted frequency counts are

$$\hat{n}_i^T = n^T\widehat{\Pr}(C^T = i) = n^T \int \hat{w}_i(a)f^T(a|\hat{\theta})da. \tag{9.17}$$

Here the weight function $\hat{w}_i(a)$ is estimated from part I of our solution and $\hat{\theta}$ is obtained from part II of our solution. We then use the Pearson goodness-of-fit χ^2 statistic, defined as

$$G = \sum_{i=1}^{I} \frac{(n_i^{\mathrm{T}} - \hat{n}_i^{\mathrm{T}})^2}{\hat{n}_i^{\mathrm{T}}}. \tag{9.18}$$

Under the null hypothesis that the model adequately explains the observed data, this statistic has a χ^2 distribution with $I - p - 1$ degrees of freedom, where I is the number of categories and p is the number of parameters used for the distribution of lifetimes in the target data.

This means simply that if we want to carry out a goodness-of-fit test at level α, let G^* be the value for $1 - \alpha$ from the inverse distribution function of a χ^2 distribution with $I - p - 1$ degrees of freedom. If $G > G^*$ then the goodness-of-fit of the model is rejected at level α.

An application of our solution

Here we will discuss the example used by Müller *et al.* (2001). For this example the reference set was made up of 744 skeletal remains using the Suchey–Brooks pubic symphysis method (Suchey *et al.* 1988). To estimate the weight functions we used a bandwidth of 8. When we look at the resulting plots for the weight functions, we note that there are four primary forms: monotone decreasing, monotone increasing, unimodal and bimodal. Because of these, we conclude that nonparametric forms are the best way to characterize the functional forms of the weight functions.

We simulate a population from a Gompertz distribution with parameters $\alpha = 0.0008$ and $\beta = 0.06$, with 300 death times. The simulation resulted in the following target sample: 12 observations for category 1; 9 for category 2; 5 for category 3; 24 for category 4; 131 for category 5; and 119 for category 6. The resulting parameter estimates are $\hat{\alpha} = 0.000758$ and $\hat{\beta} = 0.0621$.

When we estimate the average age-at-death by stage information from this model we have the following: 14.679 years old for category 1, 27.440 for category 2, 33.835 for category 3, 45.248 for category 4, 63.935 for category 5 and 73.078 for category 6. The largest difference between the theoretical average age-at-death and the estimated age-at-death is 1.2 years. With this example, the method can be shown to produce very accurate age-of-death estimates.

Finally, when we calculate the goodness-of-fit statistic we get $G = 4.695$

with 3 degrees of freedom. The corresponding *p* value is 0.196, therefore goodness-of-fit is not rejected, i.e., the estimate gives a good fit to the observed data and therefore one may proceed with the analysis.

References

Bhattacharya PK and Müller HG (1993) Asymptotics for nonparametric regression, *Sankhya A* **55**, 420–441.

Fan J and Gijbels I (1996) *Local polynomial modelling and its applications.* New York: Chapman & Hall.

Howell N (1976) Toward a uniformitarian theory of human paleodemography. In RH Ward and KM Weiss (eds.): *The demographic evolution of human populations.* New York: Academic Press, pp. 25–40.

Konigsberg LW and Frankenberg SR (1992) Estimation of age structure in anthropological demography. *American Journal of Physical Anthropology* **89**, 235–256.

Lehmann EL and Casella G (1988) *Theory of point estimation.* New York: Springer-Verlag.

Müller HG (1988) *Nonparametric regression analysis for longitudinal data.* New York: Springer-Verlag.

Müller HG, Love B, and Hoppa RD (2001) A semiparametric method for estimating demographic profiles from age indicator data. *American Journal of Physical Anthropology*, in press.

Nadaraya EA (1964) On estimating regression, *Theory of Probability and Its Applications* **9**, 141–142.

Press H, Teukolsky A, Vetterling WT, and Flannery BP (1996) *Numerical recipes in C.* Cambridge: Cambridge University Press.

Simonoff D (1997) *Smoothing methods in statistics.* Berlin: Springer-Verlag.

Suchey JM, Brooks ST, and Katz D (1988) *Instructions for the use of Suchey-Brooks system for age determination for the female's os pubis.* Instructional materials accompanying female pubic symphyseal models of the Suchey–Brooks system, distributed by France Casting (Diane France, 20102 Buckhorn Rd, Bellvue, CO 80512, USA).

Watson GS (1964) Smooth regression analysis, *Sankhya A* **26**, 359–372.

10 Estimating age-at-death distributions from skeletal samples: multivariate latent-trait approach

DARRYL J. HOLMAN, JAMES W. WOOD, AND
KATHLEEN A. O'CONNOR

Introduction

Most approaches to age estimation currently used in paleodemography and forensic science are not based on formal (or even informal) statistical methods. Instead, various *ad hoc* procedures have been developed, based frequently on simple tabulations of skeletal markers by age. The classic methods of Todd (1920) and McKern and Stewart (1957), for example, involve a nonstatistical assignment of a skeleton's age-at-death according to documented changes in the pubic symphysis. These methods produce either a nonstatistical age range or a point estimate of age, without any assessment of the error structure of the estimate based on formal probability arguments. The individual ages produced in this way are then aggregated to estimate the age-at-death distribution for an entire sample. As discussed elsewhere in this volume, the age-at-death distribution produced by this procedure will usually be biased in the direction of the age distribution of whatever reference sample was used to generate the individual estimates in the first place. In addition, we are left with little understanding of the degree of estimation error involved, either in the individual age estimates or the estimate of the aggregate-level age-at-death distribution as a whole.

In this chapter we explore some statistical methods for estimating age-at-death distributions from skeletal samples, with special emphasis on recovering the parameters of parametric models of the age-at-death distribution (see Wood *et al.*, Chapter 7, this volume). Only methods compatible with the Rostock protocol, described elsewhere in this book, are discussed. We begin by examining univariate methods – those that use a single skeletal age indicator – and then go on to examine multivariate methods. We introduce a new multivariate method for estimating a parametric age-at-death distribution from a skeletal sample. The method at least partially corrects for the correlations that almost inevitably exist among skeletal traits, and handles missing observations on particular traits.

Estimation of an age-at-death distribution

The data used for paleodemographic reconstruction of a population's age-at-death distribution are macro- and microscopic morphological indicators of age-at-death from individual skeletons. A considerable body of work has appeared over the past 80 years on the identification and quantification of age-related morphological changes in the human skeleton for use as indicators of age-at-death. Despite this work, the correlation of skeletal indicators with true chronological age, and the accuracy and reliability of most indicators, remain far from ideal (Bocquet-Appel and Masset 1982, 1985; Buikstra and Konigsberg 1985; Jackes 1992). The limitations are partly biological, and, aside from developing new and more biologically informative indicators, little can be done to improve upon them. There is considerable room, however, for improvement in the statistical methods used for paleodemographic reconstruction.

Methodological advances are needed in at least three areas. First, methods are needed that produce a target age-at-death distribution that does not mimic the age-distribution of the reference sample.[1] This "age mimicry" bias was empirically demonstrated by Bocquet-Appel and Masset (1982) and mathematically explained by Konigsberg and Frankenberg (1992; Konigsberg et al. 1997), who also proposed a statistical solution to the problem. We build on the methods of Konigsberg and Frankenberg in this chapter.

The second area concerns how age estimates are produced for individual skeletons in an archaeological target sample. Traditionally, ages have been assigned to a skeleton directly from that individual's skeletal age indicators. As discussed by Love and Müller (Chapter 9, this volume), ages produced in this way are usually biased. In most applications, accurate individual ages can be found only *after* the age-at-death distribution has

---

[1] As in the rest of this book, "reference" is used throughout this chapter to indicate an individual skeleton or sample of skeletons of known age used to calibrate our age estimation procedure. "Target" refers to the archaeological or forensic skeleton(s) whose age(s) at death we wish to estimate. These usages follow Konigsberg and Frankenberg (1992). As emphasized by Usher (Chapter 3, this volume) the "known" ages reported for many famous reference collections are often quite approximate. We ignore this problem and treat reference sample ages as if they were known without error.

been estimated for the entire target sample. Even then, the resulting age for each target skeleton should be reported as a *distribution* of probable ages, not merely a point estimate.

The third area is the development of multivariate aging methods that accommodate missing skeletal age indicators. The ideal method would allow multiple aging indicators to be combined in a way that makes statistical sense. Clearly, one motivation for developing such a method is to wring as much reliable aging information as possible from every skeleton. Another compelling motivation is that, in real skeletal collections, most if not all skeletons will be missing one or more aging indicators for taphonomic reasons.

Konigsberg and Frankenberg (1992) proposed a multivariate method for estimating age-at-death distributions using continuous age indicators. An extension to discrete age indicators was given by Konigsberg and Holman (1999). Both methods estimate a series of means from a multivariate normal (or Gaussian) distribution for the joint distribution of all age indicators, along with the entire variance–covariance matrix among indicators. Using this method with a set of 10 indicators, all distributed as multivariate normals, would require us to estimate a total of 65 parameters: 10 means, 10 variances, and 45 covariances. As the number of age indicators increases, the method becomes even more parameter-heavy, which, in turn, requires larger and larger sample sizes. In addition, numerically intensive methods must be used for multivariate integration, since the method always requires integration in one more dimension than there are age indicators. The strength of the method is that it does not require us to assume statistical independence among age indicators.

Boldsen and colleagues (Chapter 5, this volume) propose a related method, called "transition analysis", that generates an age-at-death distribution from the joint distributions of a series of skeletal age indicators. This approach makes the simplifying assumption that the indicators are independent of each other once they have been conditioned on chronological age. For 10 binary indicators, each with an independent distribution (normal, logistic, etc.), the method yields 20 parameters: 10 location parameters and 10 scale parameters. Boldsen *et al.*'s approach is considerably simpler than Konigsberg's, if only because no integration is necessary for estimating the parameters from the reference sample. Similarly, sample size is less of a problem because fewer parameters are estimated. But Boldsen *et al.*'s method comes at a price: we are required to make the possibly erroneous assumption that the indicators are independent of each other conditional on age.

In this chapter, we develop an alternative approach to estimating a multivariate age-at-death distribution – an approach we call the "latent-trait" method for reasons that will become clear presently. Our method represents something of a compromise between the two methods discussed above. Age indicators are not considered conditionally independent of each other as in Boldsen *et al.*'s transition analysis, but neither do they require estimation of the entire variance–covariance matrix as in Konigsberg's multivariate probit method. Our method also falls between the others in numerical complexity: numerical integration is required in a single dimension for parameter estimation from a reference sample and in two dimensions for recovering the age-at-death distribution from a target sample. The advantages of this method are threefold: we do not need to assume that age indicators are independent of each other, the number of parameters to be estimated grows linearly (not exponentially) with the number of indicators, and the method is numerically tractable. In addition, our model is motivated by some simple biological principles, so that some parameters may be of genuine biological interest.

Statistical age-at-death estimation can be separated logically into two distinct stages. The first stage is the generation of one (or more) standard age distributions from a known-age reference sample. The second stage is the estimation of an age-at-death distribution from some target sample, making use of the reference distribution(s) found in the first stage. Throughout this chapter, we explicitly divide every method into these two parts and provide the corresponding likelihoods for both. Maximum likelihood methods are then used to estimate parameters. The basic idea of maximum likelihood estimation is to compute a probability (or an individual likelihood) for each observation, given some underlying probability model of the process. The overall likelihood of the model, given a series of independently sampled cases, is the product of the individual likelihoods. The parameter values that globally maximize the overall likelihood are the maximum likelihood estimates (MLEs). Useful introductions to maximum likelihood estimation are provided by Edwards (1972), Pickles (1985), and Eliason (1993).

Missing skeletal observations

Because of differential preservation and recovery, few skeletons display all possible indicators of age. In almost every collection of skeletal material, there will be missing indicators for at least some of the individual skeletons. As an example, Table 10.1 shows the distribution of multiple age-at-death indicators in human skeletons from the archaeological site of Tipu in

Table 10.1. *Number of individuals in the Tipu collection by number of age-at-death indicators*

No. of age indicators	No. of individuals[a]	%[b]
1	166	31
2	152	29
3	149	28
4	45	8
5	15	3
6	5	1

[a]$N = 532$ juveniles and adults. Indicators for adults are given in Table 10.2; indicators for subadults include tooth development and eruption, epiphyseal union, diaphyseal length, and tooth wear.
[b]Percentage of individuals with the specified number of age indicators. From O'Connor 1995.

Table 10.2. *Number out of 255 adult individuals with particular aging indicators in the Tipu skeletal collection*

Age indicator	N
Cranial suture closure	143
Tooth wear	139
Auricular surface	128
Cemental annulation	37
Pubic symphysis	33
Vertebral osteophytosis	33

From O'Connor 1995.

Belize. In this case, most skeletons (318 of 532 juveniles and adults) could be aged by only one or two indicators. Only five could be aged by all six indicators. When using multivariate aging methods, missing observations for one or more indicators are likely to be the norm. Any serious multivariate aging method must be able to accommodate such missing data.

The particular adult age-at-death indicators used at Tipu are listed in Table 10.2. The skeletal material from this site is, comparatively speaking, reasonably well preserved. Nonetheless, while the pubic bone is one of the most common (and one of the best) indicators of adult age, only 33 of 255 adults had pubic bones in sufficiently good condition for aging purposes. For the Tipu collection, we would have four options for age-at-death reconstruction: we could drop the pubic bone from our suite of age indicators, we could base our age-at-death methods on only 33 skeletons

(!), we could somehow combine multiple univariate methods for different indicators, or we could use a genuinely multivariate method that accommodates the fact that the pubic bone is missing in most skeletons.

Because individual skeletons vary in the age indicators they display – and because each indicator varies in its reliability and accuracy – skeletons will differ in the quality and quantity of information they contribute to any estimate of an age-at-death distribution. Most investigators have not addressed this problem except with *ad hoc* solutions. For example, summary age-at-death, a simple unweighted average of all indicators available for an individual skeleton, is a common method for combining multiple univariate age-at-death estimates to come up with a single point estimate of individual age (Acsádi and Nemeskéri 1970). Simple averaging is clearly improper for several reasons: (a) the different age indicators do not provide exactly the same amount of information, (b) the indicators may not be independent, (c) all information about the error structure of the individual age estimates is thrown away, and (d) the age-at-death distribution for a target sample must be estimated by aggregating the individual age estimates, introducing the risk of reference sample age mimicry (Konigsberg and Frankenberg 1992).

Some researchers have advocated weighting indicators, but there is no agreed-upon, statistically valid method currently available for selecting the weights. One popular method, "multifactorial aging" (Lovejoy *et al.* 1985), weights each age indicator according to its loading on the first principal component estimated from the correlation matrix of all indicators (on the assumption that the first principal component represents true chronological age). In theory, the principal components analysis is supposed to be performed on the target sample, not the reference sample. However, principal components analysis requires complete information for each individual, and the numbers of complete individuals in most skeletal samples are far too small to support such an analysis. In the Tipu sample, for example, only five skeletons display all six indicators (Table 10.1).

The problem of missing data cannot be ignored for any real skeletal sample. It is essential, therefore, to develop a systematic multivariate method for handling missing skeletal data without resorting to *ad hoc* procedures and adjustments. In the multivariate methods we discuss below, we pay particular attention to dealing with missing data. Our general approach is to assume that data are "missing at random", by which we mean that the parameters defining the probability of an indicator being missing are independent of the parameters for the age-at-death distribution itself. This assumption may not always be a good one for skeletal data. For example, postmortem preservation of skeletal age indicators may vary with age-at-death, since the bones of very young and very old individuals often do not survive as well as those drawn from the middle portion of the age range (Walker *et al.* 1988). This differential preservation by age is potentially an important source of bias, since it is likely to result in a disproportionate number of missing observations for older adults and young children. But the assumption that data are missing at random still allows for a more satisfactory treatment of missing observations than has been possible in the past.

Univariate methods

As already mentioned, traditional methods for using age standards derived from a reference sample to compute point estimates of age-at-death for individual skeletons in a target sample can be seriously biased. There are two circumstances, however, when the traditional methods actually work (Konigsberg and Frankenberg 1992). The first is when the age indicator is almost perfectly correlated with chronological age, as in the case of annual tree rings.[2] The second circumstance is when the skeletons making up the reference sample are uniformly distributed by age. If one of these conditions is not satisfied, then the more complex procedures described below must be used in order to avoid age mimicry – bias in the estimated target age-at-death distribution reflecting the age distribution of the reference sample.

The life table method

One of the simplest procedures for generating a life table age-at-death distribution was given by Konigsberg and Frankenberg (1992). In this section, we briefly review their method in order to set the stage for the more complicated methods that follow.

We begin with a reference sample made up of N^R skeletons whose ages-at-death are known and who have been scored for a single age indicator (the superscript R denotes the reference sample). The indicator might be pubic symphysis stage, osteon count, suture closure stage, or dental root development stage. The age indicator is assumed to have m nonoverlapping states. For an indicator such as suture closure, m might be

---

[2] Cemental annulations are sometimes touted as such indicators by human osteologists, but – as the validation study presented by Wittwer-Backofen and Buba (Chapter 6, this volume) shows – their correlation with true age is actually much lower than that of tree rings.

closed or unclosed. For features of the pubic symphysis, m will usually be some larger number (e.g., six for one component of the Gilbert and McKern pubic system).

Our goal is to use this known-age reference sample to estimate an age-at-death distribution for a target sample of N^T individuals whose ages are unknown but for whom we have scored the relevant age indicator. The result of our analysis, in this particular case, will be an age-at-death distribution in the form of a life table with w discrete age intervals.

Estimating the parameters of the reference distribution

We begin by computing each element p_{ia} of the matrix P as the relative frequency in the reference sample of individuals in indicator state i given age a (where a, in this case, denotes a single age interval). This array is constructed from simple cross-tabulations. The resulting estimated elements, called $\hat{p}_{ia}$, are the probabilities of observing indicator stage i for some age a in the reference sample. We use carets "hats" ($\hat{}$) over parameters to denote values estimates from a sample – which differs from the way in which Konigsberg and Frankenberg (1992) use this notation.

Estimating the target age-at-death distribution

The probability of someone in the target population dying in the a-th life table age interval is denoted d_a. Initially we do not know the value of each d_a. The goal is to estimate the age-at-death distribution $\hat{\mathbf{d}} = \hat{d}_1, \ldots, \hat{d}_w$ subject to the constraint

$$\sum_{a=1}^{w} d_a = 1, 0 \le d_a \le 1. \tag{10.1}$$

As shown by Konigsberg and Frankenberg (1992), we can find maximum likelihood estimates of $\hat{\mathbf{d}}$ as follows. Given $\hat{p}_{ia}$, we can compute p_i, the probability of observing indicator stage i assuming a target age distribution. For convenience, we define

$$p_i = \sum_{a=1}^{w} \hat{p}_{ia} d_a. \tag{10.2}$$

Then, the likelihood function for a given $\hat{p}_{ia}$ and some target distribution d_a is

$$L = \prod_{i=1}^{N^T} p_1^{\delta_{1i}} p_2^{\delta_{2i}} p_3^{\delta_{3i}} \ldots p_n^{\delta_{ni}}, \tag{10.3}$$

where δ_{ij} is an indicator variable that is equal to 1 if the j-th target individual is in stage i and 0 otherwise. We can rewrite this likelihood as

$$L = \prod_{j=1}^{N^T} \prod_{i=1}^{n} \left(\sum_{a=1}^{w} \hat{p}_{ia} d_a \right)^{\delta_{ji}}. \tag{10.4}$$

All the life table probabilities in **d** are estimated simultaneously as the set of numerical values that maximizes the likelihood in equation (10.3) or (10.4). Additional discussion of this method, along with paleodemographic examples, can be found in Konigsberg and Frankenberg (1992) and O'Connor (1995).

As outlined by Wood *et al.* (Chapter 7, this volume), describing an age-at-death distribution with a life table is not ideal. Most human mortality distributions can be well described using five or fewer parameters, so that a parsimonious parametric model should be used in place of life tables. In what follows, we discuss methods that are fully parametric, both for the distribution of age indicators as well as for the age-at-death distribution.

A parametric univariate method

In this section we discuss univariate methods for estimating a parametric age-at-death distribution when age (*a*) is continuous. For simplicity, we initially focus on age indicators that undergo a single transition (e.g., a suture that makes a transition from opened to closed). Discussion of the more complicated "staged" indicators (which can be viewed as multivariate data) is postponed for a later section.

Estimating parameters for the reference distribution
As before, we begin with some reference sample of N^R individuals for whom exact ages-at-death are known. For each skeleton in the reference sample, we observe an indicator state. In what follows, the indicator can be either present or absent. For example, we might have recorded whether a particular suture is opened (absent) or closed (present) in a known-age reference sample of skeletons.

Following Boldsen and colleagues (Chapter 5, this volume), we will refer to the age at which the indicator went from absent to present as the "transition age". Let $f(a|\mu, \sigma)$ denote the probability density function (PDF) for the age at which the transition occurs in all human populations – the assumption of invariance discussed by Love and Müller (Müller *et al.* 2001; Love and Müller, Chapter 9, this volume). It is often reasonable to assume that $f(a|\mu, \sigma)$ is either a normal, log-normal, or logistic distribution, but it could be any parametric PDF – preferably one that somehow mimics the underlying biological processes.[3] And we will make frequent use of both the cumulative distribution function (CDF) associated with $f(a|\mu,\sigma)$,

$$F(a|\mu,\sigma) = \int_0^a f(x|\mu,\sigma)\mathrm{d}x, \qquad (10.5)$$

and the corresponding survival function:

$$S(a|\mu,\sigma) = 1 - F(a|\mu,\sigma) = \int_a^\infty f(x|\mu,\sigma)\mathrm{d}x. \qquad (10.6)$$

The goal at this point is to find $\hat{\mu}$ and $\hat{\sigma}$, the estimates of μ and σ from the reference sample. These two parameters completely describe the distribution of transition ages.

Reference samples are usually observed cross-sectionally. That is to say, the aging indicator is observed only once, at the age-at-death.[4] On the basis of the state of the indicator, the skeleton has, at the time of death, either made the transition or has not. The likelihood for a skeleton that has made the transition is constructed by specifying the probability that reference individual j aged a_j made the transition to the indicator state at some unknown age between birth and a_j. This probability is given by the entire area under the PDF to the left of age a_j, equal to $F(a|\mu,\sigma)$, the cumulative distribution at age a.

For a reference skeleton that did not make the transition by observation age a, the likelihood is the area under the PDF from age a to infinity; that is, the survival function at a, $S(a|\mu,\sigma)$. We will assume that all individuals who live long enough will eventually make the transition (an assumption that can be relaxed if needed; see Holman and Jones 1998).

An overall likelihood can be computed from a sample of N^R cross-sectionally sampled reference individuals, some who have made the transition ($\delta_j = 1$) and some who have not ($\delta_j = 0$) made the transition by the age at which they are observed, a_j. Taking the product of the individual likelihoods, we get

$$L = \prod_{j=1}^{N^R} \left[\left(\int_{a_j}^\infty f(x|\mu,\sigma)\mathrm{d}x \right)^{1-\delta_j} \left(\int_0^{a_j} f(x|\mu,\sigma)\mathrm{d}x \right)^{\delta_j} \right] \qquad (10.7)$$

---

[3] Throughout this chapter μ and σ are used to represent the location and scale parameters of a two-parameter distribution. The distribution may have more than two parameters as well. Although not strictly necessary, many of the likelihoods that follow assume that the PDF is zero for negative ages.

[4] In fact, this need not be the case. Depending on the specific age indicators being used, it might be possible to observe a living sample longitudinally. Methods for finding reference parameters from mixtures of interval-censored, right-censored, and cross-sectionally observed reference individuals are given by Wood *et al.* (1992) and Holman and Jones (1998).

$$= \prod_{j=1}^{N^R} (S(a_j|\mu,\sigma)^{1-\delta_j} F(a_j|\mu,\sigma)^{\delta_j}).$$

Estimating the target age-at-death distribution

Now assume that we have already found parameters $\hat{\mu}$ and $\hat{\sigma}$ for $f(a|\mu,\sigma)$ from an appropriate reference sample. For a target sample of N^T individuals, we want to estimate the parameters of a continuous age-at-death distribution, $g_d(a|\theta)$, where θ is a vector of parameters (for a review of parametric age-at-death distributions, see Wood *et al.*, Chapter 7, this volume). Assume that only cross-sectional observations are made on indicators of the target sample, and that these indicators denote the state at death. When $\delta_j = 0$ the j-th target subject has not yet made the transition (the trait is absent), and when $\delta_j = 1$ the j-th target subject has completed the transition (the trait is present). We can rewrite equation (10.4) for this continuous case with indicator states "absent" and "present" as

$$L = \prod_{j=1}^{N^T} \left(\int_0^\infty F(a|\hat{\mu},\hat{\sigma})^{\delta_j} S(a|\hat{\mu},\hat{\sigma})^{1-\delta_j} g_d(a|\theta) da \right). \tag{10.8}$$

Maximizing equation (10.8) over θ yields maximum likelihood estimates, $\hat{\theta}$.

Parametric methods with "stage" or "phase" data

Many traditional aging methods are based on a series of stages or phases rather than single transitions. While these methods are useful in the non-statistical context for which they were developed, they add serious complications when we adapt them for the statistical methods discussed here. When the indicator of interest is not a present/absent indicator but has ordinal states (as in pubic symphysis stages), the above parametric method must be modified.

Most adult (senescent) age-at-death indicators are based on phases or stages, including the pubic symphysis (Todd 1920; McKern and Stewart 1957; Gilbert and McKern 1973), the auricular surface (Lovejoy *et al.* 1985), ectocranial suture closure (Meindl and Lovejoy 1985), and morphological changes in the ribs (İşcan *et al.* 1984, 1985), proximal femur (Walker and Lovejoy 1985), or clavicle (Walker and Lovejoy 1985). Todd (1920) was the first to study the relationship between chronological age and metamorphosis of the articular face of the pubic symphysis in a systematic way. Using the Todd Collection,[5] Todd described 10 modal phases for

---

[5] Consisting of the skeletons of 465 indigenes from the Cleveland, Ohio, area (306 white males, 47

Table 10.3. *The Todd pubic phases (Todd 1920)*

Modal phase	Age range (years)
I	18–19
II	20–21
III	22–24
IV	25–26
V	27–30
VI	30–35
VII	35–39
VIII	39–44
IX	45–50
X	50+

adults between the ages of 18 and 50 years, each phase corresponding to a specific age range (Table 10.3). Each Todd phase is defined by several different features of the pubic symphysis scored in combination, including the dorsal plateau, ventral rampart, symphyseal face, symphyseal rim, furrows, pitting, and so on. Todd eliminated any pubic symphysis in the sample that did not conform to what he considered to be the "normal" modal phases of development. Brooks (1955) modified Todd's phases by shifting the age range for the phases covering 26–45 years downward three years to correct for a tendency to overestimate age.

McKern and Stewart (1957) used a reference sample of American soldiers killed in the Korean War to develop a three-component system for estimating age from the pubic symphysis. Although reported ages are much more accurate in this sample than in the Todd Collection, the McKern–Stewart collection has a much more restricted age distribution, with few skeletons over the age of 30 years.

Each of the three McKern–Stewart components has six stages. To estimate age, each component is ranked on a scale of 0 to 5; then a sum of scores for the three components is totaled and compared with a table of scores and associated chronological ages (Table 10.4). Although a large number of combinations is theoretically possible, only 21 of these occur with any frequency. Because of the restricted age distribution, this system does not work well for ages beyond 30 or 40 years (O'Connor 1995).

It is important to realize that most "stage" or "phase" methods are trying to code for multiple morphological changes in a variety of

white females, 90 black males, and 22 black females). While this collection covers a broad range of reported ages, ages are often poorly known and display abundant heaping at years ending in 0 or 5 (see Usher, Chapter 3, this volume).

Table 10.4. *McKern and Stewart sum of three pubic component scores (Snow 1983)*

Total score	Age range (years)	Mean age (years)
0	17	17.2
1–2	17–20	19.04
3	18–21	19.7
4–5	18–23	20.8
6–7	20–24	22.4
8–9	22–28	24.1
10	23–28	26.1
11–13	23–39	29.2
14	29+	35.8
15	36+	41.0

structures. This is clear from reading the description of the first two Todd stages:

(1) Symphysial surface rugged, traversed by horizontal ridges separated by well marked grooves; no ossific nodules fusing with the surface; no definite delimiting margin; no definition of extremities.
(2) Symphysial surface still rugged, traversed by horizontal ridges, the grooves between which are, however, becoming filled near the dorsal limit . . .. Ossific nodules fusing with the upper symphysial face may occur; dorsal limiting margin begins to develop, no delimitation of extremities; foreshadowing of ventral bevel.

(Bass 1971:155)

Clearly, this is a multifactorial indicator involving many different types of surface remodeling on the pubic symphysis, with an occasional nod toward future changes. Similarly, the McKern–Stewart method uses multiple components to assign a score. For example, scores 3 and 4 of component 3 are described as follows:

(3) The symphyseal rim is complete. The enclosed symphyseal surface is finely grained in texture and irregular or undulating in appearance.
(4) The rim begins to break down. The face becomes smooth and flat and the rim is no longer round but sharply defined. There is some evidence of lipping on the ventral edge.

(Stewart 1979:163)

These stages do *not* represent a single biological trait that changes with age in a straightforward way. Rather, the stages are based on an entire *suite* of

Table 10.5. *Stage-specific transition variables (T_1 to T_5) defined for a six-phase marker such as a McKern–Stewart pubic symphysis component*

Stage (phase)	T_1	T_2	T_3	T_4	T_5
0	0	0	0	0	0
1	1	0	0	0	0
2	1	1	0	0	0
3	1	1	1	0	0
4	1	1	1	1	0
5	1	1	1	1	1

traits that are packaged together for descriptive convenience. Unfortunately, the convenience evaporates when we try to develop formal multivariate parametric methods for age-at-death estimation. We strongly recommend that new reference age indicators be developed that are based only on single transitions (or continuous measures for continuous indicators). Our reasons are twofold. First, it makes the mathematics much easier and more logical. But, more importantly, it discourages us from developing methods that treat complex traits as if they resulted from a single process.

Estimating parameters of the reference distribution using staged indicators

For each skeleton in the reference sample, we observe an indicator variable that includes $m > 2$ ordered stages. As before, the reference sample comprises N^R skeletons of known age-at-death. One way to treat these data is to define $m - 1$ transitions that occur from one phase to the next, and use $f_1(a|\mu_1, \sigma_1), f_2(a|\mu_2, \sigma_2), \ldots, f_{m-1}(a|\mu_{m-1}, \sigma_{m-1})$ to denote the PDFs for the ages at which each transition occurs in the population. The multivariate methods described in the following sections can then be used to estimate all $m - 1$ distributions.

To estimate the distributions, we define a set of $m - 1$ stage transition variables T_2 to T_m (or T_1 to T_{m-1} if the phases are numbered from zero) that are set equal to 1 if the transition has been made for that stage and 0 if not. Consider, for example, one particular McKern–Stewart pubic symphysis component. Table 10.5 shows how to convert component phases 0 to 5 into the five transition variables T_1 to T_5. We can find the $\hat{\mu}$ and $\hat{\sigma}$ values corresponding to these transition variables by maximum likelihood using one of the multivariate methods described later in this chapter. The results can then be used to estimate the target age-at-death distribution using the corresponding multivariate method.

Alternative methods for staged indicators

Alternative methods for handling staged data that can be found in the statistical literature include the ordered probit or logit method, which treats the entire set of phases as a single ordered process. The model was introduced by McKelvey and Zavoina (1975) and McCullagh (1980), and is commonly used in the social sciences (Long 1997). An example of the method applied to the estimation of an age-at-death distribution can be found in Chapter 12 (Hermann and Konigsberg, this volume).

Multivariate methods

Independent age indicators

Now consider the case in which multiple age indicators are observed. Each individual has one or more of these indicators. Initially, we assume these indicators are completely independent of each other. Later we will discuss ways of treating nonindependence among indicators.

Estimating parameters of the reference distribution

For n independent age indicators scored in our reference sample, we can simply take the product of the individual likelihoods for each indicator. A sample of N^R reference individuals thus yields the likelihood:

$$L = \prod_{j=1}^{N^R} \left[\prod_{i=1}^{n} \left(\int_{a_j}^{\infty} f(x|\mu_i, \sigma_i)dx \right)^{(1-\delta_{ij})\varepsilon_{ij}} \left(\int_{0}^{a_j} f(x|\mu_i, \sigma_i)dx \right)^{\delta_{ij}\varepsilon_{ij}} \right], \quad (10.9)$$

$$= \prod_{j=1}^{N^R} \left(\prod_{i=1}^{n} S(a_j|\mu_i, \sigma_i)^{(1-\delta_{ij})\varepsilon_{ij}} F(a_j|\mu_i, \sigma_i)^{\delta_{ij}\varepsilon_{ij}} \right)$$

where δ_{ij} is an indicator variable that is equal to 1 if the j-th reference individual for the i-th age indicator is present and 0 if it is absent. The indicator variable ε_{ij} denotes that the age indicator is available for scoring. It is set to 0 when the i-th age indicator is missing for the j-th individual, and 1 if it is not. This, in effect, yields a likelihood of 1 for each missing observation so that it makes no contribution to the overall likelihood.

It is important to realize that equation (10.9) assumes that the probability of each transition is independent of all other transitions in the same individual. If some age indicators are correlated, then estimates for the μ

and σ values could be biased. The degree of bias is an empirical question for any combination of age indicators and reference sample.

Estimating the target age-at-death distribution

The extension for estimating the age-at-death distribution in the target sample is straightforward. Again we assume indicators are independent, and we have estimated the parameters $\hat{\mu}$ and $\hat{\sigma}$ for the distributions $f_i(a|\mu_i, \sigma_i), i = 1 \ldots n$, from the reference sample. The transition indicator δ_{ij} is now equal to 1 if the j-th target individual has made transition for age indicator i, and 0 otherwise. The likelihood is a straightforward multivariate extension of equation (10.8), in which we place all the independent reference distributions inside the integral:

$$L = \prod_{j=1}^{N^T} \int_0^\infty g_d(a|\theta) \prod_{i=1}^n (S_i(a|\hat{\mu}_i, \hat{\sigma}_i)^{(1-\delta_{ij})\varepsilon_{ij}} F_i(a|\hat{\mu}_i, \hat{\sigma}_i)^{\delta_{ij}\varepsilon_{ij}}) da. \qquad (10.10)$$

Missing age indicators are handled by setting ε_{ij} to 0.

Non-independent indicators: the full multivariate method

Estimating parameters of the reference distribution

The full method for handling multiple age indicators is to treat them as following some multivariate distribution that includes all covariance terms. If, for example, the indicators are assumed to be multivariate lognormal, then we use a multivariate log-normal distribution, including all covariances. For n independent age indicators, let $\mathbf{m}$ be the array of n means $(\mu_1, \mu_2, \ldots, \mu_n)$ and $\mathbf{V}$ the $n \times n$ variance–covariance matrix. For a sample of N^R reference individuals, the likelihood is

$$L = \prod_{j=1}^{N^T} \int_{a_j(1-d_j)\varepsilon_j}^{a_j/(d_j\varepsilon_j)} f(\mathbf{x}|\mathbf{m}, \mathbf{V}) d\mathbf{x}. \qquad (10.11)$$

Note that this likelihood requires us to integrate the array of ages over all dimensions of the multivariate distribution $\mathbf{f}(\mathbf{a}|\mathbf{m}, \mathbf{V})$. The array $\mathbf{d}_j$ consists of n indicator variables for the j-th individual: element δ_{ij} is equal to 1 if the i-th transition has occurred in that individual, and 0 if it has not occurred. Then $\mathbf{1} - \mathbf{d}_j$ is the array of complements of $\mathbf{d}_j$ and ε_j is a vector of n indicators denoting missing observations (ε_{ij} is 0 if missing, 1 if not). The upper limit of integration is set to infinity whenever an observation is missing *or* the age indicator is absent (but not missing) in any given dimension. The lower limit of the integral goes to 0 for a missing indicator or when the age indicator is present in a dimension. In this way, a missing age indicator results in a marginal likelihood of 1 (integration from 0 to infinity in that dimension). When the indicator is not missing, the limits of integration in one dimension will be from a_j to infinity if the transition has not been made, and from 0 to a_j if the transition has been made. This method of estimating $\hat{\mathbf{m}}$ and $\hat{\mathbf{V}}$ is identical to multivariate probit analysis (Bock and Gibbons 1996; Chib and Greenberg 1998; Konigsberg and Holman 1999).

There are two practical difficulties with this full multivariate method. First, it is extremely numerically intensive. Multivariate integration over more than about five dimensions takes a great deal of computing time, even using very fast computers. To circumvent this difficulty, one of several methods of stochastic integration can be used, such as the Gibbs sampler or the Markov chain Monte Carlo method (see Konigsberg and Holman 1999; Herrmann and Konigsberg, Chapter 12, this volume). These methods make it feasible to integrate multivariate integrals to fairly high dimensions.

The second difficulty is posed by the number of parameters that must be estimated. As the number of age indicators increases, the number of parameters that must be estimated grows as $(n^2 + 3n)/2$. For example, with two indicators we estimate two means, two variances, and one covariance term – a total of five parameters. For five indicators we must estimate 20 parameters (5 means, 5 variances, 10 covariances). And for 10 indicators there are 64 parameters to estimate. If we wanted to use 20 indicators (e.g., by observing the emergence of all the deciduous teeth), we would need to estimate 230 parameters! Alas, as the number of indicators grows, the reference sample size needed to estimate the parameters with any certainty increases. In response, we might be tempted to reduce the number of indicators we use for age estimation by throwing out data – not an appealing strategy.

Estimating the target age-at-death distribution
Estimation of the target age-at-death distribution for the multivariate case uses all the information from the full multivariate distribution $\mathbf{f}(\mathbf{a}|\mathbf{m}, \mathbf{V})$. If we have already estimated $\hat{\mathbf{m}}$ (the n means) and $\hat{\mathbf{V}}$ (the $n \times n$ variance–covariance matrix) from the reference sample, we can find the likelihood for the N^T target individuals as a simple multivariate extension of equation (10.8):

$$L = \prod_{j=1}^{N^\mathrm{T}} \int_0^\infty g_d(a|\theta) \int_{a(1-d_j)\varepsilon_j}^{a/(d_j\varepsilon_j)} \mathbf{f}(\mathbf{x}|\hat{\mathbf{m}}, \hat{\mathbf{V}})\mathrm{d}\mathbf{x}\mathrm{d}a. \tag{10.12}$$

Nonindependent indicators: the latent-trait method

The latent-trait method is intended as a compromise between the extremes of assuming that age indicators are independent of each other and trying to estimate the full multivariate distribution. The method is based on a model of a particular type of nonindependence among age indicators, one that is of much lower dimensionality than the full variance–covariance matrix. Integration is required over only one dimension for finding parameters from the reference sample, and two dimensions for finding the age-at-death distribution from the target sample. The major advantage of this model as compared with the full multivariate model discussed in the previous section is that the number of parameters increases linearly with the number of age indicators, not as the square of that number.

The method is based upon a simple biological model for the underlying developmental or senescent process that affects the skeletal indicators of interest. For simplicity, we discuss the method assuming that the indicators are developmental (growth-related) rather than senescent in nature. For concreteness, we use the first emergence of various deciduous teeth as our example of the skeletal indicators of interest. The principles apply equally well to senescent traits.

The method supposes that each child has its own individual growth rate z, and that the value of z acts to accelerate or decelerate emergence of all the child's teeth simultaneously (Figure 10.1). In a child with a low value of z – and thus a slow underlying growth trajectory – all teeth will emerge later, on average, than in a child whose z value is high. Under this model, the correlations among the various emergence times *within* a child reflect both the child's age and the value of its underlying growth parameter z_j.

The effect of z can be different for each tooth. For some teeth z may have almost no effect, for others the effect may be strong. The different effects of z can be seen as different slopes across z for the teeth in Figure 10.1. We use a series of parameters β_{zi} to describe the strength of association between latent trait z and age indicator i.

Although the model assumes that each child has its own unique growth trait, we do not attempt to measure the value of z for each child. This value is not directly observable, but rather is concealed or "latent".[6] We assume

---

[6] We use "latent trait" in a biological sense to denote a continuous unmeasurable trait that affects a series of binary indicators. Konigsberg and Herrmann (Chapter 11, this volume) use the term "latent variable" in the statistical sense to denote an underlying continuous variable that is revealed as a binary or staged indicator. Thus the method we discuss here is a latent-variable model (for a series of binary indicators) for which each indicator is also affected by an additional latent trait, z.

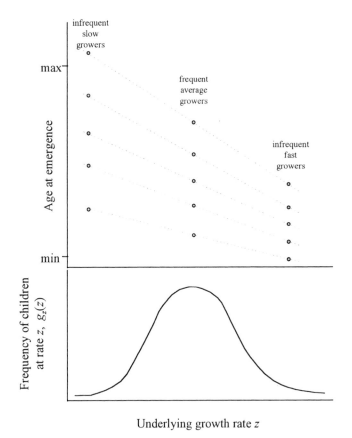

Figure 10.1. (*Upper panel*) The relationship between latent growth rate variable z and the average age at which a child will emerge five deciduous teeth. (*Lower panel*) The distribution of z among children in the population.

that the trait has a particular parametric distribution among children – a distribution whose parameters are initially unknown. The lower panel of Figure 10.1 shows a hypothetical distribution of z among children in a population. Even though we cannot measure the z value for each child, we can estimate the entire distribution of z values among children, as well as the average effect of the latent trait on the emergence of each tooth.

The method controls for correlations among age indicators in a way similar to that of models of shared frailty and some random effects models (e.g. Hougaard 1986; Klein *et al.* 1999). The effect of z on the PDF $f_i(a|\mu_i, \sigma_i, z, \beta_{zi})$ or the survival function $S_i(a|\mu_i, \sigma_i, z, \beta_{zi})$ of transition times for the i-th aging indicator, can be modeled in one of two standard ways.

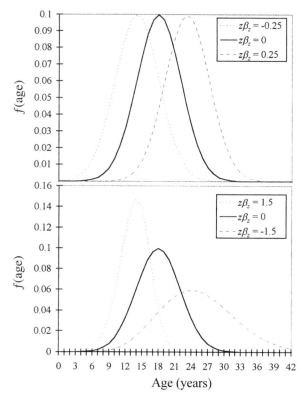

Figure 10.2. The effect of $z\beta_z$ on the distribution of times to transition. The distribution of the latent trait z is normal with $\mu = 18$ and $\sigma = 4$. (*Upper panel*) Accelerated failure time model in which $z\beta_z$ shifts the distribution rigidly to the left or right. (*Lower panel*) Proportional hazards model, in which $z\beta_z$ changes both the mean and the variance of the distribution.

The first is by using an accelerated failure time model, in which the effect of z is either to accelerate or decelerate the time to the transition (Klein *et al.* 1999). One common specification for an accelerated failure time model is $f_i(a|\mu_i, \sigma_i, z, \beta_{zi}) = f_i[a|\mu_i \exp(z\beta_{zi}), \sigma_i]$, in which β_{zi} simply shifts the mean time to emergence up or down without changing the variance (Figure 10.2, top panel). A second standard way to model the effects of z is to assume that it increases or decreases the hazard of making the transition at each age. If a proportional hazards model is specified, the effect of z on the PDF of transition times is $f_i(a|\mu_i, \sigma_i, z, \beta_{zi}) = f_i(a|\mu_i, \sigma_i)S_i(a|\mu_i, \sigma_i)^{\exp(z\beta_{zi}) - 1}e^{z\beta_{zi}}$ and the effect of z on the SDF is $S_i(a|\mu_i, \sigma_i, z, \beta_{zi}) = S_i(a|\mu_i, \sigma_i)^{\exp(z\beta_{zi})}$. Under this specification both the mean and the variance of times to emergence change with different values of β_{zi} (Figure 10.2, lower panel).

The distribution of z must be specified parametrically – for example, as a gamma or normal distribution, both of which are often used in this kind of analysis. In the examples presented below, we use a normal distribution for z, which we denote $g_z(z|\mu_z, \sigma_z)$. The parameter μ_z is constrained to equal 0, and we estimate the σ_z parameter along with the arrays μ and σ for the n age indicators. When more than two age indicators are used, an array of $n-1$ β_{zi} parameters is found as well, each β_{zi} telling us something about the strength of association between z and the i-th age indicator. The value of β_{zi} is constrained to equal 1, so that the other β parameters model the effect of z on the corresponding age indicators *relative* to its effect on the first age indicator.

Estimating parameters of the reference distribution

For a sample of N^R reference individuals and n age indicators, we need to modify equation (10.9), which assumed independence among all the aging indicators. We now want to estimate the function $g_z(z|0, \sigma_z)$ that describes how z varies among individuals. In addition, the distribution for each age indicator, $f_i(a|\mu_i, \sigma_i)$ or $S_i(a|\mu_i, \sigma_i)$, has a new parameter β_{zi} that describes how strongly the indicator is affected by the individual's underlying growth trajectory z. The necessary likelihood is

$$L = \prod_{j=1}^{N^R} \int_{-\infty}^{\infty} g_z(z|0, \sigma_z) \prod_{i=1}^{n} \left(\int_{a_i}^{\infty} f_i(x|\mu_i, \sigma_i, z, \beta_{z_i}) dx \right)^{(1-\delta_{ij})\varepsilon_{ij}} \tag{10.13}$$

$$\times \left(\int_0^{a_j} f_i(x|\mu_i, \sigma_i, z, \beta_{z_i}) dx \right)^{\delta_{ij}\varepsilon_{ij}} dz$$

$$= \prod_{j=1}^{N^R} \int_{-\infty}^{\infty} g_z(z|0, \sigma_z) \prod_{i=1}^{n} [(S_i(a_j|\mu_i, \sigma_i, z, \beta_{z_i}))^{(1-\delta_{ij})\varepsilon_{ij}} F_i(a_j|\mu_i, \sigma_i, z, \beta_{z_i})^{\delta_{ij}\varepsilon_{ij}}] dz.$$

The latent-trait method can be used for either developmental or senescent traits. When both types of trait are available in the reference sample, it is conceivable that distributions for two separate latent traits (one for growth and one for senescence) can be estimated.

Estimating the target age-at-death distribution

We assume that the parameters $\hat{\mu}$, $\hat{\sigma}$, $\hat{\beta}_z$, and $\hat{\sigma}_z$ have already been estimated from the reference sample. The likelihood for the target sample is then an extension of equation (10.10), to which we add integration over the distribution of z. The likelihood for N^T target individuals is

$$L = \prod_{j=1}^{N^T} \int_0^\infty g_d(a|\theta) \int_{-\infty}^\infty \hat{g}_z(z) \tag{10.14}$$

$$\times \prod_{i=1}^n [S_i(a|z, \hat{\beta}_{z_i}, \hat{\mu}_i, \hat{\sigma}_i)^{(1-\delta_{ij})\varepsilon_{ij}} F_i(a|z, \hat{\beta}_{z_i}, \hat{\mu}_i, \hat{\sigma}_i)^{\delta_{ij}\varepsilon_{ij}}] dz \, da.$$

Application

In this section, we present an illustrative analysis using the latent-trait method. The dataset was provided by Lyle Konigsberg, who uses it in Chapter 11. Reference and target distributions were by partitioning a sample of 737 known-age males, each scored by the Suchey system. A target sample of 149 target individuals was drawn according to a Gompertz–Makeham distribution with parameters $\alpha_1 = 0.01$, $\alpha_2 = 0.001$, and $\beta_g = 0.1$, and the reference distribution encompassed the remaining 588 individuals.

In our attempts to retrieve parameters for the age-at-death distribution of the dataset, we treated the six pubic phases as a series of five transitions representing five correlated age indicators, modeled as being log-normally distributed. Maximum likelihood estimates of the reference and target parameters were found by the latent-trait method using equations (10.13) and (10.14), and for comparison we estimated the corresponding models assuming independence among traits by equations (10.9) and (10.10). A proportional hazards specification was used to model the effect of z on the age indicator distributions. Parameters were estimated by numerically maximizing the log-likelihood using *mle* version 2.0 software (Holman 2000). Numerical integration was performed by 30-point trapezoidal approximations. Estimates of the standard errors were found by the method of Nelson (1982), which involves inverting a numerical approximation of Fisher's information matrix.

The latent-trait model used to estimate the multivariate reference distribution has five μ and σ parameters, four β parameters, and one σ_z parameter. The resulting parameter estimates are given in Table 10.6. The σ_z parameter was not well estimated for the reference sample and the β parameters were not significantly different from zero. It appears that the transition times between different phases are relatively independent. To further explore this issue, we also fit the 10-parameter multivariate independent model given by equation (10.9) obtaining a log-likelihood of -671.83 for the reference sample. The Akaike information criterion (AIC) can be used to select between the two models (Akaike 1973, 1992; Burnham and Anderson 1998). The difference in AIC is 117, suggesting the latent-trait model does provides a better fit to the data.

Table 10.6. *Parameter estimates for the reference distribution of 587 individuals found by the latent-trait method. The log-likelihood is −608.09*

Parameter	σ_z	μ_1	μ_2	μ_3	μ_4	μ_5	σ_1	σ_2	σ_3	σ_4	σ_5	β_2	β_3	β_4	β_5
Estimate	0.13	3.06	3.21	3.29	3.63	4.38	0.10	0.10	0.11	0.20	0.33	−10.7	−13.2	−10.5	−15.0
SE	0.28	0.01	0.03	0.02	0.03	0.11	0.04	0.04	0.03	0.05	0.09	20.4	26.2	22.1	33.8

SE, standard error.

Table 10.7. *Parameter values used to simulate the example target sample,
and parameter estimates for the target age-at-death distributions for the
target sample. Log-likelihoods for the known-age model and the latent-trait
model were* -607.77 *and* -222.61, *respectively*

Parameter	Simulation parameter[a]	Known-age estimates[b] (SE)	Latent-trait estimates[c] (SE)
α_1	0.01	0.013 (0.003)	0.012 (0.006)
α_2	0.001	0.00009 (0.00012)	0.00007 (0.0006)
β_g	0.1	0.11 (0.02)	0.13 (0.15)

SE, standard error.
[a]Parameter value used to simulate the target sample (see Chapter 11).
[b]Parameters recovered by direct estimation of known ages in the simulated target sample.
[c]Parameters recovered by the latent-trait method.

The parameter estimates derived from the reference sample by the latent-trait model were used, in turn, to estimate the parameters of a Gompertz–Makeham age-at-death distribution using data from the target sample. The Gompertz–Makeham model has three parameters, α_1, α_2, and β_g (for details, see Wood et al., Chapter 7, this volume). Parameter estimates for the resulting age-at-death distribution are given in Table 10.7. Additionally, target ages were provided for the target sample, so we could estimate the parameters of the Gompertz–Makeham directly from the known target ages (Table 10.7). The parameters recovered by the latent trait model were very close to the parameters used for the simulation as well as the parameters estimated from the known ages of the target sample. Clearly, the β_g parameter was not well estimated by the latent-trait method for the target sample. Nevertheless, the difference in AIC between the latent-trait model and the multivariate independent model was 14.52, indicating that latent-trait model fits somewhat better than the model assuming independence.

Age-at-death distributions estimated from known ages and by the latent-trait method are shown in Figure 10.3. The distributions recovered from the known ages and by the latent-trait method are not significantly different, but we note that the standard errors recovered by the latent trait method are quite large.

We conclude that the latent-trait model does a reasonable, though not perfect, job of recovering the parameters in these simulated age-at-death

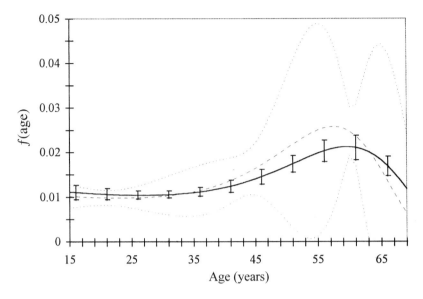

Figure 10.3. Age-at-death distribution for the target sample based on estimated parameters in Table 10.7. The solid line (± 1 standard error bar) shows the distribution recovered directly from the known ages of the target sample. The dashed line is the target distribution recovered by the latent-trait method using pubic symphysis indicators, and dotted lines are ± 1 standard error.

distributions. One of the difficulties of the estimates presented here is that the standard errors may have been poorly estimated by errors introduced in the numerical integration. Methods that use Markov chain Monte Carlo for the integration and bootstrapped estimates of parameter uncertainty would be useful refinements of the method.

Conclusions

We have presented a method for estimating an age-at-death distribution from multivariate skeletal data with possible missing values. The method adheres rigorously to the Rostock Manifesto outlined in other parts of this book. Thus the method complements those used by Konigsberg and Herrmann (Chapters 11 and 12) and Love and Müller (Chapter 9). It is also consistent with methods found elsewhere in the recent paleodemographic literature (Konigsberg and Frankenberg 1992; Konigsberg and Holman 1999; O'Connor 1995).

We would argue that skeletal data, by their nature, absolutely demand multivariate treatment. But three additional criteria must be met for any multivariate method to be of use to the practicing paleodemographer. First, the method must not assume that traits are statistically independent within an individual (for biological reasons, skeletal traits are unlikely to meet this assumption). Second, the number of parameters to be estimated must not grow as an exponential function of the number of traits (paleodemographic samples are too small to support estimation of a large number of parameters). Third, the method must be able to accommodate missing data for some skeletons (imperfect preservation almost inevitably results in missing data). We have developed the latent-trait method in response to these demands. Although it is a method of intermediate computational complexity – two nested integrals appear in the likelihood for the parameters of the age-at-death distribution – even this degree of complexity may require stochastic methods of integration such as the Markov chain Monte Carlo methods used in Chapter 11 (Konigsberg and Herrmann, this volume). Nonetheless, the latent-trait approach represents a major gain in practicality over methods that estimate the full variance–covariance matrix among age indicators – and a major gain in realism over methods that assume that indicators are independent.

The usefulness of this method (or any other multivariate method) rests, in part, on the development of true multivariate reference samples. The ideal reference sample would include numerous binary and continuous indicators from many parts of the skeleton, maximizing the chance that at least one indicator would be available for any skeleton. We eschew the notion of developing any stage or phase indicators – as we argued earlier, staged traits are likely to reflect multiple semi-independent processes that would be better coded as a series of binary traits or as a continuous trait.

Acknowledgments

We thank Jesper Boldsen, Rob Hoppa, Lyle Konigsberg, Brad Love, George Milner, Hans-Georg Müller, Bethany Usher, and Jim Vaupel for helpful comments and discussion. This research was supported in part by F32-HD07994 and NICHD Population Center grant 1-HD28263.

References

Acsádi G and Nemeskéri J (1970) *History of human life span and mortality.* Budapest: Akadémiai Kaidó.

Akaike H (1973) Information theory and an extension of the maximum likelihood principle. In BN Petrov and F Csaki (eds.): *Second international symposium on information theory.* Budapest: Hungarian Academy of Sciences, pp. 268–281.

Akaike H (1992) Information theory and an extension of the maximum likelihood principle. In S Kotz and N Johnson (eds.): *Breakthroughs in statistics.* New York: Springer-Verlag, pp. 610–624.

Bass WM (1971) *Human osteology: a laboratory and field manual of the human skeleton.* Columbia, MO: Missouri Archaeological Society.

Bock RD and Gibbons RD (1996) High-dimensional multivariate probit analysis. *Biometrics* **52**, 1183–1194.

Bocquet-Appel JP and Masset C (1982) Farewell to paleodemography. *Journal of Human Evolution* **11**, 321–333.

Bocquet-Appel JP and Masset C (1985) Paleodemography: resurrection or ghost? *Journal of Human Evolution* **14**, 107–111.

Brooks ST (1955) Skeletal age at death: the reliability of cranial and pubic age indicators. *American Journal of Physical Anthropology* **13**, 567–597.

Buikstra JE and Konigsberg LW (1985) Paleodemography: critiques and controversies. *American Anthropologist* **87**, 316–333.

Burnham KP and Anderson DR (1998) *Model selection and inference: a practical information-theoretic approach.* New York: Springer-Verlag.

Chib S and Greenberg E (1998) Analysis of multivariate probit models. *Biometrika* **85**, 347–361.

Edwards AWF (1972) *Likelihood.* London: Cambridge University Press.

Eliason SR (1993) *Maximum likelihood estimation: logic and practice.* Newbury Park, CA: Sage Publications.

Gilbert BM and McKern TW (1973) A method for aging the female os pubis. *American Journal of Physical Anthropology* **38**, 31–38.

Holman DJ (2000) *mle: a programming language for building likelihood models.* Version 2 (Software and manual). (Website: http://faculty.washington.edu/~djholman/mle/)

Holman DJ and Jones RE (1998) Longitudinal analysis of deciduous tooth emergence. II. Parametric survival analysis in Bangladeshi, Guatemalan, Japanese and Javanese children. *American Journal of Physical Anthropology* **105**, 209–230.

Hougaard P (1986) A class of multivariate failure time distributions. *Biometrika* **73**, 671–678.

İşcan MY, Loth SR, and Wright RK (1984) Age estimation from the rib by phase analysis: white males. *Journal of Forensic Science* **29**, 1094–1104.

İşcan MY, Loth SR, and Wright RK (1985) Age estimation from the rib by phase analysis: white females. *Journal of Forensic Science* **30**, 853–863.

Jackes MK (1992) Paleodemography: problems and techniques. In SR Saunders and MA Katzenberg (eds.): *Skeletal biology of past peoples: research methods.* New York: Wiley-Liss, pp. 189–224.

Klein JP, Pelz C, and Zhang M (1999) Modeling random effects for censored data by a multivariate normal regression model. *Biometrics* **55**, 497–506.

Konigsberg LW and Frankenberg SR (1992) Estimation of age structure in anthropological demography. *American Journal of Physical Anthropology* **89**, 235–256.

Konigsberg L and Holman DJ (1999) Estimation of age at death from dental emergence and implications for studies of prehistoric somatic growth. In RD Hoppa and CM FitzGerald (eds.): *Human growth in the past: studies from bones and teeth.* Cambridge: Cambridge University Press, pp. 264–289.

Konigsberg LW, Frankenberg SR, and Walker RB (1997) Regress what on what? Paleodemographic age estimation as a calibration problem. In RR Paine (ed.): *Integrating archaeological demography: multidisciplinary approaches to prehistoric population.* Carbondale, IL: Southern Illinois University Press, pp. 64–88.

Long JS (1997) *Regression models for categorical and limited dependent variables.* Thousand Oaks, CA: Sage.

Lovejoy CO, Meindl RS, Pryzbeck TR, and Mensforth RP (1985) Chronological metamorphosis of the auricular surface of the ilium: a new method for the determination of adult skeletal age at death. *American Journal of Physical Anthropology* **68**, 15–28.

McCullagh P (1980) Regression models for ordinal data. *Journal of the Royal Statistical Society* **42**, 109–142.

McKelvey RD and Zavoina W (1975) A statistical model for the analysis of ordinal level dependent variables. *Journal of Mathematical Sociology* **4**, 103–120.

McKern T and Stewart TD (1957) *Skeletal age changes in young American males.* Analyzed from the skeletal standpoint of age identification. Technical report EP-45. Natick, MA: US Army Quartermaster Research and Development Center.

Meindl RS and Lovejoy CO (1985) Ectocranial suture closure: a revised method for the determination of skeletal age at death based on the lateral-anterior sutures. *American Journal of Physical Anthropology* **68**, 57–66.

Müller HG, Love B, and Hoppa R (2001) A semiparametric method for estimating demographic profiles from age indicator data. *American Journal of Physical Anthropology*, in press.

Nelson W (1982) *Applied life data analysis.* New York: John Wiley and Sons.

O'Connor KA (1995) The age pattern of mortality: a micro-analysis of Tipu and a meta-analysis of twenty-nine paleodemographic samples. Doctoral Dissertation, Department of Anthropology, State University of New York.

Pickles A (1985) *An introduction to likelihood analysis.* Norwich: Geo Books.

Snow CC (1983) Equations for estimating age at death from the pubic symphysis: a modification of the McKern–Stewart method. *Journal of Forensic Sciences* **28**, 864–870.

Stewart TD (1979) *Essentials of forensic anthropology, especially as developed in the United States.* Springfield, IL: C. C. Thomas.

Todd TW (1920) Age changes in the pubic bone. I. The male white pubis. *American Journal of Physical Anthropology* **3**, 285–339.

Walker PL, Johnson JR, and Lambert PM (1988) Age and sex biases in the preservation of human skeletal remains. *American Journal of Physical Anthropology* **76**, 183–188.

Walker RA and Lovejoy CO (1985) Radiographic changes in the clavicle and proximal femur and their use in the determination of skeletal age at death. *American Journal of Physical Anthropology* **68**, 67–78.

Wood JW, Holman DJ, Weiss KM, Buchanan AV, and LeFor B (1992) Hazards models for human population biology. *Yearbook of Physical Anthropology* **35**, 43–87.

11 Markov chain Monte Carlo estimation of hazard model parameters in paleodemography

LYLE W. KONIGSBERG AND NICHOLAS P. HERRMANN

Introduction

In the early 1990s Konigsberg and Frankenberg wrote "A future direction that we expect to see in anthropological demography and paleodemography is the incorporation of uncertainty of age estimates into reduced parameterizations of life table functions. For example, hazards analysis, which reduces the mortality parameters to a small set, has recently been used in a number of anthropological demography studies" (Konigsberg and Frankenberg 1992:252). At the time we were writing we lacked the appropriate reference sample data for such an endeavor, as well as a number of the requisite statistical/computational tools. Today, neither of these issues is particularly problematical. Consequently, in this chapter we present some newer methods exploiting available reference sample data. The structure of this chapter is as follows. First, we discuss methods for modeling the dependence of an ordinal categorical variable on age. We then discuss the modeling of survivorship for archaeological human remains, and show how hazard model parameters can be estimated from an ordinal categorical variable using traditional maximization of the log-likelihood. We follow this presentation of methods with a brief example of estimating the parameters in a Gompertz–Makeham model using pubic symphyseal data and the method of maximum likelihood. We then turn to using a specific Markov chain Monte Carlo (MCMC) method known as the Gibbs Sampler to show how more general problems in hazard model and age estimation can be attacked. After another brief example, we discuss extensions to the use of MCMC in paleodemography, and close with a brief discussion of various critiques of previous methods.

Modeling the dependence of a discontinuous "age indicator" on age

One of the key elements of the discussion from the Rostock Workshops was the importance of appropriately modeling the dependence of "age indicators" on age-at-death when doing any form of demographic reconstruction or age estimation. Following the notation from the Workshops, we write a single "age indicator" as C, for "character". The character can take any of $1, ..., I$ values, each represented as c_i. For example, in the Suchey–Brooks pubic phase system, the character states are c_1, c_2, c_3, c_4, c_5, and c_6. Our first task, then, is to find $\Pr(C(A) = c_i | A = a)$, which is the probability that an individual would be in the i-th state of the character conditional on their age being exactly $A = a$ years. In Chapter 9 (Love and Müller, this volume), it was assumed that the character states are polychotomous, in other words, that they are mutually exclusive but unordered alternative states of the character. In Chapter 5 (Boldsen *et al.*, this volume), it was assumed that the character is an ordinal categorical variable. In this chapter we also make this stronger assumption, in other words that the "phases" within an age determination system do represent ordered states.

Since Boldsen and colleagues assume that the character states are ordinal categorical, they apply logistic regression analysis. In this chapter we use the closely related model of probit regression. In the statistical literature the probit (or the comparable logit) when applied to ordinal dependent data, is generally referred to as an "ordinal probit model" (Johnson and Albert 1999b), an "ordered probit model" (Powers and Xie 2000), or a "cumulative probit model" (Long 1997). This model can be written as

$$\Pr(C(A) = c_i | a = A) = \Phi(\alpha_i - \beta \times A) - \Phi(\alpha_{i-1} - \beta \times A), \tag{11.1}$$

where $\Phi(\cdot)$ is standard normal integral, α is a set of intercepts with α_0 equal to negative infinity and α_I equal to positive infinity, and β is a slope. The method of maximum likelihood can be used on a reference sample in order to estimate the parameters $\alpha_1, ..., \alpha_{i-1}$ and β. In addition to proprietary software, there are a number of freely available programs that can be used to fit the ordinal probit model:

> tda, which is available from
> ftp://ftp.stat.ruhr-uni-bochum.de/pub/tda/,
> nkotp from ftp://k7moa.gsia.cmu.edu/nkotp.zip and see

http://k7moa.gsia.cmu.edu/nkotp.htm for documentation,
and MIXOR from http://www.uic.edu/~hedeker/mix.html

Following Boldsen and coworkers' terminology, the ordinal probit model can also be written in terms of the mean "age to transitions" and the standard deviation of the transition distributions, so that equation (11.1) becomes

$$\Pr(C(A) = c_i|A = a) = \int_{-\infty}^{a} f(A|\mu_{i-1},\sigma)\mathrm{d}A - \int_{-\infty}^{a} f(A|\mu_i,\sigma)\mathrm{d}A, \quad (11.2)$$

where $f(A = a|\mu,\sigma)$ is the normal probability density function at variate value a with mean μ and standard deviation σ.

The representation of the ordinal probit in equation (11.2) makes clear one particular problem, which is that the integration across age starts at negative infinity. There are two ways to circumvent this problem. The first, and simplest, way is to measure age in a logarithmic scale, or equivalently to let the "age to transition" distributions be log-normal rather than normal (see Holman *et al.*, Chapter 9, this volume). The second way is to allow the standard deviations for transitions to vary by phase, so that equation (11.2) becomes

$$\Pr(C(a) = c_i|A = a) = \int_{-\infty}^{a} f(a|\mu_{i-1},\sigma_{i-1})\mathrm{d}A - \int_{-\infty}^{a} f(A|\mu_i,\sigma_i)\mathrm{d}A. \quad (11.3)$$

In our experience, the standard deviations for transitions between early phases are generally so small relative to the means that the integrals from negative infinity to zero (across age) are negligible. Equation (11.3) does, however, produce a different problem, which is that some of the calculated probabilities for being in a particular phase at a particular age can be negative. To circumvent this problem, we set any calculated probabilities to zero and renormalize (i.e., divide the probability of being in a particular phase at a particular age by the sum of the probabilities of being in each phase at that age).

Both models that we have discussed (the log-normal model and the separate standard deviation model) are supported in CatReg (US Environmental Protection Agency 2000), a collection S+ routines available from

http://www.epa.gov/ncea/catreg.htm and
http://www.stat.uiuc.edu/~simpson/papers.html

In CatReg the separate standard deviation model is referred to as an "unrestricted cumulative" probit, while in Hedeker *et al.*'s (1999) terminology this is referred to as a "thresholds of change model". In general, we

Table 11.1. *Maximum likelihood estimates of means and standard deviations in years (and associated standard errors) for transition ages between Suchey–Brooks phases (N = 588)*

Transition	Mean	SE (mean)	Standard deviation	SE (sd)
I/II	21.02	0.24	2.20	0.23
II/III	25.74	0.45	5.29	0.47
III/IV	28.62	0.55	6.84	0.60
IV/V	40.22	0.84	11.37	0.86
V/VI	69.97	2.27	19.34	1.99

have not been able to fit the separate standard deviation model in CatReg, or in MIXOR, because the occurrence of negative probabilities early in the optimization of the total log-likelihood causes severe numerical problems. We have written our own software, which uses a tensor method (Chow *et al.* 1994) for maximizing the log-likelihood, and which replaces negative probabilities with positive values near zero. In our experience this method has almost always converged properly, and yields answers identical to the "unconstrained cumulative" probit in CatReg when that program has converged properly. Table 11.1 contains maximum likelihood estimates for the cumulative ordinal probit separate standard deviation model. This table was formed using 588 of the original 737 cases from Suchey's dataset. The "loss" of 149 cases is because we have held them out as test cases, to be discussed below.

Modeling survivorship

Hazards analysis has rapidly begun to supplant the use of life tables in anthropological demography (Gage 1988; Wood *et al.* 1992), though applications in paleodemography have been less numerous (see Wood *et al.*, Chapter 7, this volume). In this chapter we will initially use a Gompertz–Makeham hazard model to represent adult mortality, and will then switch later in the chapter to a Weibull distribution. The Gompertz–Makeham survivorship can be written as:

$$S(A = a) = \exp\left[-\alpha_1 a + \frac{\alpha_2}{\beta}(1 - \exp(\beta a)) \right], \tag{11.4}$$

where A is reported age minus 15 years (we only consider individuals 15 years old or older) and α_1, α_2, and β are three parameters to be estimated from the data on reported ages. The hazard of death is

$$h(a) = \alpha_1 + \alpha_2 \times \exp(\beta a), \tag{11.5}$$

and the probability density function is then the product of the hazard with the survivorship. The log-likelihood of the three parameters conditional on observed ages-at-death is

$$\ln L(\alpha_1, \alpha_2, \beta \,|\, a) = \sum_{j=1}^{n} \left[\ln(\alpha_1 + \alpha_2 \exp(\beta a_j)) + \alpha_1 a_j \right. \tag{11.6}$$
$$\left. + \frac{\alpha_2}{\beta}(1 - \exp(\beta a_j)) \right],$$

where again the probability density function for age is

$$f(a \,|\, \theta) = h(a \,|\, \theta) S(a \,|\, \theta), \tag{11.7}$$

where we use θ to represent the hazard parameters.

Modeling survivorship concurrent with the dependence of a discontinuous "age indicator" on age

Combining equations (11.3) and (11.7) we can write the log-likelihood for the hazard parameters conditional on the observed phase data as

$$\ln L(\theta \,|\, \mathbf{c}) = \sum_{i=1}^{I} \left[n_i \times \ln \left(\int_{A=0}^{\omega} P(C_i \,|\, A) f(A \,|\, \theta) dA \right) \right], \tag{11.8}$$

where n_i are the elements of a vector that holds the counts for numbers of individuals observed to be in the i-th of the I phases. Here the reference sample information provides the probabilities that individuals in the target sample are in their observed phases, though we must treat the conditioning on age across an integral containing the probability density function for age derived from the hazard parameters. Equation (11.8) can be maximized by searching across the hazard parameters until a local maximum is found. We have used both a tensor method (Chow *et al.* 1994) and simulated annealing (Goffe *et al.* 1994) to find maximum likelihood estimates. For the integration across age shown in equation (11.8) we have used routines from QUADPACK (Favati *et al.* 1991).

Example of estimating Gompertz–Makeham parameters from pubic symphyseal data

In our first example we estimated the Gompertz–Makeham parameters and their associated variance–covariance matrix by explicitly maximizing the log-likelihood shown in equation (11.8). Our example was drawn from

Suchey's 737 known-age males, with the pubic symphysis scored by Suchey on her six-phase system. Specifically, we formed a "biased bootstrap" sample from Suchey's data to serve as a target sample, and treated the remaining cases as the reference sample. For the target sample we started with α_1, α_2, and β equal to 0.01, 0.001, and 0.1, respectively, and determined how many deaths we would need at each age in order to get a sample of about 150 individuals. In the end we drew 149 individuals with the resulting Gompertz–Makeham parameters of 0.014, 4.63 × 10^{-4}, and 0.1165. To make these draws we sorted Suchey's data on ascending age, randomly permuted individuals within each yearly age class, assigned the requisite number of cases to the target sample and the remaining cases in the age class to the reference sample. As a consequence of using this method for forming the reference and target samples, we know that issues of interobserver error in scoring and differences in aging across samples are circumvented. However, the age-at-death structures for the target and reference samples are radically different, as is shown in the empirical survivorship (see Figure 11.1). Consequently, it should be easy to determine whether there are problems of "age mimicry" occurring when we estimate the hazard parameters for the target sample. The mean ages and standard deviations for transitions in the reference sample of 588 individuals are reported in Table 11.1.

We maximized the log-likelihood shown in equation (11.8) using both simulated annealing (Goffe *et al.* 1994) to assure that we had identified a global maximum and the tensor method (Chow *et al.* 1994) (starting from the simulated annealing solution) to obtain the asymptotic variance–covariance matrix for the hazard parameters. The number of cases in each of the phases for the target sample was 15 in phase I, 6 in phase II, 5 in phase III, 32 in phase IV, 65 in phase V, and 26 in phase VI. Table 11.2 contains the actual Gompertz–Makeham parameters and their variance–covariance matrix estimated from the real ages, as well as the comparable estimates from the phase data. Figure 11.1 shows the 95% confidence interval around the survivorship estimated from the actual ages for the 149 individuals, and estimated from the phase data. For comparison, the figure also shows the survivorship from the reference collection of 588 skeletons. The figure shows quite clearly that it is possible to recover unbiased estimates of the actual hazard parameters, but that confidence intervals on survivorship (or the hazard or probability density function) are necessarily larger when estimated from skeletal data rather than directly from age. Konigsberg and Holman (1999) make a similar point in regard to estimating skeletal growth parameters when ages are estimated rather than known. Similarly, Konigsberg and Frankenberg (1992:251) noted that "the assumption that ages are known (when they are not) will lead to false

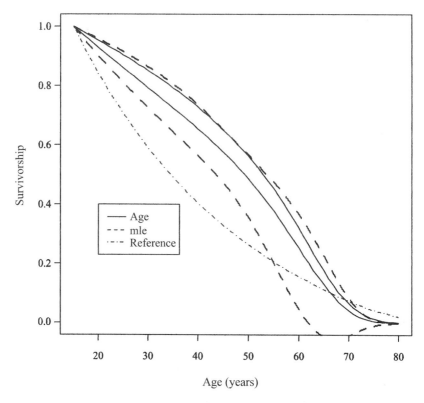

Figure 11.1. Ninety-five percent confidence intervals around survivorship for actual age from a target sample (solid lines, Age) and for survivorship from age estimated from Suchey–Brooks pubic symphyseal faces (dashed lines, mle). For comparison, the reference sample survivorship is shown (dotted/dashed line, Reference). The target sample was drawn using a Gompertz–Makeham model of mortality, and the model was estimated from phase data using maximum likelihood estimation (mle).

power in tests and confidence intervals that are too small". Conversely, when the ages are known (but we do not know them) the actual confidence intervals should be narrower than the ones we estimate from estimated ages.

Gibbs sampling

There is an alternative strategy for fitting hazard models to paleodemographic ("age indicator") data, which is to use MCMC methods. MCMC methods have become increasingly popular over the last few years, and are

Table 11.2. *Estimated Gompertz–Makeham hazard parameters and variance–covariance matrix using actual ages for 149 individuals and observed pubic symphyseal phase data*

Parameter	Estimate	Covariance matrix		
Age data				
α_1	0.014508	9.272400E-06		
α_2	0.000392	−7.928000E-07	1.542100E-07	
β	0.119995	3.928259E-05	−8.045600E-06	4.285446E-04
Phase data				
α_1	0.013701	1.232958E-05		
α_2	0.000595	−8.309787E-07	1.684148E-07	
β	0.11636	8.039658E-06	−3.657529E-06	1.663518E-04

covered extensively in the statistical literature (Gelman *et al.* 1995; Gilks *et al.* 1996; Gamerman 1997; Johnson and Albert 1999; Robert and Casella 1999). The advantage of these methods is that they replace the integrations shown in equation (11.8) with Monte Carlo simulation. While equation (11.8) only contains a twofold integral (one for the normal "transition" and one across the age-at-death distribution), "multifactorial" (i.e., multivariate) ordinal applications will require $p + 1$ levels of integration (where p is the number of "age indicator" traits). For example, Konigsberg and Holman (1999) fit a hazard model from deciduous dental eruption data. As they considered 10 teeth, to fit such a model by maximizing equation (11.8) would have required an iterative search across a likelihood calculated from numerous 11-dimensional integrations. This is true because the likelihood requires integration for every observed pattern of dental eruption in their example. As an alternative to these excessive calculations, Konigsberg and Holman used an MCMC method to fit a hazard model. In this section we describe and implement a MCMC method for estimating a hazard model from a single ordinal categorical age "indicator".

The particular MCMC method we describe here has been referred to in the literature as a "Gibbs Sampler". In Gibbs sampling we alternately sample from full posterior distributions so as to obtain estimates for marginal distributions. In paleodemographic analysis, typically we will be interested in summarizing the marginal distributions for hazard parameters, though in some situations we might be interested in the marginal distributions of age-at-death for each individual. The method is certainly flexible enough that either kind of information can be obtained, so we do not make as strong a distinction between these two pursuits (estimating hazard models versus estimating ages-at-death) as was originally made at the Rostock workshops. The Gibbs Sampler method applied to a single ordinal categorical age "indicator" fits very comfortably within the "transition analysis" paradigm described by Boldsen and colleagues (Chapter 5, this volume), so we will style our presentation after their work.

Simulating transition ages

We start by assuming that we actually know the values for the hazard parameters in a particular hazard model, and that we know everyone's age-at-death. While these appear to be enormous assumptions, we simply make these assumptions to serve as starting values for the Markov chain that we will simulate. As the first few hundred runs of the chain will be discarded (as a "burn-in" or "de-memorization"), the starting values we choose have no practical effect on the outcome of the MCMC. In the first pass through the data we simulate the ages at transition for each individual, where each individual has two ages at transition, an earlier and a later one. The earlier simulated age is for the age at which the individual is presumed to have made the transition into the observed phase, while the later age is for the age at which we presume they would have moved into the next higher stage had they not died. To simulate these transition ages we sample out of truncated normal distributions, so that the transition into the observed phase must occur prior to our current guess at the individual's age, while the transition into the next phase must occur after our current guess at the individual's age. Figure 11.2 shows this graphically for an example where an individual is observed to be in phase IV in the Suchey–Brooks system, our current guess at their age is 30.0 years, and the normal distributions for transition ages come from the reference sample information in Table 11.1. Simulation from truncated normal distributions is a straightforward matter using the "inversion method" of sampling (see Buck *et al.* 1996). Although analytical solutions are not available for the normal, there are fast numerical routines for evaluating tail areas and finding z-deviates that correspond to particular tail areas. These can be combined in order to simulate from truncated normal distributions. Appendix 11.1 gives a brief "R" function for simulating from doubly truncated normal distributions. To truncate only from the left we can pick a very high value for the right, and to truncate only from the right we pick a very low value for the left. For individuals in the first or last phase it is only necessary to simulate one transition age, as for the first phase they are assumed to have entered at birth, while for the last phase they will remain in the phase in perpetuity.

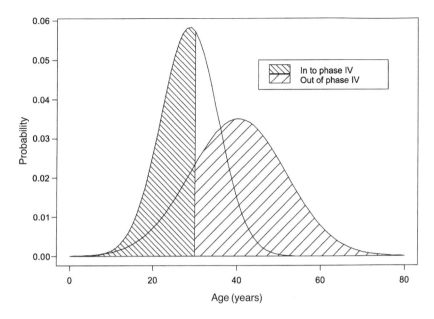

Figure 11.2. Graphical representation of simulating "transition ages", where the individual is assumed to be 30 years old and in phase IV of the Suchey–Brooks system. The normal distributions are taken from the parameters in Table 11.1. Ages should be simulated from the truncated normals represented by the "hatching".

Simulating ages-at-death

Now that we have simulated transition ages we can simulate individual ages-at-death. These individual ages must fall between the transition ages, and should follow the assumed probability density function for age-at-death specified by the value of the hazard parameters. For the remainder of the chapter we will use a simpler hazard model than the Gompertz–Makeham, specifically we will use the two-parameter Weibull model. For an individual we need to sample from the Weibull truncated at the left by the transition age into the observed phase and truncated at the right by the transition age into the next higher phase. Simulation from a doubly truncated Weibull can also be handled using inversion sampling.

Simulating the Weibull parameters

Starting from the ages-at-death simulated in the step above it is possible to simulate the two Weibull parameters from their posterior distributions.

Dellaportas and Smith (1993) described in detail how to use adaptive rejection sampling (Gilks 1992, 1996; Gilks and Wild 1992; Gilks *et al.* 1995) to make these simulation draws. We give an abbreviated account here. The log-likelihood for the Weibull model can be written as:

$$\ln L(v, \psi \mid T) = \sum_{j=1}^{n} [\ln(\psi) - \psi \times \ln(t_j) + \psi \times \ln(v) - t_j^{\psi} v^{-\psi}], \qquad (11.9)$$

where v is a scale parameter and ψ is a shape parameter. As with the Gompertz–Makeham, we can also include a known "shift" or location so that the exposure to risk of death starts at later than age 0. We use a different parameterization of equation (11.9) that assures that log-likelihood curves are concave (down). As in Dellaportas and Smith (1993), we write a new parameter v that is equal to $-\psi \times \ln(v)$, and is constrained to be less than 0 (while ψ must be greater than 0). Equation (11.9) then becomes

$$\ln L(v, \psi \mid T) = \sum_{j=1}^{n} [\ln(\psi) + (\psi - 1) \times \ln(t_j) + v - t_j^{\psi} \exp(v)], \qquad (11.10)$$

which has partial first derivatives

$$\frac{\partial \ln L(v, \psi \mid T)}{\partial v} = n - \sum_{i=1}^{n} [t_j^{\psi} \exp(v)] \qquad (11.11a)$$

$$\frac{\partial \ln L(v, \psi \mid T)}{\partial \psi} = \frac{n}{\psi} + \sum_{j=1}^{n} [\ln(t_j)(1 - t_j^{\psi} \exp(v))]. \qquad (11.11b)$$

These derivatives are used in finding a lower and upper "envelope" for sampling v and ψ. Differentiating again leads to the second derivatives, which are:

$$\frac{\partial^2 \ln L(v, \psi \mid T)}{\partial v^2} = -\sum_{i=1}^{n} [t_j^{\psi} \exp(v)] \qquad (11.12a)$$

$$\frac{\partial^2 \ln L(v, \psi \mid T)}{\partial \psi^2} = -\frac{n}{\psi^2} - \sum_{j=1}^{n} [t_j^{\psi} \ln(t_j)^2 \exp(v)]. \qquad (11.12b)$$

Both of these quantities are negative, showing that the posterior log-distributions are concave. Log-concavity is required for adaptive rejection sampling (without a Metropolis-Hastings step).

Table 11.3. *Estimated Weibull hazard parameters and variance–covariance matrix using actual ages for 150 individuals and observed pubic symphyseal phase data*

Parameter	Estimate	Covariance matrix	
Age data			
v	31.08	2.1989	
ψ	1.8657	0.01568	0.0170
Phase data (*mle*)			
v	30.08	4.1027	
ψ	1.8531	-0.0449	0.0381
Phase data (*Gibbs Sampler*)			
v	29.69	3.9715	
ψ	1.8369	-0.0456	0.0374

Example of estimating Weibull parameters from pubic symphyseal data

In our second example we fit a Weibull model using both traditional maximization of the log-likelihood (as in our previous example) and the Gibbs Sampler described above. This allows us to compare these two methods, as well as determine their ability to recover the generating Weibull parameters. For the generating Weibull parameters we use v ("scale") equal to 33.22 and ψ ("shape") equal to 1.75. These values are taken from the mortality over age 15 years from Model West 1 for males (Coale and Demeny 1966). We sampled 150 deaths from the Suchey data as in our previous example, with a resulting v ("scale") equal to 31.08 and ψ ("shape") equal to 1.86 (see Table 11.3). Although we re-estimated the transition age means and standard deviations shown in Table 11.1 using the remaining 587 cases, these values were so similar to those from Table 11.1 that we do not present them here.

Table 11.3 contains the estimated v and ψ parameters and their variance–covariance matrix from direct maximization of the log-likelihood in the tensor algorithm. For the Gibbs Sampler, also shown in Table 11.3, we started by assuming that everyone was 30 years old, that v was equal to 20.0, and that ψ was equal to 2.0. For the adaptive rejection sampling of the Weibull hazard parameters we used FORTRAN routines available from the Medical Research Council at Cambridge, see

http://www.mrc-bsu.cam.ac.uk/Research/Projects/ars.shtml

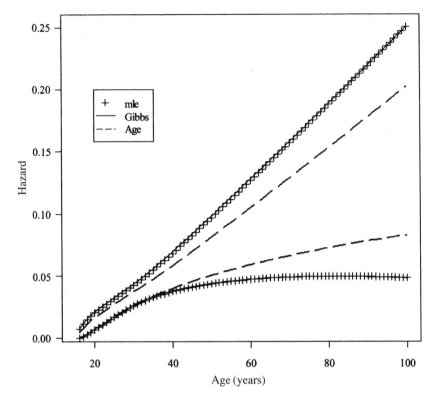

Figure 11.3. Ninety-five percent confidence intervals around the hazards for actual age from a target sample (dashed lines, Age), for survivorship from age estimated from Suchey–Brooks pubic symphyseal faces using maximum likelihood estimation ("plus" symbols, mle), and using the Gibbs Sampler (solid lines, Gibbs). The target sample was drawn using a Weibull model of mortality.

These routines can also be downloaded in single precision form from statlib (see http://lib.stat.cmu.edu/apstat/), and were originally published in the journal *Applied Statistics* (Gilks and Wild 1992). After an initial 300 iterations to "de-memorize" the starting values, we retained the next 10 000 iterations, and used the output v and ψ parameters to calculate their averages and variance–covariance matrix. Table 11.3 shows that traditional maximization of the log-likelihood and the Gibbs Sampler give nearly identical results. Further, these methods do an excellent job of recovering the actual Weibull parameters. Figure 11.3 shows a comparison of the 95% confidence intervals around the hazards from the actual age data, and from maximum likelihood and Gibbs Sampler estimation using the phase data. These intervals are indistinguishable between the maximum likelihood and Gibbs Sampler methods, both of which give wider confidence intervals than are obtained using actual age.

Extensions of the MCMC method for hazard model estimation

In this closing section we consider a number of possible extensions to the Gibbs Sampler method that we have described. In particular, we consider multivariate extensions, where the integrations required for ordinal categorical traits rapidly become prohibitively expensive using traditional maximization of the likelihood. We also consider complications in the "age estimator" data, as well as the use of more complicated hazard models to represent prehistoric mortality.

Multivariate age estimation

For binary age indicators, such as Holman *et al.* discuss in Chapter 10 (this volume), the extension to multivariate data is immediate. When the observed skeletal indicators are binary, single transition ages (rather than two ages) must be simulated. For individuals in the second stage we simulate the age at which they moved into this stage, while for individuals in the first stage we simulate the age at which they would move into the second stage if they had survived. Because the data from the binary indicators are presumably dependent, even after conditioning on age, we need to condition the transition age for one trait on the transition ages for all other observed traits within the individual. Konigsberg and Holman (1999) present an example of hazard model (and age) estimation in the binary multivariate setting, using as their example dental eruption of 10 deciduous teeth.

For multivariate ordinal categorical data we need to modify our approach rather considerably. The problem with maintaining the straight "transition age" approach is that we now need to condition each indicator on all other indicators, and if the traits are not binary then we will have two ages per indicator. Rather than maintain the "transition age" paradigm, we suggest treating the ordinal categorical data as latent traits (see e.g., Johnson and Albert 1999:127–130). Each trait can then be modeled using a standard normal integral to replace equation (11.2) with:

$$\Pr(C(a) = c_i | A = a) = \int_{z = \frac{a - \mu_i}{\sigma}}^{\frac{a - \mu_{i-1}}{\sigma}} \phi(z|0, 1)dz, \tag{11.13}$$

and dependence between traits can be handled by allowing for nonzero correlations. In this setting it would generally be reasonable to measure age on a logarithmic scale. Rather than simulate directly from equation (11.13), the logical approach now is to simulate the latent-trait value and then sample directly from the posterior distribution of age for each individual. The posterior is formed as the product of the probability density function at z with the current probability density function for age-at-death (as in equation 11.8). This is often a difficult distribution from which to simulate directly. We have had some success using an independence Metropolis sampler. Specifically, we sample an age from a uniform distribution between 0.0 and ω, and write this proposal age as a_m (for age to move to). We have the previous guess at the age, which we write as a_c (for current age estimate). We can then form an acceptance ratio AR as

$$AR = \min\left(\frac{\Pr(c_i|a_m) \times f(a_m|\theta)}{\Pr(c_i|a_c) \times f(a_c|\theta)}, 1\right). \tag{11.14}$$

After forming the acceptance ratio, we sample from a uniform distribution between 0 and 1. If the random deviate is less than the acceptance ratio, then we accept the move to the new age (a_m). If the random deviate is greater than the acceptance ratio, then we remain with our current estimate (a_c).

Mixed and missing data

There are two additional complications we have not yet considered. The first complication is that we may have data not only from ordinal categorical variables, but also from continuous variables. This is a "mixed data" setting. As an example of a continuous variable, the second Rostock workshop saw considerable discussion of cementum annulations. While these data take only integer values, if the annulations do generally equal the number of years lived since tooth eruption, then these data are better treated as continuous. For continuous variables we can model the data using a linear model regressing the continuous variable on age. This is analogous to our description of the latent-trait approach above, but now we do not have to simulate a latent trait because the actual trait value is observed. The independence Metropolis sampler can again be used for the continuous traits and, consequently, ordinal categorical and continuous traits can be handled together.

The second complication is one of which paleodemographers are painfully aware: the high frequency of missing data. Any of the simulation approaches we have described can easily accommodate incomplete datasets. In the latent-trait approach, unobserved, ordinal categorical data are simulated by conditioning on other traits, but they are not truncated. For continuous data that are unobserved, the variables are conditioned on latent-trait values and observed continuous variables.

More complex hazard models

While the parameters in many hazard models have full conditional densities that are log-concave, and consequently can be sampled easily using adaptive rejection, other models do not meet this criterion. In particular, the Gompertz–Makeham model has some convexities for the log densities. We have, for simplicity's sake, avoided such models here. Gilks (Gilks *et al.* 1995; Gilks 1996) shows how a Metropolis-Hastings step can be added to adaptive rejection sampling so that one can make draws on densities that are not log-concave. In the future we will extend our work to include these more complicated hazard models.

Whither now?

It was our naive hope with the publication of Konigsberg and Frankenberg's (1992) initial work on anthropological age estimation that much of the rancor (e.g., Bocquet-Appel and Masset 1982, 1985; Van Gerven and Armelagos 1983; Buikstra and Konigsberg 1985; Bocquet-Appel 1986; Greene *et al.* 1986) surrounding paleodemography would disappear. While possibly the skirmishes have diminished, the war still appears to wage, at least in some quarters. Our current methods fit fairly comfortably within the approaches taken during the Rostock workshops, and are clearly within the parameters established within the most recent review of paleodemography (Milner *et al.* 2000). When a specific critique of the methods proposed by Konigsberg and Frankenberg (1992) appeared in the *American Journal of Physical Anthropology* (Bocquet-Appel and Masset 1996) we chose not to comment in print at that time. By 1996, we had largely switched from using life tables to using hazard models, and so our comments would not have been relevant. We spelled out in our 1992 article that we expected to see paleodemography move in the direction of hazards analysis, so we make no apologies here for leading people "astray" with our

1992 use of life tables. As some people have continued to use life table approaches in paleodemography, we do need to comment briefly here on some of the possible pitfalls that arise in following this approach.

First, we should comment very briefly on Bocquet-Appel and Masset's (1996) critique. We have programmed the "iterative proportional fitting procedure" (IPFP) that Bocquet-Appel and Masset describe, as well as the "iterated age-length key" (IALK) (Kimura and Chikuni 1987) that we used previously (Konigsberg and Frankenberg 1992), and a similar expectation maximization (EM) log-linear model from the fisheries literature (Hoenig and Heisey 1987). Provided the same convergence criteria are used, the IPFP and the IALK yield identical results, so clearly they are the same algorithm. The EM log-linear method that Hoenig and Heisey presented is preferable to the IALK because the former includes the IALK as a special case where the reference sample is very large (technically, infinite in size). The difference between the IALK and the method presented in Hoenig and Heisey points out a shortcoming of many of the approaches in this volume, including our own work. We, as others here, have ignored the sampling variance that comes from the reference sample. In a full MCMC approach, this variance could be included by estimating the probit model simultaneously with estimating hazard parameters (for examples of MCMC estimation of probit models, see Albert and Chib 1993; Chib and Greenberg 1998; Johnson and Albert 1999).

Bocquet-Appel and Masset's chief critique of the IALK (and hence their identical IPFP) is that they believe the method is incapable of recovering anything other than the mean age-at-death. This is not an argument based in logic, but instead based on simulation work they have done. As the IALK is a maximum likelihood method, to reject it out of hand we must either critique the necessary assumptions (principally, Howell's (1976) "uniformitarian assumption") or reject the underlying statistical premise of likelihood estimation. Beyond this it is also important to realize that there are contexts in which the IALK is not identified, and consequently is doomed to failure. For example, Jackes (2000:435) has attempted to fit a life table with 17 age classes using only the six Suchey–Brooks phases and the IALK, and notes that the method "is shown to be completely ineffective in replicating the real age-at-death distribution". An examination of her figure 15.7 shows that many of the estimated age classes have zero frequencies and, consequently, her solution falls on boundaries of the likelihood space. Fienberg's (1977) "Result 2" states that in order for there to be a unique likelihood solution the parameters must fall in the interior of the parameter space. Clearly, Jackes has attempted to estimate a model that is not identified. She could have avoided this pitfall either by reducing the number of age classes or by switching to a hazard model. As should be obvious from the results in our chapter, as well as other chapters in this volume, such models are identified, provided they are not excessively parameterized.

In a recent review of paleodemography, Chamberlain (2000:108) writes that "the approach advocated by Konigsberg and Frankenberg . . . cannot be recommended". He continues that the method "is computationally difficult, and it relies on the target series being an unbiased sample of its parent population". This first point is debatable (we have written an "R" function in under 10 lines that fits Hoenig and Heisey's EM). The second point is not true. One can always try to estimate a hazard model or life table on a biased sample, and then show that the results do not fit reasonable expectations for human mortality. An interesting aspect of Chamberlain's review is that he uses Bayesian estimation by assuming some prior age distribution and updating this with the likelihood to obtain a posterior age distribution. This is a cruder form of what Di Bacco *et al.* (1999) have suggested. They take a fully Bayesian approach by starting from an uninformative prior on hazard model parameters, and then updating these using the likelihood from the target and reference sample information. Their likelihood (in their equation 20) is specified in the same manner as ours (our equation 11.8). The difference in approach is between Bayesian estimation and maximum likelihood estimation, a philosophical debate that we should best avoid here.

Acknowledgments

We thank Wally Gilks for providing us with source code for adaptive rejection and adaptive rejection Metropolis-Hastings sampling. Many of the ideas reflected here grew out of discussions with Jesper Boldsen, Darryl Holman, and Jim Wood, who are thanked, but should remain blameless (at least for our foibles). We also benefited greatly from the discussions in Rostock. We thank Rob Hoppa and Jim Vaupel for organizing the workshops, and all the participants for their helpful comments. The University of Tennessee generously provided travel funds for the second workshop. This work was supported in part by the National Science Foundation (SBR-9727386).

Appendix 11.1

"R" function for simulating deviates from a doubly truncated normal distribution

```
function (ndev=1,mu=0,sd=1,left=-1,right=1)
{
Fl<-pnorm(left,mu,sd)      # Get cumulative distrib. up to left truncation
Fr<-pnorm(right,mu,sd)     # Get cumulative distrib. up to right truncation
p<-runif(ndev)*(Fr-Fl)+Fl  # Simulate ndev uniforms between F(L) and F(R)
qnorm(p,mu,sd)             # Invert the random deviates
}
```

"R" function for simulating deviates from a doubly truncated Weibull distribution

Note that "R" has intrinsic functions for the distribution and quantile functions in a Weibull, which would presumably be faster than the explicit code below. The function below allows for a "shift" in case the hazard only applies to a particular age and above. The symbol "b" below is equivalent to v in the text, and "c" is equivalent to ψ.

```
function (ndev=1,b=30,c=2,shift=15,left=20,right=25)
{
  Sl<-exp(-((left-shift)/b)^c)   # Get Survivorship until age "left"
  Sr<-exp(-((right-shift)/b)^c)  # Get Survivorship until age "right"
  p<-runif(ndev)*(Sl-Sr)+Sr      # Simulate uniform between survivorships
  b*(log(1/p)^(1/c))+shift       # Invert
}
```

References

Albert JH and Chib S (1993) Bayesian analysis of binary and polychotomous response data. *Journal of the American Statistical Association* **88**, 669–679.

Bocquet-Appel J-P (1986) Once upon a time: palaeodemography. *Mitteilungen der Berliner Gesellschaft für Anthropolgie, Ethnologie und Urgeschichte* 7, 127–133.

Bocquet-Appel J-P and Masset C (1982) Farewell to paleodemography. *Journal of Human Evolution* 11, 321–333.

Bocquet-Appel J-P and Masset C (1985) Paleodemography: resurrection or ghost? *Journal of Human Evolution* 14, 107–111.

Bocquet-Appel JP and Masset C (1996) Paleodemography: expectancy and false hope. *American Journal of Physical Anthropology* 99, 571–583.

Buck CE, Cavanagh WG, and Litton CD (1996) *Bayesian approach to interpreting archaeological data.* New York, NY: John Wiley & Sons.

Buikstra JE and Konigsberg LW (1985) Paleodemography: critiques and controversies. *American Anthropologist* **87**, 316–333.

Chamberlain A (2000) Problems and prospects in paleodemography. In M Cox and S Mays (eds.): *Human osteology in archaeology and forensic science*. London: Greenwich Medical Media, pp. 101–115.

Chib S and Greenberg E (1998) Analysis of multivariate probit models. *Biometrika* **85**, 347–361.

Chow T, Eskow E, and Schnabel R (1994) Algorithm 739: a software package for unconstrained optimization using tensor methods. *ACM Transactions on Mathematical Software* **20**, 518–530.

Coale AJ and Demeny P (1966) *Regional model life tables and stable populations*. Princeton, NJ: Princeton University Press.

Dellaportas P and Smith AFM (1993) Bayesian inference for generalized linear and proportional hazards models via Gibbs sampling. *Applied Statistics* **42**, 443–459.

Di Bacco M, Ardito V, and Pacciani E (1999) Age-at-death diagnosis and age-at-death distribution estimate: two different problems with many aspects in common. *International Journal of Anthropology* **14**, 161–169.

Favati P, Lotti G, and Romani F (1991) Algorithm 691: improving QUADPACK automatic integration routines. *ACM Transactions on Mathematical Software* **17**, 218–232.

Fienberg SE (1977) *The analysis of cross-classified categorical data*. Cambridge, MA: MIT Press.

Gage TB (1988) Mathematical hazard models of mortality: an alternative to model life tables. *American Journal of Physical Anthropology* **76**, 429–441.

Gamerman D (1997) *Markov chain Monte Carlo: stochastic simulation for Bayesian inference*. New York: Chapman & Hall.

Gelman A, Carlin JB, Stern HS, and Rubin DB (1995) *Bayesian data analysis*. London: Chapman & Hall.

Gilks WR (1992) Derivative-free adaptive rejection sampling for Gibbs sampling. In JM Bernardo, JO Berger, AP Dawid, and AFM Smith (eds.): *Bayesian statistics 4*. New York: Oxford University Press, pp. 641–649.

Gilks WR (1996) Full conditional distributions. In WR Gilks, S Richardson, and DJ Spiegelhalter (eds.): *Markov chain Monte Carlo in practice*. New York: Chapman & Hall, pp. 75–88.

Gilks WR and Wild P (1992) Adaptive rejection sampling for Gibbs sampling. *Applied Statistics* **41**, 337–348.

Gilks WR, Best NG, and Tan KKC (1995) Adaptive rejection Metropolis sampling within Gibbs sampling. *Applied Statistics* **44**, 455–472.

Gilks WR, Richardson S, and Spiegelhalter DJ (eds.) (1996) *Markov chain Monte Carlo in practice*. New York: Chapman & Hall.

Goffe WL, Ferrier GD, and Rogers J (1994) Global optimization of statistical functions with simulated annealing. *Journal of Econometrics* **60**, 65–99.

Greene DL, Van Gerven DP, and Armelagos GJ (1986) Life and death in ancient populations: bones of contention in paleodemography. *Human Evolution* **1**, 193–207.

Hedeker D, Mermelstein RJ, and Weeks KA (1999) The thresholds of change model: an approach to analyzing stages of change data. *Annals of Behavioral Medicine* **21**, 61–70.

Hoenig JM and Heisey DM (1987) Use of a log-linear model with the EM algorithm to correct estimates of stock composition and convert length to age. *Transactions of the American Fisheries Society* **116**, 232–243.

Howell N (1976) Toward a uniformitarian theory of human paleodemography. In RH Ward and KM Weiss (eds.): *The demographic evolution of human populations.* New York: Academic Press, pp. 25–40.

Jackes M (2000) Building the bases for paleodemographic analysis: adult age estimation. In MA Katzenberg and SR Saunders (eds.): *Biological anthropology of the human skeleton.* New York: Wiley-Liss, pp. 417–466.

Johnson VE and Albert JH (1999) *Ordinal data modeling.* New York: Springer-Verlag.

Kimura DK and Chikuni S (1987) Mixtures of empirical distributions: an iterative application of the age-length key. *Biometrics* **43**, 23–35.

Konigsberg LW and Frankenberg SR (1992) Estimation of age structure in anthropological demography. *American Journal of Physical Anthropology* **89**, 235–256.

Konigsberg L and Holman D (1999) Estimation of age at death from dental emergence and implications for studies of prehistoric somatic growth. In RD Hoppa and CM FitzGerald (eds.): *Human growth in the past: studies from bones and teeth.* New York: Cambridge University Press, pp. 264–289.

Long JS (1997) *Regression models for categorical and limited dependent variables.* Thousand Oaks, CA: Sage.

Milner GR, Wood JW, and Boldsen JL (2000) Paledemography. In MA Katzenberg and SR Saunders (eds.): *Biological anthropology of the human skeleton.* New York: Wiley-Liss, pp. 467–497.

Powers DA and Xie Y (2000) *Statistical methods for categorical data analysis.* New York: Academic Press.

Robert CP and Casella G (1999) *Monte Carlo statistical methods.* New York: Springer-Verlag.

US Environmental Protection Agency (2000) *CatReg Software Documentation.* Research Triangle Park, NC: Office of Research and Development, National Center for Environmental Assessment, EPA. EPA/600/R-98/053F.

Van Gerven DP and Armelagos GJ (1983) Farewell to paleodemography? Rumors of its death have been greatly exaggerated. *Journal of Human Evolution* **12**, 353–360.

Wood JW, Holman DJ, Weiss KM, Buchanan AV, and LeFor B (1992) Hazards models for human population biology. *Yearbook of Physical Anthropology* **35**, 43–87.

12　*A re-examination of the age-at-death distribution of Indian Knoll*

NICHOLAS P. HERRMANN AND LYLE W. KONIGSBERG

Introduction

A majority of prior paleodemographic studies have focused on the estimation of population structure utilizing individual age range estimates derived from a variety of age indicators and compiled into a life table (Johnston and Snow 1961; Weiss 1973; Mensforth 1990). General population parameters from the life table are then compared among populations or with model mortality schedules (e.g., Coale and Demeny 1966). Recent research has demonstrated that age-at-death distributions derived from these types of age estimation method are biased as a result of an *a priori* assumption equating the age-at-death distributions of the reference and skeletal samples (Bocquet-Appel and Masset 1982, 1996; Konigsberg and Frankenberg 1992, 1994).

In this chapter, we will provide a case study based on an extension of the statistical methods detailed in Konigsberg and Herrmann (Chapter 11, this volume) using pelvic age indicator data from the large Archaic skeletal sample from Indian Knoll (15Oh2), Kentucky. This well-preserved skeletal series offers a unique opportunity to test these new methods. We compare the age-at-death distribution derived from this new approach with mortality data collected by several researchers from the Indian Knoll series. Our comparison illustrates differences between the earlier techniques, specifically life table based analyses, and our new method, which utilizes modeled hazard parameters and unbiased age estimates.

Indian Knoll history

The Indian Knoll skeletal series represents over 1100 individuals. The burial sample is one of the largest North American hunter–gatherer skeletal collections from a single site. Occupation of the site spans from the Archaic to Mississippian cultural periods defined in the Eastern

Woodlands of North America. The burial sample dates primarily from the Middle to Late Archaic Periods. Five calibrated radiocarbon dates of midden debris and individual burials span an interval from 5500 BC to 1500 BC (Winters 1974; Herrmann and Fenton 2000).

Two major excavations were undertaken at the site. In the fall and winter of 1915–16, Clarence B. Moore identified and recovered portions of 298 burials (Moore 1916). The second, more extensive, investigation was conducted in 1939 under the auspices of the Works Progress Administration (WPA, Webb 1946). Large-scale excavations were initiated at Indian Knoll and several other shell middens along the Green River drainage. Dr William S. Webb coordinated the fieldwork and logistics of the entire program, but field supervisors directed excavations at each site. Webb's goal at Indian Knoll was to supplement C. B. Moore's earlier work with controlled excavations. Webb was unsure whether intact cultural deposits were still present, given Moore's substantial prior investigations. Much to the surprise of field investigators and Webb a majority of the site remained undisturbed. The WPA investigations resulted in the recovery of thousands of stone tools, worked bone objects, shell beads, and 880 human burials (Figure 12.1).

The skeletal collection from Indian Knoll has been the focus of numerous osteological studies. Moore (1916) provided basic burial data and descriptions of the artifacts recovered during his investigations. The extensive WPA excavations were summarized in two publications. Webb (1946) described the archaeological material and mortuary practices at the site, and Charles E. Snow (1948) reported on the skeletal remains recovered during Moore's excavations and the WPA investigations. Webb provided simple burial demographic data and contextual information in the "Indian Knoll" monograph (Webb 1946). The age and sex determinations provided in Webb's publication were derived from Snow's skeletal analysis. In "Indian Knoll skeletons", Snow (1948) provided a basic age-at-death distribution of the burial sample, described unique pathologies, tabulated metric and discrete observations, and presented a detailed typological analysis of the complete crania. Although it was not specified in his publication, Snow appears to have based age determinations on a combination of cranial suture closure, dental attrition, and the extent of skeletal pathology. He provided information on pubic symphysis morphology employing Todd's (1920, 1921) method, but it does not appear that he relied on these data when estimating ages. Thirteen years after the initial analysis, Francis E. Johnston and Snow re-evaluated the original age estimates in the light of new and refined aging methods, McKern and Stewart's three component pubic symphysis system, and a standardized

Figure 12.1. Location of Indian Knoll within the Eastern United States.

dental attrition technique (Johnston and Snow 1961). The new age-at-death distribution significantly increased the number of individuals over 30 years old as compared to Snow's original assessments, but the number of adults over 50 years old decreased from four individuals to one.

Since Johnston and Snow's reanalysis, the Indian Knoll collection has served as an excellent comparative sample for numerous researchers examining issues of subsistence change. Typically, these researchers compare the mortality profile and the pattern of pathological lesions of the Indian Knoll collection to various skeletal series from later horticulturists or maize agriculturists. Blakely (1971) compared data from Indian Knoll to the Mississippian Dickson Mounds sample, Cassidy (1972) contrasted it with the Fort Ancient Hardin Village series, and Kelley (1980) examined the Northern Plains Mobridge and Southwestern Grasshopper Pueblo collections relative to Indian Knoll. The primary problem with these prior studies is that age estimates are based on biased methods. Assigned age ranges are often too restrictive or unrealistic given the available age indicators. The use of the 5- or 10-year age range in life table construction unknowingly truncates realistic age range estimates. Numerous additional studies have been conducted on Indian Knoll in the 20 years since Kelley's research. Often previous age estimates are utilized with some modification or adult ages are evaluated in reference to very broad age categories for comparative purposes.

Material and methods

In this study, we reconstructed the age-at-death distribution of Indian Knoll. We employed methods outlined in Chapter 11 (this volume), using two pelvic aging methods: Todd's 10-stage pubic symphysis system and Lovejoy and colleagues' (1985) eight-phase auricular surface approach. In order to complete the age-at-death distribution, Kelley's (1980; n.d.) interval-censored age estimates for individuals below 18 are combined with the adult age-at-death distribution based on the pelvic indicators.

Herrmann recorded pubic symphysis and auricular surface data from available adult burials ($n = 472$) in the skeletal collections housed at the William S. Webb Museum of Anthropology at the University of Kentucky and the Smithsonian Institution. Observations of the two age indicators were independently assessed during different data collection periods. Todd's (1920, 1921) original descriptions, supplemented by Buikstra and Ubelaker's (1994) written descriptions and drawings, were used to assess the pubic symphysis. Auricular surfaces were scored based on Lovejoy et al.'s (1985) original descriptions. Our reference dataset consists of individuals ($n = 745$) from the Terry Collection, housed at the Smithsonian Institution in Washington, DC. Konigsberg directed the collection of age data from this series, including auricular surface and pubic symphysis stage information. Herrmann assessed over 95% of the pelvic indicators in the reference series. Consequently, interobserver error is not an issue in this study.

Mathematical approach

For Indian Knoll we will fit a four-parameter Siler model with survivorship and hazard functions specified as

$$S(a) = \exp\left(-\frac{\alpha_1}{\beta_1}(1 - e^{-\beta_1 a}) + \frac{\alpha_3}{\beta_3}(1 - e^{\beta_3 a}) \right), \qquad (12.1a)$$

$$h(a) = \alpha_1 \exp(-\beta_1 a) + \alpha_3 \exp(b_3 a). \qquad (12.1b)$$

Here a is a random variate representing an exact age at death, α_1 and β_1 are parameters that represent the juvenile component of mortality, and α_3 and β_3 represent the senescent component (Wood *et al.* 1992). We do not include a "baseline" hazard parameter (α_2), as in our experience this parameter is rarely estimable from paleodemographic data. In the following we will represent the set of hazard parameters as θ.

Building on equation (11.13) presented by Konigsberg and Herrmann (Chapter 11, this volume), we model the probability that an individual who is exact age A will be in the j-th and k-th phases of the pubic symphysis and auricular surface as

$$\Pr(c_j, c_k | A = a) = \int_{z_1 = \frac{a - \mu_j}{\sigma_1}}^{\frac{a - \mu_{j-1}}{\sigma_1}} \int_{z_2 = \frac{a - \mu_k}{\sigma_2}}^{\frac{a - \mu_{k-1}}{\sigma_2}} \phi(z_1, z_2) dz_1 \, dz_2, \qquad (12.2)$$

where $\phi(z_1, z_2)$ represents a standard bivariate normal probability density function with one "free" parameter (a correlation coefficient r). The parameters that specify this model (the mean "age to transitions," the common within-character standard deviations, and the correlation coefficient between the two characters) were estimated with age measured on a logarithmic scale using our reference sample.

For Indian Knoll we have data on 891 individuals. From dental development/eruption and epiphyseal closure, we consider 509 of these individuals, which includes the 472 assessed, as being ≥ 18 years old at the time of their death. The joint probability that one of the 891 individuals would be ≥ 18 years old at time of death and be in the j-th and k-th phases of the pubic symphysis and auricular surface conditional on the hazard parameters is

$$\Pr(a \geq 18.0 \cap c_j, c_k | \theta) = S(18.0|\theta) \int_{a = 18.0}^{\omega} \Pr(c_j, c_k | a) \frac{f(a|\theta)}{S(18.0|\theta)} da \qquad (12.3)$$

$$= \int_{a = 18.0}^{\omega} \Pr(c_j, c_k | a) f(a|\theta) da.$$

The division by survivorship to age 18.0 in the first line is so that the probability density function for age-at-death $(f(a|\theta))$ will integrate to 1. This term cancels with the probability of surviving to age 18.0 years, as shown in the second line. For individuals where one characteristic cannot be observed, we use the marginal for the other characteristic, and when neither characteristic is observable we replace the probability for the "observed" phases with 1.

For the 382 remaining individuals who are judged to have died at less than 18 years of age, we have interval-censored age estimates. If o_i and e_i represent the left- and right-censored ages for the i-th individual, then the joint probability for an individual dieing between 0 and 18 years and between o_i and e_i is

$$\Pr(a \leq 18.0 \cap o_i \leq a \leq e_i|\theta) = \Pr(a \leq 18.0)\Pr(o_i \leq a \leq e_i|a \leq 18.0)$$

(12.4)

$$= (1 - S(18.0|\theta))\frac{S(o_i|\theta) - S(e_i|\theta)}{1 - S(18.0|\theta)}$$

$$= S(o_i|\theta) - S(e_i|\theta).$$

Combining the probabilities from equations (12.3) and (12.4) we can write the total log-likelihood for the hazard parameters conditional on the observed data as

$$\ln L(\theta|\mathbf{C}, \mathbf{o}, \mathbf{e}) = \sum_{i=1}^{382} \ln(S(o_i|\theta) - S(e_i|\theta))$$

(12.5)

$$+ \sum_{m=1}^{509} \ln\left(\int_{a=18.0}^{\omega} \Pr(c_m|a)f(a|\theta)\mathrm{d}a\right).$$

We find the maximum likelihood estimates for the hazard parameters using simulated annealing ("SIMANN" as described by Goffe et al. (1994)) to first identify a global maximum for the log-likelihood function, followed by maximization using a tensor method (subroutine "TENSOR" as described by Chow et al. (1994)) in order to estimate the Hessian and ensure that the simulated annealing had converged properly.

Occasionally, the transition ages derived from the probit model for the early stages of ordinal aging systems are extremely low. These low transition ages present serious problems for estimating model parameters. To overcome this obstacle we compressed stages in both the Todd and auricular systems. Stages 1 through 4 in the Todd method were combined, and phases 1 and 2 of the auricular method were grouped. In both cases the early stage transition ages are well below the adult range as defined for this study (18 years). The combined stages provide more appropriate transition ages for these early stages. The transition ages on a log scale are provided in Table 12.1.

Table 12.1. *Transition ages on a log scale, individual standard error estimates, common standard deviation by indicator, indicator correlation, and log-likelihood derived from the Terry Collection age data (n = 745)*

Transition	Estimate (log age)	SE
Pubic symphysis		
1[a]/2	2.8670	0.0548
2/3	3.1974	0.0396
3/4	3.3396	0.0343
4/5	3.4679	0.0302
5/6	3.9367	0.0237
6/7	4.4287	0.0373
SD	0.4724	0.0258
Auricular surface		
1[b]/2	2.9350	0.0452
2/3	3.3481	0.0298
3/4	3.5920	0.0233
4/5	3.8257	0.0204
5/6	3.9227	0.0204
6/7	4.3275	0.0286
SD	0.3973	0.0191
ln L = − 2189.2080		
	r	SE
Indicator correlation	0.4271	0.0347

SD, standard deviation; SE, standard error.
[a]Includes Todd stages 1–4.
[b]Includes auricular phases 1–2.

Comparative samples

Three prior paleodemographic reconstructions of Indian Knoll serve as comparative data (Table 12.2). These studies span a period of methodological advances in age estimation in physical anthropology. Snow's (1948) original life table is the initial dataset. Johnston and Snow's (1961) reanalysis of Indian Knoll serves as the second profile. Finally, Kelley's (1980, n.d.) paleodemographic reconstruction is the third comparative sample.

The age-at-death profiles by Snow (1948) and Johnston and Snow (1961) represent basic life tables. Snow's sample consists of the burials from the WPA, collections from Moore's initial investigations (housed at the Smithsonian Institution), and disturbed remains from Moore's excavation

Table 12.2. *Paleodemographic samples for the analysis of Indian Knoll*

Researcher(s)	Sample size	Adults	Reference date
Snow	1161	602	1948
Johnston and Snow	873	512	1961
Kelley	840	474	1980, n.d.
Present study	891	509	Present study

recovered during the WPA excavations. Our age-at-death distribution for Snow's 1948 publication is based on the combined totals of these three samples with some modifications.[1] Johnston and Snow's data are directly from the 1961 published life table with no modifications. Kelley's profile is derived from individual interval-censored age estimates (Kelley 1980, n.d.).

For each of the comparative samples, we also will fit a four-parameter Siler model with survivorship and hazard functions as described in formula (12.1). The Siler parameters are estimated in *mle Version 2.0.5* (Holman 2000) using a simulated annealing method. Once again we do not include a "baseline" hazard parameter (α_2). The life table data by cohort are entered in the model as simple frequencies with a beginning and ending age. For Kelley's interval-censored ages, we interpreted point ages (i.e., 14 years old) as one-year intervals (13.5–14.5 years). For general classifications we defined a range encompassing the entire interval. For example, an individual aged as "adult" is treated as age 18 to 120 years. If Kelley aged an individual as "45 +", then this individual is treated as 45 to 120 years.

Standard error estimation

Age-specific survivorship and standard errors for each Siler model were generated in *R Version 1.1.1* (Ihaka and Gentleman 1996) using the parameter estimates and covariance matrix. The upper age limit of the output was truncated at 80 years, given the extremely low survivorship at this age in all models. These data were then imported in a spreadsheet and the survivorship for each analysis bounded by ($\pm$)1 standard error is plotted for comparative purposes.

---

[1] We have reduced the count estimate in the disturbed area for the age range 4–12 from 100 to 50. Also, we do not include the "decayed" remains ($n = 33$). Finally, Snow's (1948) numbers in Table 5 sum to 1244 individuals not 1234. Based on a comparison with the individual burial data it appears the mistake is in the "Infant to 3 year" age group.

	Stage	.	1	2	3	4	5	6	7	8	9	10	Total
	.	0	6	7	3	2	4	7	3	0	0	1	33
	1	9	21	22	2	1	1	0	0	0	0	0	56
	2	11	4	10	9	11	6	6	3	1	0	0	61
	3	8	1	3	6	7	12	13	12	12	4	0	78
Auricular Surface	4	22	0	0	1	4	8	26	12	17	9	8	107
	5	15	0	0	1	1	5	10	3	13	6	1	55
	6	1	0	0	0	0	1	0	1	0	1	1	5
	7	20	0	0	0	0	1	2	4	9	10	10	56
	8	7	0	0	0	0	0	1	1	2	2	8	21
	Total	93	32	42	22	26	38	65	39	54	32	29	472

(Table header: Pubic Symphysis)

Figure 12.2. Contingency table of observed age indicators from Indian Knoll. Missing data are represented in the "." column.

Results

The observed data matrix for the Indian Knoll sample is provided in Figure 12.2. Both auricular surface and pubic symphysis scores are available from 346 of the 472 adults observed. Thirty-three of the adults evaluated from Indian Knoll are missing auricular surfaces, and 93 adults lack pubic symphyseal surfaces. As expected, preservation of the auricular surface is better than the pubic symphysis. The polychoric correlation of auricular surface phase and pubic symphysis stage is 0.80 with a 95% confidence limit from 0.76 to 0.84.

The parameters of the infant mortality component (α_1 and β_1) for all the models are quite similar. However, the parameters of the senescent mortality component (α_3 and β_3) are more variable, as expected. These nuances are indicative of different methods employed by each researcher. Each model's parameter estimates are provided in Table 12.3. Subadult age estimates for all the studies are based on a variety of dental development standards (see Meredith 1946; Hunt and Gleiser 1955; Moorrees *et al.* 1963a,b). Although potentially biased, these standards provide consistent and relatively narrow age estimates, reducing variation between studies.

Differences in the senescent mortality component result in marked variation in adult survivorship between the methodological approaches. A plot of the hazard functions clearly shows the differences between the paleodemographic analyses (Figure 12.3). The competing hazard model produces a classic shape with a high infant mortality, a low juvenile and young adult hazard, and increased adult mortality. We focus on the variation in the adult range between the studies. The present research

Table 12.3. *Estimated Siler model parameters for each study*

Parameter	Snow	Johnston and Snow	Kelley	Present study
α_1	0.3333	0.3487	0.3715	0.3326
β_1	1.0791	1.1236	1.0773	1.1221
$\alpha_2{}^a$	0	0	0	0
α_3	0.0094	0.0056	0.0069	0.0092
β_3	0.0838	0.0969	0.0844	0.0690

[a]Not estimated.

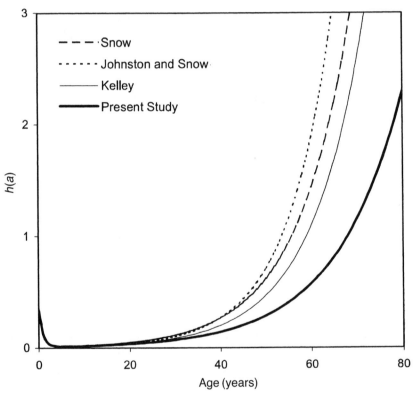

Figure 12.3. Plot of the hazard functions for each paleodemographic reconstruction of the Indian Knoll series.

exhibits the lowest hazard of death across the adult interval as compared with the other studies.

In Figure 12.4, survivorship intervals are plotted relative to age for each paleodemographic reconstruction of the Indian Knoll sample. The inter-

Table 12.4. *General comparison of age-specific survivorship by researcher, based on estimated Siler model parameters*

	Age-specific survivorship			
Age (years)	Snow	Johnston and Snow	Kelley	Present study
18	0.4943	0.5578	0.5284	0.5358
30	0.2049	0.2692	0.2737	0.2959
40	0.0475	0.0332	0.0695	0.1038
50	0.0005	0.0005	0.0029	0.0129

vals represent 1 standard error as derived from the Siler model parameter estimates and covariance matrix. Adult survivorship gradually increases across the four methods. This increase is associated with the addition of new age indicators and reassessment of earlier age estimates. Survivorship based on the present study is high across the entire adult interval as compared with Kelley and Snow, and it outpaces Johnston and Snow after age 26 years. A simple breakdown of survivorship by 10-year increments clearly demonstrates the increase (Table 12.4). The confidence interval of our approach in the midadult range (25–45 years) does not overlap with Snow's original data, but the other two profiles overlie the lower boundary of the confidence interval. It is important to note that the confidence intervals of the method proposed here provide a more realistic range of the actual age-at-death distribution. In contrast, the standard errors in the prior studies produce narrow bands suggesting a false accuracy in age assessment.

Discussion

The age-at-death distributions presented here are not dramatically differ-ent. One primary distinction in the studies presented is the adult aging methods employed by each researcher. Auricular surface aging was not available to earlier physical anthropologists. Some would argue that this fact alone would explain the slight differences evident in the results. It should be noted that the earlier age-at-death reconstructions are based on biased adult aging standards that fail to account for the actual variation in age estimation. For example, had we used the simple 5- to 10-year ranges assigned to the auricular surface phases in our age estimates (Lovejoy *et al.* 1985), then the age-at-death distribution would have been quite different. However, the distribution would have been biased.

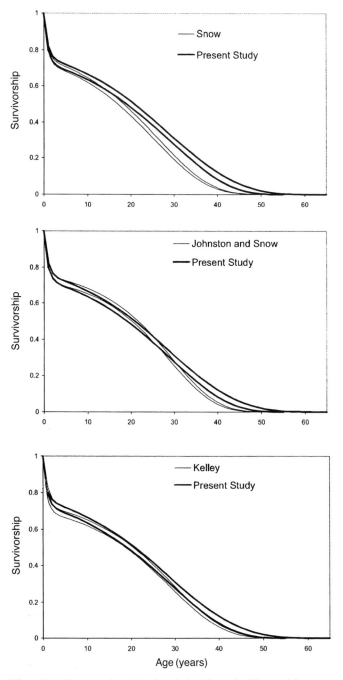

Figure 12.4. Three survivorship plots derived from the Siler model parameters comparing the present study with those of Snow, Johnston and Snow, and Kelley, respectively. The lines represent upper and lower bound of 1 standard error.

Variation in the Siler model parameters is greatly reduced in these earlier studies through the assignment of narrow age ranges and the application of life table analysis. In paleodemographic studies employing life tables, the adult age range is divided into 5- or 10-year intervals. Typically, each observed individual is placed within one of these age ranges. Individuals are placed in each cohort on the basis of the estimated age range or midpoint age estimate. Small adult age cohorts in the life table produce unrealistic error intervals for the age-at-death distribution. The new methodological approach proposed here overcomes this bias providing statistically accurate intervals.

Conclusions

This study demonstrates the extension of the proposed analytical methods to a bivariate age indicator model using age indicator data from the large prehistoric skeletal sample from Indian Knoll. The results clearly show differences between the current study and past paleodemographic reconstructions of the Indian Knoll series. Prior research inappropriately assigned biased age estimates to individuals and reduced true age variation through the use of life tables. These problems are typical in prior paleodemographic research and are the focus of numerous critiques (Bocquet-Appel and Masset 1982, 1996; Konigsberg and Frankenberg 1992; Konigsberg *et al.* 1997). Although not significantly different from previous survivorship curves, the new Siler model distribution and confidence interval provides a more realistic range of variation in the age-at-death distribution. On the basis of paleodemographic observations derived from this study, we have a clearer picture of mortality and longevity of the hunter–gatherer population that once occupied Indian Knoll.

Acknowledgments

We wish to thank the organizers of the Rostock workshops, Rob Hoppa and James Vaupel, for the opportunity to participate. Sissel Schroeder and Mary Powell of the William S. Webb Museum of Anthropology and David Hunt at the Smithsonian Institution National Museum of Natural History allowed access to the Indian Knoll collections. We also thank Jim Fenton, Allen Tackett, Sherri Turner, and Ben Auerbach who helped in the collection of age data from the Indian Knoll series in Lexington, Kentucky. The

W.K. McClure Fund from the University of Tennessee Center for International Education and the William M. Bass Endowment from the University of Tennessee Forensic Anthropology Center provided travel grants for Nicholas Herrmann. A National Science Foundation grant supported reference data collection (NSF Grant SBR-9727386).

References

Blakely RL (1971) Comparison of the mortality profiles of Archaic, middle Woodland, and middle Mississippian skeletal populations *American Journal of Physical Anthropology* **34**, 43–54.

Bocquet-Appel J-P and Masset C (1982) Farewell to paleodemography. *Journal of Human Evolution* **11**, 321–333.

Bocquet-Appel J-P and Masset C (1996) Paleodemography: expectancy and false hope. *American Journal of Physical Anthropology* **99**, 571–583.

Buikstra JE and Konigsberg LW (1985) Paleodemography: critiques and controversies. *American Anthropologist* **87**, 316–33.

Buikstra JE and Ubelaker DH (1994) *Standards for data collections from human skeletal remains.* Research Series no. 44. Fayetteville, AS: Arkansas Archeological Survey.

Cassidy CM (1972) Comparison of nutrition in pre-agricultural skeletal populations. Ph.D. dissertation, Department of Anthropology, University of Wisconsin.

Chow T, Eskow E, and Schnabel R (1994) Algorithm 739: a software package for unconstrained optimization using tensor methods. *ACM Transactions on Mathematical Software* **20**, 518–530.

Coale AJ and Demeny P (1966) *Regional model life tables and stable populations.* Princeton, NJ: Princeton University Press.

Goffe, WL, Ferrier GD, and Rogers J (1994) Global optimization of statistical functions with simulated annealing. *Journal of Econometrics* **60**, 65–99.

Herrmann NP and Fenton JP (2000) A report on new radiocarbon dates and recent investigations at three Green River Archaic sites. Paper presented at the Kentucky Heritage Council Annual Meeting, Bowling Green, Kentucky.

Holman, DJ (2000) *mle: a programming language for building likelihood models.* Version 2. Website: http://faculty.washington.edu/~holman/mle

Hunt EE and Gleiser I (1955) The estimation of age and sex of preadolescent children from bone and teeth. *American Journal of Physical Anthropology* **13**, 479–487.

Ihaka R and Gentleman R (1996) R: a language for data analysis and graphics. *Journal of Computational and Graphical Statistics* **5**, 299–314.

Johnston FE and Snow CE (1961) The reassessment of the age and sex of the Indian Knoll skeletal population: demographic and methodological aspects. *American Journal of Physical Anthropology* **19**, 237–244.

Kelley MA (1980) Disease and environment: a comparative analysis of three early

American Indian skeletal collections. Ph.D. dissertation, Case Western Reserve University, Cleveland.

Kelley MA (n.d.) Pathology inventory for Indian Knoll, Oh2. Unpublished manuscript on file at the William S. Webb Museum of Anthropology, the University of Kentucky, Lexington.

Konigsberg LW and Frankenberg SR (1992) Estimation of age structure in anthropological demography. *American Journal of Physical Anthropology* **89**, 235–256.

Konigsberg LW and Frankenberg SR (1994) Paleodemography: "Not Quite Dead". *Evolutionary Anthropology* **3**, 92–105.

Konigsberg LW, Frankenberg SR, and Walker RB (1997) Regress what on what?: paleodemographic age estimation as a calibration problem. In Paine RR (ed.): *Integrating archaeological demography: multidisciplinary approaches to prehistoric population.* Occasional Paper no. 24. Carbondale, IL: Center for Archaeological Investigations, pp. 64–88.

Lovejoy CO, Meindl RS, Pryzbeck TR, and Mensforth RP (1985) Chronological metamorphosis of the auricular surface of the ilium: a new method for the determination of age at death. *American Journal of Physical Anthropology* **65**, 15–28.

Meredith HV (1946) Order and age of eruption for the deciduous dentition. *Journal of Dental Research* **25**, 43–66.

Mensforth RP (1990) Paleodemography of the Carlston Annis (15Bt5): a late Archaic skeletal population. *American Journal of Physical Anthropology* **82**, 81–99.

Moore CB (1916) Some aboriginal sites on the Green River, Kentucky. *Journal of the Philadelphia Academy of National Sciences* **16**, 431–487.

Moorrees CFA, Fanning EA, and Hunt EE (1963a) Formation and resorption of three deciduous teeth in children. *American Journal of Physical Anthropology* **21**, 205–213.

Moorrees CFA, Fanning EA, and Hunt EE (1963b) Age variation of formation stages for ten permanent teeth. *Journal of Dental Research* **42**, 1490–1502.

Snow CE (1948) Indian Knoll skeletons. *The University of Kentucky, Reports in Anthropology* **4**(3, part 2), 367–555.

Todd TW (1920) Age changes in the pubic bone. I. The male white pubis. *American Journal of Physical Anthropology* **3**, 285–334.

Todd TW (1921) Age changes in the pubic bone. *American Journal of Physical Anthropology* **4**, 1–70.

Webb WS (1946) Indian Knoll, Site Oh2, Ohio County, Kentucky. *The University of Kentucky, Reports in Anthropology* **4**(3, part 1), 115–365.

Weiss KM (1973) Demographic models for anthropology. *Society for American Archaeology, Memoirs* **27**; *American Antiquity* **38**, 1–186.

Winters HD (1974) Introduction to the new edition. In WS Webb: *Indian Knoll.* Knoxville, TN: University of Tennessee Press, pp. v–xxvii.

Wood JW, Holman DJ, Weiss KM, Buchanan AV, and LeFor B (1992) Hazards models for human population biology. *Yearbook of Physical Anthropology* **35**, 43–87.

Index